AF679907

The

Poseidon Initiative

by

Thomas Velsun

The Poseidon Initiative

Copyright © Henry Thomas Jones

All rights reserved.

This novel is a work of fiction. Names, characters, places, events, and incidents are either products of the author's imagination or are used fictitiously. Any resemblance to actual persons, living or dead, or actual events is purely coincidental. Please don't copy, share, or use any part of this book without written permission from the author. Short quotes for reviews are okay if credit is given.

About the Author:

Thomas Velsun lives with his wife in coastal Florida. He's a former Army officer and a veteran of the Vietnam War. After leaving the Military he spent forty years in business and retired from a large global technology company.

The knowledge gained from his three college degrees from three different major universities (a BS in Math and Accounting, an MS in Engineering, and an MBA) has contributed heavily to his success in business and to his grasp of the subject matter in his novels.

During his business career, he completed special projects with various government agencies in Washington DC, including the FBI,CIA,US Mint, and IRS. He has participated in special projects with RAND Corporation (a think tank formed after World War II to continue the activities of various experts accumulated during the war years). He has worked in many different areas in the United States and in foreign countries. He has researched many conspiracy theories and has included selected subject matter from some of them in his novels.

He's a former athlete and maintains fitness with daily workouts involving weightlifting. He also enjoys playing golf and tennis.

The Poseidon Initiative

Chapter 1

Colt Randall, the leading field agent for Boswic Corporation (Boswic), dashed toward the bulletproof glass doors at the front entrance of the headquarters building in Tampa, Florida. Boswic, a private military company, provided support for Homeland Security in special situations.

Feeling the warm sunshine against his back on this clear December day, Colt enjoyed the soothing effect. Based on the information he had just received, he was thankful for the extra comfort.

The Russians had established a new spy base in Nicaragua, and they were in the process of establishing another one in the western hemisphere on La Orchila Island in the Caribbean Sea, about 200 miles northeast of Caracas.

Russia had obtained permission from Venezuela to build an air base for their TU 160 Blackjack Bombers on the island. Colt figured the base would also include a sophisticated spying operation, but there was much more to be concerned about.

According to an earlier CIA report, the Russians had developed a huge underwater missile carrying a nuclear warhead. They had named the missile 'Poseidon.' It was 65 feet long and 6.5 feet wide. The warhead was reported to be a large thermonuclear bomb capable of creating a radioactive tsunami to swamp any targeted coastal city in the United States.

Colt, along with his partner Linda Martinez, soon rushed through the open doorway of the main conference room to attend an urgent briefing from CIA Agents.

Harlan Pierce, Jim Boxer, and three other people sat around the large table. Harlan was the Executive Director of Boswic and Jim was the Vice President. Three other people sat alongside them. Colt and Linda quickly eased into two of the empty seats.

Blake Morgan, the primary Boswic tactics analyst, sat beside Harlan and Jim. Paul Collins, head of a terrorist threat investigation unit at the CIA, was there along with Nick Wallace, a CIA technology specialist who reported to Paul.

No introductions were necessary. Everyone had worked extensively together before.

Paul scanned the faces around the table. "In addition to the update we gave you involving the existence of the Poseidon underwater missiles, we've received some more disturbing news. The Russians and Chinese are coordinating closely, and the Chinese are in the process of using some of their latest technology innovations to improve the missiles. An attack is believed to be imminent. " He gestured to Nick.

"NSA intercepted a call into the Washington DC area," Nick said. "The call originated from a group of tiny islands between Finland and Sweden. NSA hasn't yet identified the exact locations of any of the participants in the call."

"What was the problem in identifying the exact locations?" Colt asked. "NSA usually doesn't have any trouble determining that."

"I don't know all the technical details, but I know there

are a lot of islands in the archipelago just off the western shore of Finland," Nick said. "At least we know the general locations of the people on both ends of the discussion, and we've decrypted enough of the conversation to identify the voice prints of two of the people involved."

Colt started to ask a question just as Nick gave the answer he was seeking.

"Ivan Titov, a Russian military leader, and Denis Andreev, a Russian expert on international banking, were both on the call," Nick said. "There were more people on the call, but NSA hasn't yet been able to identify the others."

"Could we tell who was on which end of the call?" Colt asked.

"Titov was in the area near Finland and Andreev was in the Washington DC area, probably with one of their moles," Nick said. "We know several other people were on each end of the call. NSA is hoping to be more specific after they complete additional analysis." He hesitated for several seconds.

Harlan gestured impatiently for Nick to continue. "What else do you know?"

"The Poseidon underwater missile was mentioned several times," Nick said. "Some of the voices in the conversation had Chinese accents. La Orchila was mentioned. Some new Russian and Chinese supercomputers were mentioned on the call along with a lot of other interesting things we need to investigate…" He hesitated and glanced at Paul.

"We know Ivan Titov owns some of those islands off Finland's western shore," Paul said. "He has at least two of them set up with security cameras, motion detectors, no-trespassing signs, boat piers, helipads, swimming pools draped with camouflage netting, and housing for a small army."

"Does he actually have a small army there?" Jim asked.

"Maybe," Paul said. "Black speedboats packed with

men dressed in camouflage fatigues have been seen docking at some of the piers."

"Why would he want to fortify those islands?" Colt asked.

"That's something we need to find out," Paul said. He glanced toward Colt and Linda. "In fact, there're a lot of things we need to find out, and we think Boswic can help us. That's why we're having this meeting."

Colt now had no doubt he and Linda had a new mission coming up.

Linda looked directly at Nick. "You mentioned some new supercomputers. How do they fit into all this?"

"I'll give you a little background information first," Nick said. "We think China is supplying the technology for the Poseidon underwater missile as well as for Russia's newest computer. The Chinese team who developed the Sunway Taihulight apparently has also developed a quantum computer. The Sunway achieved a speed of 93.01 petaflops. A petaflop is a thousand trillion floating point operations per second, and the quantum computer is a billion times faster than the Sunway. We're talking about unbelievable speeds."

"What in the hell are they planning to do with a quantum computer?" Harlan asked.

"That's something we need to find out. Nick and Blake will take the lead on that," Paul said. He gestured for Nick to continue.

Blake looked at Nick and held up a hand. "We need to tell them something about the technology involved with a quantum computer."

"It operates on the Superposition Principle. That relates to atoms being in several different energy states at once," Nick said. "It can act on all variable states simultaneously and carry out numerous computations in parallel. That makes it unbelievably fast."

No one commented. Colt figured everyone was waiting for Nick to continue.

"A quantum computer has molecules which interact with one another as qubits," Nick said. "Each molecule consists of the nuclei from five fluorine atoms and two carbon atoms. The atoms obviously function in a way to produce incredible speed."

Harlan grunted. "I think that's all I want to know about the technology. I still want an answer to my question."

"Okay," Paul said. "The answer is we don't know what they plan to do with the quantum computer, but we can give you some guesses. We think they'll use it to evaluate all their options as they analyze mountains of data to develop their latest military strategies. We know both Russia and China want to dominate us." Paul looked directly at Harlan. "We also think they'll use it to hack into as many of our computer systems as they can. With all that speed, a quantum computer can bypass our safeguards."

"Think they'll try to hack into our banking systems and steal our money?" Jim asked.

Paul gestured to Nick.

"We think that's a real possibly. That's probably why Denis Andreev was on the call," Nick said. "We're developing some quantum computers too. If we have them ready soon enough, we can use them for defense. And defense can be viewed in a lot of ways. The Russians might even plan to use some version of a quantum computer in their guidance system for their Poseidon Missiles."

"How can they do that?" Linda asked.

"Right now, I'll just tell you the CIA has a lot of people working on getting all the necessary answers," Nick said.

Paul nodded. "All the other intelligence agencies are also working with us on that. You might know a missile was developed for our submarines back in the time frame of 1965-1971 that we named the Poseidon C3. The Russian Poseidon missile is an entirely different animal so don't get confused as we discuss a lot more details in the future. Our Poseidon missiles were only about five feet in diameter and were only launched from submarines."

Colt nodded. "So, what do we need to do first?"

"That's why we're here. We need to come up with some good suggestions," Paul said. "My boss plans to form a team to take some immediate action. Boswic will be part of the team. An elite taskforce will be created." He looked at Colt and Linda. "The two of you will be on that taskforce."

"When can we expect to go into action?" Harlan asked.

"A lot of different agencies are investigating the threats we know about and will be making recommendations. The President will likely make the critical decisions about the specifics," Paul said. "For those of us in this room, I think we'll need to concentrate on the activities in the archipelago next to Finland. My guess is we'll also need to concentrate on what could happen on the island of La Orchila. It's well out into the Caribbean, 200 miles northeast of Caracas to be exact. Its location makes it an ideal spot to launch Poseidon Missiles toward several major cities in the United States."

"Are we going to get support from the Navy?" Linda asked.

"Probably," Paul said, "but I've been advised the President wants to avoid an official confrontation between the United States and Russia or China if possible. That's why our taskforce will take the lead." He narrowed his eyes as he looked around the table. "We'll see how things develop as we go forward."

Colt gave a slow nod. He felt sure he could make some accurate guesses.

Chapter 2

On an unnamed island just off the western shore of Finland, Ivan Titov sat in a conference room at his new base of operations and looked at his second in command, Sergei Nikitin, who sat across the table from him.

"The Kremlin has issued the orders to proceed with The Poseidon Initiative," Ivan said.

"So, we're going to receive big paychecks now?" Sergei asked.

Ivan nodded slowly. "And we'll keep receiving big paychecks if we perform our duties correctly."

"The Kremlin assured you of that?"

"Yes, all the top people."

"And Denis will take care of the funding?"

"That why he's in Washington. He's working with some of our moles who have close connections to China. He told me everything looks good for going forward at a fast pace."

"Will we operate from here or from La Orchila?"

"The Kremlin will decide as things progress. They're still working out some of the details."

"How many Poseidon Missiles do we have?"

"Five, the first three are 65 feet long and 6.5 feet wide. They each have a 2-megaton warhead. The last two are 80 feet long and 8 feet wide. Each one of them will carry a much larger warhead, maybe up to 100 megatons."

Sergei leaned forward. "Where are they?"

"The three older ones are on La Orchila Island at our combined bomber base and spy center. We'll probably launch them from there."

"What about the other two?"

"They're in China undergoing improvements. The Chinese technicians are retrofitting them to carry the larger warhead."

Sergei narrowed his eyes and didn't comment.

Ivan leaned back in his chair and pondered their current situation. He knew China had provided much of their advanced technology and he knew Chinese experts were trying to make any improvements they could to several key weapons Russia would be using. He was aware China wanted to conquer the United States as much as they did, and he wondered if there would be some competition later. He gave a mental shrug and decided not to worry about that now.

"Are you ready for this?" Sergei asked.

Ivan narrowed his eyes. "Are you asking if I'm ready to help execute The Poseidon Initiative?"

Sergei nodded slowly.

"Of course, why wouldn't I be?"

"It looks like we're going to be responsible for the point of the spear, so to speak. That's a huge undertaking."

Ivan looked directly at Sergei. "We've known this was coming for quite some time. We both have the qualifications to do what we need to do. And we're getting large paychecks to lead the activity at the launch site. Are you getting cold feet?"

"No, I'm just thinking what we're going to do is a huge undertaking, probably the biggest strike ever unleashed on mankind."

Ivan held a fist high in the air. "And that's good. Cheers for Mother Russia to be the dominating country on the planet."

Sergei pursed his lips and leaned forward. "China might have something to say about that."

"That's not anything we need to worry about right now. Getting the United States out of the way is our focus and China is our partner in doing that. Our leaders in the Kremlin can worry about all the other stuff later. How we continue to partner with China will be something they'll have to work out after we've gotten the United States out of the way."

Sergei raised his arms slightly with both palms out. "Like whether we're the dominant country on the planet or whether we share power with China?"

Ivan shrugged. "I'm sure it's something like that. But that's not our concern."

A brief silence ensued.

"I'm just thinking of the enormity of what we have ahead of us," Sergei said.

Ivan gave a short laugh. "Not a good thing to worry about. You should concentrate on our next step and execute properly. That's all we need to do. A lot of other people are looking ahead and doing the proper planning. We just need to follow orders and make good tactical decisions."

Chapter 3

Colt Randall sat in his desk chair at Boswic and stared at the computer screen in front of him. The threat matrix continued to expand. Due to his former Delta Force experience and his success on recent projects, he knew he would be expected to provide expert help in several areas.

As he studied the information on the computer screen, his phone buzzed and he glanced at the caller ID. It was his boss, Jim Boxer.

Colt answered.

"Harlan just received an interesting phone call," Jim said.

Expecting Jim to continue, Colt waited.

"Get Linda and come down to Harlan's office. We'll discuss it," Jim said. He disconnected.

As soon as Colt and Linda walked through the doorway to Harlan's office, Jim waved them toward the round conference table in the corner. The table had seating for six.

Colt and Linda eased into a couple of empty chairs across from Harlan and Jim.

Harlan leaned forward. His intense gaze focused on

Colt. "Jim told you about the phone call?"

Colt gave a slight shrug. "He didn't give any details. He just mentioned Linda and I should come down here and discuss it."

Harlan grunted and narrowed his eyes. "The caller told me we were continuing to meddle around in dangerous territory. He warned me about Boswic constantly getting in the way of the Power Elite and he mentioned we would suffer the consequences."

"Do you know who called? Linda asked.

"Not yet," Harlan said. "The FBI is working on it."

"Did he give any specifics?" Colt asked.

"No, but he emphasized we should know who we were messing around with and if we wanted to stay alive we had better wise up and get the hell out of the way," Harlan said.

"Wow, what a jerk." Linda glanced at the others around the table. "I would like to get him out of our way. If we find out who he is, I hope I get the opportunity."

Colt looked directly at Harlan. "Do you know where the call came from?"

"No," Harlan said, "but I've called NSA. They're looking into the situation. They also sent some information they thought we should be aware of. I printed it a few minutes ago."

Harlan looked at a sheet of paper in front of him and started reading. "An elite cabal of wealthy individuals has been called the Establishment, the Invisible Government, the Illuminati, the Secret Brotherhood, the Power Elite, and several other things. These could be separate organizations, interrelated, or all one and the same." He looked at Colt and Linda. "Blake has been studying some aspects of these organizations."

"Shouldn't he join us?" Colt asked.

Harlan glanced at Jim.

"I know you decided to keep this discussion just among the four of us to start with." Jim looked at Harlan and made a slight gesture with his palms up. "But Colt has a good point."

Harlan removed his phone from a pocket and punched a button.

"Come join us in my office," Harlan said into his phone.

In less than a minute, Blake occupied one of the two previously empty chairs at the table. Harlan gave him a quick update and then asked, "What do you think?"

"I have an opinion there's a powerful covert influence involved in all our government decisions. I'm thinking about the Bilderberg Society in particular," Blake said. "No matter who or what the caller was referencing we need to be more aware of a lot of things relating to secret power structures."

Colt noted Blake clinched a fist as he talked.

Blake scanned the faces around the table. "Are all of you familiar with the Knights Templar?"

"Didn't they raid Solomon's Temple and abscond with great wealth?" Colt asked.

"Yes," Blake said. "Long story short, they eventually hooked up with the Free Masons and the inner core of that group evolved into the Illuminati. Over the last few years, I've completed extensive research on the Illuminati. They're a well-organized group of Power Elite. They're referenced by a lot of different names, and they're sometimes referred to as the Establishment."

"Was your original research for some specific purpose?" Linda asked.

"It started with my dissertation for my PhD," Blake said. "A lot of my professors were conspiracy buffs."

Jim grunted. "I guess we're well into that area now."

"The Bilderberg Society has an annual, unofficial, invitation-only conference of around 150 people from North America and Western Europe. About a third of them are from government and the rest are from finance, industry, and education," Blake said. "All, of course, are people of influence."

"What do they do at the conference?" Harlan asked.

"In broad terms, they discuss major problems facing the United States and Western Europe," Blake said, "and then come up with some type of action plan."

"Do you have specifics on any of the action plans?" Colt asked.

"I've never been able to come up with any details," Blake said. "They keep everything very secretive and they seem to have powerful resources at their disposal."

"Do you have any details on their nature of their resources?" Harlan asked.

"There are thousands of significant pieces to the puzzle," Blake said. "Academia seems to be a big player. Princeton and Georgetown's Institute for the Study of Diplomacy are both part of that picture." He leaned forward and explained.

Harlan narrowed his eyes. "So, the Bilderberg Society and our Federal Reserve System are both believed to be active in the overall conspiracy."

Blake nodded.

"Have we been doing anything that would involve the Federal Reserve?" Colt asked.

"Jim and I have recently looked into some large international money pipelines," Harlan said. "We might have stumbled into some sensitive areas. I'm not saying the Federal Reserve is part of, or even connected to any of this, but they're connected to various large international money flows involving the World Bank and the International Monetary Fund."

"Are we getting into areas where we don't belong?" Colt asked.

"Someone seems to think so," Harlan said. He looked at Blake. "Go continue your research and collect some more details. We'll all get back together tomorrow morning."

Blake stood and left quickly.

Colt felt a little apprehension creeping into his thoughts.

They were getting into some areas he wasn't familiar with, but he knew he was probably about to learn a lot more about conspiracies, secret societies, and international money flow.

Chapter 4

On his island base off the west coast of Finland, Ivan Titov sat in his office and looked across his desk at Sergei Nikitin. "Are you ready to move forward?"

"What's our initial strategy?" Sergei asked.

"That depends on the Kremlin, but I think we should ease into things as much as we can," Ivan said. "It would be foolish to rush and make a big mistake."

"Is all of our necessary funding in place?"

"Denis tells me it's all set," Ivan said. "He told me most of it is well disguised and routed through different facets of the World Bank. I didn't ask for any details."

Sergei nodded slowly and then asked, "Has the Kremlin made a decision yet about which location we'll use for our primary base of operations to launch the Poseidon Missiles against the United States?"

"No, but they've made some recommendations about a few things we need to take care of before we get fully into the project."

Sergei narrowed his eyes. After a short hesitation, he asked, "And what are these things?"

"I understand there's a long list of items the Kremlin is putting together," Ivan said. "I'm told one item on the list will be to eliminate Colt Randall."

"How are we going to do that?"

"We use our best assassin Stephan Zak as a starter."

"Is he in the United States?"

"He's actually in Tampa as we speak."

Sergei leaned forward. "Exactly what do you have in mind?"

"Due to our previous encounters with Randall, we have a pretty good profile on him. We also have detailed information about his schedule and office hours."

"Did we get the information from our moles in Washington?"

Ivan grinned. "Yep, they're doing their job."

"Do you think Stephan can eliminate Randall?"

"Remember, Stephan's our best."

"I don't think Randall has ever lost an encounter with any of our previous assassins and they were all real good."

"Eliminating him probably isn't an immediate problem. We'll likely be able to ease into it."

Sergei tilted his head slightly and stared at Ivan.

"I've already called Harlan Pierce and given him a warning about Boswic intruding in sensitive areas. As a starter Stephan will simply reinforce that warning. He won't try to kill Randall during this initial meeting."

"I'm surprised the Kremlin wouldn't insist Randall be eliminated sooner rather than later."

"Their first priority is to provide cover for our activity in kicking off The Poseidon Initiative. They want to create a lot of misdirection. Randall feeling personally under siege will be part of a smokescreen they want to generate." Ivan looked directly at Sergei. "The Kremlin wants all the entities in the United States who might be involved in trying to prevent any of our missile launches to be concerned about a wide range of threats."

Sergei frowned. "Are some of Russia's chess masters who're working with the Kremlin influencing the strategy being developed?"

"I didn't ask."

Sergei hesitated for a moment and then leaned forward. "That sounds like something they would recommend, but it shouldn't cause us any problems. When is Stephan going to personally give Randall the warning?"

"Real soon and it needs to be up close and personal to have the right impact," Ivan said.

A brief silence ensued.

Sergei narrowed his eyes. "When we get ready to kill Randall, using a sniper to shoot him as he's leaving the Boswic offices might be our smartest move."

"Our moles tell me that won't work," Ivan said. "They tell me Boswic has technology that will sound an alarm if a rifle is within 400 yards of the property."

"Are they sure about that?"

Ivan shrugged. "We'll check more into that later. Right now, it's best for us to go along with the current strategy we've been given."

"So, this time we're just going to warn Randall to back off?"

"That's the plan for now. Like I mentioned, the Kremlin wants to create enough distraction to provide some significant cover for our upcoming activities in preparing to launch our Poseidon Missiles."

Chapter 5

The next morning, Colt, Linda, and Blake sat with Harlan and Jim at the round conference table in Harlan's office.

"We have something new to consider," Blake said. "The Russians and the Chinese are both suddenly pouring a lot of money into Jamaica. Most of it is going to their respective embassies there."

"How much money are we talking about?" Harlan asked.

"Each country has spent over five hundred billion so far," Blake said, "and our Federal Reserve System has ties to some of it."

Jim leaned forward. "Are you sure about that?"

"Yes," Blake said. "Many of the owners of the Federal Reserve can be classified as international powers. And I'm convinced several shadow groups still have connections to some of these owners."

Colt narrowed his eyes. "Which shadow groups?"

"The Illuminati and the Freemasons to name a couple," Blake said. "There are more."

"Do you know what's going on?" Colt asked.

"Maybe," Blake said. "There's a lot to consider. From my research I've recently found that a lot of dislocated facts tie together. They even bring logic to the farfetched notion that the powers behind the world's central banks destroyed the Titanic on purpose."

"That's a good one," Colt said. "How did you come up with something like that?"

"It's not far-fetched if you look at all the facts," Blake said. "The founders of our Federal Reserve System met on Jekyll Island in November of 1910. After their meeting, they worked toward getting Congress to legally establish the Federal Reserve Bank."

"What does that have to do with the Titanic?" Colt asked.

"I'm getting to that," Blake said. "There are a lot of dislocated facts that need to be tied together. I'm trying to summarize."

As Colt waited for Blake to continue he noticed Blake's eyes had narrowed a lot and Blake had made a fist with his right hand.

"Several mercantile tycoons who were opposed to the creation of the Federal Reserve System were onboard the Titanic for the maiden voyage," Blake said. "The Titanic sank on April 15, 1912, and some onboard who opposed the creation were eliminated. Members of Congress who would be voting to establish the Federal Reserve had been properly warned."

"The Federal Reserve was established in 1913, right?" Linda asked.

"With the proper messages sent to the opposition, the Federal Reserve Act passed Congress on December 23, 1913," Blake said. "Congressmen at that time were well aware they would be in great danger if they opposed it."

There was a moment of silence.

"If there's any truth to that, our involvement in any investigation of irregular activities within the Federal Reserve System could turn out to be a big problem for us," Harlan said.

Jim looked at Blake. "Do you know if any descendants of these ruthless bastards are still carrying on the work of their fathers?"

"I've never found any direct evidence of that," Blake said, "but it's a fact some members of the families of many of the original owners are still in place."

Harlan studied Blake for a few moments. "I want you to do a lot more checking on this. We need to know more about the territory we're getting into."

Jim nodded. "We need to know as much as possible about all the subtleties of the Federal Reserve and more about any owners who could be lurking behind the scenes. They could even be involved in some aspect of the funding for the launch of the Poseidon Missiles."

"I've heard a lot of stories over the years about many of the conspiracy theories regarding the Federal Reserve," Colt said, "but I never took these theories seriously before now."

"Yeah, we need to take them seriously. There are things I haven't mentioned," Blake replied. "Lincoln needed money to finance the Civil War. The international bankers at the time offered him loans at 24% to 36%. Long story short, Lincoln rejected their offer and decided to print U.S. Treasury notes, debt and interest free."

Harlan grunted and looked directly at Blake. "The bankers of that time didn't like that, did they?"

"Of course not," Blake said, "and they took drastic action. After Lincoln's death, Congress passed a new banking act and all currency became interest-bearing debt instruments again, making members of the Establishment of that era very wealthy."

Harlan nodded slowly. "I guess all that was predictable."

"That's right," Blake said. "And basically, the same thing happened with President Kennedy. On June 4, 1963, President Kennedy issued Executive Order 11110. It called for a new currency to be issued by the United States

Treasury. This would bypass the Federal Reserve."

Linda shook her head slowly. "Kennedy was assassinated in Dallas on November 22, 1963, and the new currency was soon withdrawn from circulation."

Blake nodded.

"And there's a lot more," Blake said. "My research indicated Reagan discussed taking some drastic action against the Fed and was shot soon after. He was lucky to have survived. I'm convinced his shooting was connected to his planned action against the Federal Reserve. There are certain people in the ownership of the Federal Reserve who don't want a big source of their money and power cut off."

"So where does all this leave us?" Colt asked. He looked at Harlan and Jim.

"In one damned big mess," Harlan said. "We already know the FBI is concerned a world-wide conspiracy could be preparing to operate here in Tampa. Everything we've discussed, including the Russian nuclear threat, could be connected and every part of it needs a huge money flow. We have a lot to investigate and we need to continue, even if we might be stepping on the toes of some powerful people."

Colt grunted. "Yeah and we need to stay on full alert for adverse reactions from those people as we go forward." He looked at Blake. "So how is the money flow from Russia and China into their embassies in Jamaica connected to what you just mentioned?"

"I was getting to that," Blake said. He looked slowly around the table. "I don't know the answer to that yet, but I'm continuing to investigate. Jamaica would be a great place to launch Poseidon Missiles to threaten the United States. The fact that both Russia and China are involved with the missiles and they're both suddenly pouring big money into that location is a red flag. The fact that our Federal Reserve is currently involved in that money flow is definitely another red flag."

Harlan nodded. "We have a lot to be concerned about."

Chapter 6

On his island base off the west coast of Finland, Ivan Titov sat in his plush office chair and looked across his desk at Sergei Nikitin.

"We're not staying here and we're not going to La Orchila Island," Ivan said. "I just found out a few minutes ago."

"Where then?"

"Jamaica."

"What's wrong with La Orchila? It seems like the perfect spot to launch our underwater missiles."

"It would be except for one thing," Ivan said, "too many coral reefs."

Sergei stared at Ivan and didn't comment.

"China is supplying a lot of advanced technology for Russia's construction of the air base there," Ivan said. "They were going to help construct our missile launch site too."

"How does that relate to the coral reefs?"

"While they were building the air base, the Kremlin originally planned to create a structure that would allow us to launch the missiles from deep underwater, the Poseidon

Missile can travel at a depth of 3,280 feet," Ivan said, "but they decided to build the structure in Jamaica instead."

"Don't we have submarines capable of launching the missiles?"

"I haven't been in any meetings on the subject, but our bosses told me that option isn't the best for right now. And they reminded me getting the missiles launched is going to be our job."

"They want us to actually launch the missiles?"

"Supervise the crew that will do it," Ivan said. "The Kremlin wants to be sure the launches are undetectable. They want to launch the missiles at a very low depth. With the assistance of the Chinese, they were going to build an advanced structure for the launches on La Orchila. However, the island has too many huge coral reefs for it to be practical to do that."

"Doesn't Jamaica have coral reefs too?"

"Yes, but I'm told the reefs aren't a problem where our bosses are building our advanced structure for carrying out the mission," Ivan said.

"How long before the structure will be finished?"

"I understand the completion is close. I don't know all the technical details, but I'm told we need to start preparing to move in."

"When did you find this out?"

Ivan glanced at his watch and said, "Twenty minutes ago, just before you came over for our meeting."

Sergei shook his head slowly. "Some things are moving faster than I anticipated. Do you know the exact location of our launch site?"

"Not yet, but I know it's somewhere around Kingston."

Sergei gave a slight grin. "Well at least we'll have some civilization around us."

"We have an embassy in Kingston and so do the Chinese. I'm told both embassies will be useful in helping to hide our activity while we're preparing for the missile launches."

"How will the embassies be useful?"

"I don't know those details yet, but we can make some good guesses." Ivan leaned forward and looked directly at Sergei. "And again, I'm told we need to get ready to move to Jamaica real soon."

Sergei gave a slight shrug. "We could be in worst places."

There was a brief silence.

Ivan narrowed his eyes. "I have some more news."

Sergei raised an eyebrow.

"Stephan is in the Boswic parking lot as we speak. When Colt Randall walks out of the building, Stephan's ready to confront him."

"Do we know when that's going to be?"

"Within the next ten minutes if Randall is on his usual schedule."

Chapter 7

As he left the Boswic headquarters building, Colt scanned the surrounding area like he always did. He immediately noticed a man walking toward him from the visitor parking lot.

The man wore a light blue shirt under a navy-blue sports coat. His casual slacks were grey. Colt studied him while he walked closer. He looked Russian and bulging muscles made the man's coat and slacks a tight fit.

Colt stayed on high alert and prepared to take action if he needed to.

When the man drew to within about twenty feet of Colt he stopped and grinned.

Staying on high alert, Colt stood motionless and waited for the man to speak.

"So, you're Colt Randall," the man said. "I've heard you were a tough guy to deal with."

"Who's telling you that?"

"Let's just say you're well known to my employers."

"And they are?"

"You don't need to know who they are," the man said.

"What you do need to know is if you don't quit meddling, you're going to die."

"Meddling in what?"

The man continued to grin. "You know very well what I mean. I don't have time to explain any further."

Colt kept his balance on both feet and stood ready for action. He could feel his 9mm Glock 19 in the holster toward the back of his right hip.

"Do you have any message other than to quit meddling?" Colt asked.

"My employers are disturbed about what you and your Boswic pals are continuing to stick your noses into."

"And you'll give me no specifics?"

The stranger pursed his lips and looked down. Colt got the impression he was undecided about something.

Colt remained on high alert. He figured the stranger might be trying to catch him off guard and then try to eliminate him.

However, that didn't make any sense, Colt thought. They were in a public place in broad daylight and there were cameras recording everything.

"Are you going to give me any additional details about what your employers are disturbed about?" Colt asked. He kept his gaze fixed on the stranger.

The stranger hesitated a few moments and then said, "I keep telling you that you already know."

Colt didn't comment.

"For some reason, they want to give you a warning and a chance to live longer," the stranger said. He shrugged. "And they wanted me to emphasize this is your final warning."

Colt remained silent and stayed ready for anything.

"The message has been delivered," the stranger said. "We've talked long enough."

"An argument could be made about how clear your message has been."

The stranger made no comment. He turned and started walking away.

"Hold it right there," Colt said. He contemplated what to do next. The stranger hadn't broken any laws, but Colt was reluctant to let him walk off.

The stranger stopped and turned slowly toward Colt. He narrowed his eyes and stared at Colt.

"I need something specific," Colt said. "Otherwise, your warning does no good."

A slight grin tugged at the corners of the stranger's mouth. He widened his stance slightly and appeared to crouch just a little. He jiggled the fingers on his right hand.

Colt returned his stare and remained silent.

The stranger's grin expanded. "Do you want to file a complaint?"

Colt made no comment.

"I've done nothing wrong. I was hired to deliver a message and I did my job."

"You didn't deliver any real message. You just make a lot of vague threatening comments."

"I did what I was paid to do," The stranger said. "I'm going to leave now. If you attack me in any way, I'll retaliate. It will be self defense." His grin remained pasted on his face.

Colt felt it was clear the stranger wanted to either intimidate or eliminate him.

The stranger continued to grin like the Joker in the old Batman stories.

Colt figured the stranger had a strong urge for the elimination part, but he needed Colt to initiate the action so he wouldn't violate his instructions.

The stranger gave Colt one of those 'I'm better than you are' looks. He somehow flashed an even bigger grin than his previous one.

Remaining on full alert, Colt watched the stranger slowly move his right arm further from his side. He knew the stranger wanted him to feel like a coward if he did nothing.

Deep down, Colt hoped the stranger would draw.

Continuing to grin, the stranger looked directly into Colt's eyes and gave him an 'I dare you' look.

Colt figured the stranger was under strict orders to not draw on him without a real good excuse, self defense being one.

The stranger stood completely still. He now seemed more comfortable. He had apparently fought off any flash of temptation.

Colt fought with some temptation too. He didn't want to let the stranger just walk away. He knew the stranger had cleverly backed him into a corner. This was complicated.

The stranger continued to grin.

Colt fought back a strong urge and decided to do nothing.

The stranger seemed disappointed. He hesitated for a few seconds then turned and walked away, appearing to have no concern about being shot in the back.

Chapter 8

At his small military base on his private island off the western shore of Finland, Ivan sat across from Sergei at the small round conference table in his office.

"It looks like Stephan did okay," Ivan said. "He reported he delivered the required message emphatically and he thinks it will give Randall a lot to think about for quite some time."

"Will it be enough to create a real distraction from what we're getting ready to do?" Sergei asked.

"Stephan thinks so and so does the Kremlin."

There was a brief silence.

"So, what's our next step here?" Sergei asked.

Ivan leaned forward and put his elbows on the table. "Our next step here is to pack up and go to our new headquarters."

"Down in Jamaica, around Kingston?"

"Yep, everything's still the same as I told you earlier."

"I've been thinking more about all that," Sergei said. "Maybe launching our Poseidon Missiles from Bermuda would be better. I think it has a better tactical location than Kingston."

"Bermuda is even worse than La Orchila on the coral reefs," Ivan replied. "That's how Bermuda stays so protected from hurricanes."

Sergei nodded slowly and then asked, "Are any of the Poseidon Missiles already in Jamaica?"

"Not yet," Ivan said. "The three that were stored in La Orchila are in route. They'll be in Jamaica before we arrive."

"What about the new ones in China?"

"I'm told we'll get them in Jamaica as soon as they're ready to use."

Sergei regarded Ivan carefully. "Think we'll use all the older ones before the new ones are shipped from China?"

"It probably depends on how things progress."

"Aren't we making the decisions?"

"We see how that evolves."

"Didn't you tell me we're the head of the spear?"

"For immediate activity once we get into action," Ivan said. "I don't think we'll need to make any of the strategic decisions. We'll just be making tactical decisions."

Sergei narrowed his eyes and didn't comment.

"Once we get set up at our new headquarters I don't think we're going to make any decisions about where the targets are located or when we're going to strike them," Ivan said. "Those decisions will be made elsewhere, probably in the Kremlin."

"What involvement will China have in making those decisions?"

"I don't know and I haven't asked."

"So, we're just going to carry out our orders from the Kremlin when we receive them?"

"Right," Ivan said. "We're going to constantly receive a lot of intelligence, and we'll stay in close communication with our bosses."

"So, we'll all be discussing things often as we move

forward?"

"Yes, details will probably be constantly changing. You and I will be expected to make the necessary adjustments and execute properly when we receive specific orders."

Sergei nodded slowly.

"There will be a large number of people in Moscow who will be constantly working to make sure we're provided all the resources we'll need," Ivan said.

There was a brief silence.

"It's going to be interesting to see what kind of decisions our bosses make on launching the missiles." Sergei took a deep breath, exhaled slowly, and leaned back in his chair. "There's quite a difference between a 100-megaton warhead and a 2-megaton warhead."

"You have a point there," Ivan said.

Sergei narrowed his eyes. "I'm guessing China will have a large influence on most decisions the Kremlin makes."

Ivan narrowed his eyes and suddenly seemed occupied with his own thoughts.

Chapter 9

The next morning Colt and Linda sat in a conference room at Boswic along with Harlan, Jim, and Grant Winston, Special Agent in Charge (SAC) of the Tampa FBI office.

"Colt, I want to compliment you on your restraint," Grant said. "You did the right thing."

Colt raised an eyebrow and didn't comment.

"The man's name is Stephan Zak," Grant said. "He's a well-known assassin in some circles, but he has no pending charges in the United States."

Colt leaned forward. "You can't find some reason to arrest him?"

"Not at this time," Grant said, "but we have some men looking for clues as to where he is right now."

"Do you know who he's working for?" Harlan asked.

"Not for sure, but we can make a good guess," Grant said. "NSA intercepted another phone call from one of the islands off the west cost of Finland into the Washington area. The villains have advanced technology, but NSA can decrypt various words here and there. We picked up several names."

Harlan leaned forward. "Probably Ivan Titov and Denis Andreev are two of them, right?"

"Right," Grant said. "And they picked up several more. Titov has a partner up there with him on his island, Sergei Nikitin." He looked directly at Colt. "NSA picked up enough words from the call to put together a good bit of information. It looks like Titov and Nikitin wanted Zak to give you that warning."

"Why?" Colt asked.

"That's not yet clear," Grant said, "but you and Linda were both mentioned in the phone conversation."

"We'll plan to stay alert," Colt said. He glanced at Linda.

Linda gave a slight nod.

Colt noted she didn't seem overly concerned.

There was a brief silence.

Harlan motioned for Grant to continue.

Grant leaned forward. "Gold was one of the topics in the call. The Federal Reserve Bank of New York was mentioned."

"Are Titov and Andreev involved with the gold part?" Jim asked.

"Most likely," Grant said. "And there's something else of real interest. Titov and Nikitin have acquired a supercomputer."

Jim leaned forward. "Is it being used for hacking?"

"Maybe," Grant said. "There are some things we need to figure out. This whole puzzle fits neatly into the reasons we have you under contract."

Jim narrowed his eyes. "Exactly what do you expect us to do?"

"Along with providing some expert firepower to help us deal with pending threats, help us root out some active elements of various secret societies involved in the threats," Grant said. "Also, Blake should be able to provide some expert help on the additional analysis we need."

Harlan nodded slowly.

Jim leaned forward toward Grant. "Do you think this secret society stuff might be the stimulus behind the warnings we're receiving?"

"My staff thinks there's a connection," Grant said. "I hope you'll allow Blake to do a lot of consulting with them."

Colt noticed that Harlan seemed to be deep in thought.

Within a few more seconds, Harlan pressed a button on the phone in front of him. "Come to the main conference room immediately."

Harlan disconnected and looked directly at Grant. "We need a quick start on putting the pieces of this puzzle together."

Grant pressed his lips together and nodded.

In less than a minute, Blake appeared in the doorway. Harlan waved him toward an empty chair at the conference table.

After giving a brief explanation, Harlan said, "You've been doing a lot of research. We want all the facts you consider relevant to what I just mentioned."

Blake grunted, "That might take a while."

Harlan hesitated for a moment. "Summarize."

"No one knows for absolute certainty," Blake said. "But it's likely the Federal Reserve Bank of New York has the biggest gold supply in one place in the world. However, we don't own all of it."

Colt nodded. "I understand foreign investors own most of it."

"That's correct," Blake said. "The U.S. can only claim about 5% of it. There are 5,000 metric tons of gold in the vault in New York. That's supposed to be 500 metric tons more than Fort Knox."

"Are you trying to make any particular point?" Jim asked.

"Not really," Blake said, "just trying to provide some

perspective relating to the gold supply." He looked at Harlan. "You mentioned that could be part of the current puzzle."

Harlan made an impatient gesture "Go ahead and finish summarizing the facts you think are relevant to the current situation."

"If the Russians begin using a lot of their gold supply we'll know something big is going on they need to finance," Blake said. "We'll need to stay alert for that."

After a little more discussion, Harlan turned toward Grant. "Let's get back to the intercepted phone call. How many assassins were mentioned?"

"Two," Grant said, "Stephan Zak and Ludvig Glinka."

"Know much about Glinka?" Jim asked.

"Not yet," Grant said, "but we have several analysts doing extensive research on him." He glanced at Blake. "You should probably join some of their discussions."

Blake nodded and made a note.

A brief silence ensued.

Harlan looked at Grant. "Are your people still trailing Zak?"

"Haven't lost him yet," Grant said. "He's still in the local area."

"Are you getting any direct help from NRO on that?" Harlan asked.

Colt knew the NRO (National Reconnaissance Office) designed, built, and operated the reconnaissance satellites of the United States government. An agency in the Department of Defense, it coordinated collection and analysis of information from both airplane and satellite reconnaissance by the military services and the CIA. The FBI was a primary recipient of data concerning activity in the United States.

"Quite a bit," Grant said. "I won't go into all the details right now."

Harlan gave a slow nod.

"We know Titov and Nikitin are both billionaires and

we know they're smart," Grant said, "but we think there's a higher intellectual layer involved in what they're doing. We're convinced something real big is going on and it probably involves launching some of Russia's Poseidon Missiles."

Harlan grunted and drummed his fingers on the table for a moment. "This whole thing is beginning to look like one gigantic challenge."

Grant nodded. "It's shaping up to be the most complex puzzle I've ever been involved with." He scanned the faces around the table. "Do any of you play chess?"

Harlan narrowed his eyes. "What does chess have to do with any of this?"

Grant looked directly at Harlan. "I've always been a chess enthusiast, and I think it's a good mental exercise to help anyone's thinking. After ten moves in chess, a tree-diagram of options has around 170 million branches. I think we're dealing with something like that."

"I play chess and I agree with everything you just mentioned," Blake said.

Harlan grunted and turned slightly toward Grant. "Do you think Titov and Nikitin are involved in all this stuff we're looking at, the Federal Reserve stuff, the gold aspect that just came up, and any other aspects of funding an attack on the United States?"

"Definitely," Grant said, "and I think at least one attack on the United States could very well involve Poseidon Missiles."

"Launched from where?" Linda asked.

"Probably from Jamaica," Grant said. "That's something we need to confirm as quickly as we can. We have an extremely complex problem to resolve. That's why I mentioned the chess aspect."

"And which of the millions of options should we concentrate on?" Colt asked.

Grant leaned forward. "All of them."

"How can we do that?" Harlan asked. An expression of exasperation dominated his face.

Grant elaborated for several minutes.

Jim rubbed his chin and appeared thoughtful. "If we don't stop this thing pretty soon, we'll have an even bigger problem."

Harlan nodded. "We need to figure out what's connected and what's not. This is going to take all the resources the United States has. We're all going to have to work closely together to make fast progress."

Everyone was silent for a few moments.

Narrowing his eyes, Harlan stared hard at Grant. "Does the FBI have a lot of available information from other intelligence agencies on this matter?"

"Yes," Grant said. "Cooperation seems to be at a peak level. We need to keep it there and we need Boswic to join in full time."

Harlan raised an eyebrow and nodded slowly. No one working for Boswic made any comments.

"I'll let all of you take a little time to get your minds around this situation," Grant said. "Good luck and we'll stay in close touch." He stood, shook hands, and turned toward the door.

Knowing some timely action would be necessary, Colt figured he and Linda would be making a trip to Jamaica in the near future.

Chapter 10

On his island off the western shore of Finland, Ivan Titov leaned back in his desk chair and thought about what was ahead.

And there was a lot to think about.

The new quantum computer would be installed in their new headquarters in Jamaica. He wasn't sure why the Kremlin didn't prefer to keep it in Moscow, but he figured he would find out later. He knew Denis Andreev would be joining them in Jamaica to be directly involved in all the financial maneuvering. Maybe they thought it was necessary for Denis to have firsthand access to the quantum computer?

He figured if he, Sergei, and Denis executed correctly in getting the gold, the CIA would never know what they had done. Neither would the FBI or anyone else, especially the Federal Reserve and the United States Mint.

The Poseidon Initiative needed a lot of funding and, in addition to the quantum computer, his team would also use a new supercomputer supplied by the Chinese to support that purpose too. Denis Andreev would work closely with the scientists and technicians on their team to that end.

The Federal Reserve would never know a lot of their money was stolen. The Fed's records would show the money flowing to several dummy corporations who would be camouflaged by fake activities with the World Bank.

The dummy corporations would appear as legitimate organizations involved in international projects run by corporations established by Russia and China.

Ivan knew the chess masters in Moscow who were developing the strategy would consider all possible countermoves the Americans would make.

Ivan laughed. He was confident the Americans would never figure out all the details of the plan his team would be using. His team would have too many options and they would use the new computers to thoroughly analyze all the options and always select the optimal one.

From his perspective, life was good and he planned on it getting better.

The American Federal Reserve System was created in 1913 as a response to prior financial panics and bank runs.

Ivan chuckled. They were now going to get a run they would never detect, until it was too late.

He remembered the Federal Reserve advertised four duties: The first was to conduct the nation's monetary policy by influencing monetary and credit conditions in the economy. Next the Fed supervised and regulated banking institutions to ensure the soundness of the nation's systems. Then they maintained stability by containing systemic risk.

Lastly, they provided financial services to depository institutions and played a major role in operating the nation's payments system.

Ivan continued to chuckle.

This last role of the Federal Reserve System would be the one his team would take full advantage of. The new transactions the Fed would be handling would look like normal business. The dummy corporations Moscow and

Beijing had set up would officially be providing the funding his team needed under the guise of doing necessary work for the Chinese Embassy and the Russian Embassy in Jamaica.

His team would receive billions of dollars to finish construction of some new approved infrastructure in Jamaica. However, that infrastructure would secretly be used for launching the Poseidon Missiles.

Soon he would have it all set up.

"Is there something amusing?" Sergei asked as he walked through the doorway into Ivan's office.

"Your timing is perfect. I was sitting here reviewing our strategy and tactics for our new corporation's activity. Many of them will require your expertise as well and that of Denis Andreev."

"Is he going to start meeting with us in person?"

"Once we get setup in Jamaica."

"Do we have a schedule yet?" Sergei asked.

"There are a lot of variables being worked out," Ivan said. "I'm told by the Kremlin we'll get a schedule soon."

"Any new issues I should know about?"

"Nothing specific," Ivan said. "I received the usual intelligence briefing. It has to do with maintaining leverage against the Americans. I didn't get any new details. I'm told we don't need to worry about our master plan, just follow orders. I was reminded we're being paid very well to make the necessary tactical decisions as things progress."

"Do you have any more details on where all the money is coming from?"

"Why does that matter as long as we get the money?"

Sergei shrugged.

"Are you worried about getting paid?" Ivan asked.

"Do we have the responsibility of paying any of the people who'll be working for us?"

Ivan laughed.

"What's so funny?"Sergei asked.

Ivan leaned forward. "Why are you suddenly worried

about the funding?" We know Denis will be handling that and he's going to be on our team in Jamaica."

"People who don't get their money can get pretty vicious. Do you think we're going to be directly responsible for making sure everyone in Jamaica who works on The Poseidon Initiative gets paid?"

"Don't worry. Everyone will get paid, especially us."

Sergei leaned forward. "Randall is still around and we know he can screw everything up."

"He probably won't be involved in any of the money situation; besides he's going to be eliminated real soon anyway."

"Maybe."

"Why are you so skeptical all of a sudden?" Ivan asked.

"I've been reviewing things too and I think we need to be real careful we don't leave a lot of loose ends that could cause us some big problems later on."

"Don't forget, we're not responsible for developing the strategy. We just have to follow orders. We need to develop the specific tactics we'll use, and then execute," Ivan said.

"This is a huge undertaking, and our tactics might need to cover a really broad area at times."

"That's why Denis is on our team to take care of our funding in Jamaica and the hacking into the Federal Reserve System," Ivan said.

"Also, our team is responsible for making sure the underwater missiles are launched successfully. We have a lot of responsibility for a huge variety of technical, financial, and security aspects."

"I think we can handle it," Ivan replied. "Are you still game?"

"Of course," Sergei said, "but we'll need to be extremely careful."

Ivan nodded slowly. "I'm sure we will be."

"This will never work unless the plans and the execution are both perfect."

Ivan continued to nod. “We’ll check and doublecheck everything constantly.”

Sergei hesitated for a moment and then gave a thumbs-up.

Chapter 11

Colt sat beside Linda in a conference room at Boswic. They both looked across the large table at Blake.

"Jim told me NSA had intercepted some more phone calls and funding was being discussed for launching Poseidon Missiles," Colt said. "Since Linda and I are going to be the primary field agents from Boswic involved in all of this, Jim suggested we have another discussion with you on the financial aspects of what Russia and China will probably want to do."

"How is that relevant to what your responsibilities will be?" Blake asked.

"Jim thinks it's good for us to have a better understanding of the whole scope of what we're getting into," Linda said. "Colt and I read your paper covering multiple aspects of global financing. Jim wants us to stay updated on your thinking in that regard." Linda gave a slight shrug. "We all know there must be a big money flow going to support the latest activity by Russia and China we've discovered. It could come in handy for Colt and me to be more aware of some additional aspects of that."

Blake nodded and leaned forward. "I have new concerns about the powers in the ownership hierarchy of the Federal Reserve. There seems to be more collusion between the World Bank and our Federal Reserve System than I previously thought. The financial aspects are too complicated to get into any level of detail with you."

Colt narrowed his eyes. "Try us. Linda and I need to know what's going on."

Blake hesitated.

"You can summarize a lot of the details." Colt leaned forward.

"The FBI has teamed with the CIA to beef up security at the World Bank," Blake said. "The FBI is concentrating on the domestic considerations. The CIA has been looking into all the international aspects."

"How does that relate to our Federal Reserve System?" Linda asked.

"Remember, I told you it was complicated," Blake said. "Let's just say it looks like the main pipeline for funding any big project for launching Poseidon Missiles goes through the World Bank via the IMF and our Federal Reserve System is involved in a part of that."

Colt narrowed his eyes. "Go on and give us some more details. Linda and I already know a little bit about this stuff."

"You have to back off and look at the big picture to even get a hint of what's going on," Blake said. "We'll call the big picture the global financial system."

Colt and Linda remained silent.

Blake leaned forward. "Speaking globally, the most prominent international financial institutions are the IMF, the World Bank, and the WTO."

"And the WTO is the World Trade Organization?" Colt asked.

Blake nodded. "They negotiate international trade agreements and settle trade disputes. Money, of course, is always involved. That's one way they get into the mix of international financing. The World Bank and the IMF do their things, and the details are really complicated."

"Doesn't the World Bank have a lot of different components?" Linda asked.

"Yes," Blake said. "That's one way this gets complicated. It's often referenced as the World Bank Group. It's composed of five different international organizations. They're referred to as agencies, IBRD, IDA, IFC, MIGA, and ICSID. They all play a part in this."

"And you're telling us some of the global money flow has a connection to our Federal Reserve System?" Colt asked.

Blake nodded. "There's a reason why the money is in United States dollars." He went on to give more details.

Linda stared at Blake. "Before you give us any more details, I'd be interested in knowing the full names of those five agencies you mentioned. Just knowing those initials isn't really that useful."

"IBRD stands for International Bank for Reconstruction and Development. IDA stands for International Development Association," Blake said. "Actually, when someone is referring to the World Bank, they're generally referring to those two agencies."

Linda and Colt both nodded and took notes.

"IFC stands for International Finance Corporation, MIGA stands for Multilateral Investment Guarantee Agency, and ICSID stands for International Centre for Settlement of Investment Disputes." Blake focused his gaze on both Linda and Colt. "Does that help any?"

"A little," Linda said. "At least I know reconstruction is a major subject within the World Bank Group."

"I can see the potential for creating a lot of confusion." Colt gave a slight shrug. "And that would fit into what the Russians and Chinese would want to do to mask financing any major construction activity anywhere in the world."

"The Federal Reserve Bank of Chicago has an international finance conference every year," Blake said. "They invite researchers and policymakers from a lot of different countries." He looked directly at Colt. "The World Bank Group provides financial assets and advice to countries for the purposes of economic development and eliminating poverty. A few insiders can throw a good smoke screen over selected financing, especially dealing with work done for embassies."

Colt shook his head slowly. "Like the Russian Embassy and the Chinese Embassy in Jamaica."

Blake nodded.

There was a brief silence.

"Getting on to another aspect of this," Blake said. "A quantum computer was mentioned in some of the intercepted calls. It's going to be used by both Russia and China to move the money around on some new joint projects they're planning."

"The quantum computer the CIA informed us about?" Colt asked.

Blake nodded. "And the Chinese will also be using one of their new supercomputers to handle some of the financial transactions."

"Would you brief us on how the Chinese supercomputer works?" Linda asked.

Blake smiled. "I'm not sure you two want to hear the details."

"Go on," Colt said. "We could use a little more insight into the technical details involved in this. Nick will probably refer to some of them in his future briefings to us. It will be a good thing if we understand more of what he tells us without having to ask a lot of questions."

Blake hesitated a moment and then said, "The new Chinese supercomputer is based on a Field-Programmable Gate Array. The technology is commonly referred to as FPGA. It facilitates running complex algorithms a lot faster.

The primary programming language for the advanced algorithms is Java. A lot of experts started out with C++ and then flattened it down to a Java code."

"What's the speed of the new supercomputer?" Linda asked.

"Do you know what a FLOP is?" Blake smiled.

"We've heard what Nick mentioned about it," Linda said.

Blake looked at Colt.

"It wouldn't hurt to go over it again," Colt said.

"FLOP stands for floating point operation," Blake replied. "FLOPS are how many per second. It's our primary measure of speed right now."

Colt narrowed his eyes. "If I remember correctly, the computer geeks I knew when I was in college talked about MIPS."

"That stands for millions of instructions per second," Blake said. "We quit using that terminology a long time ago. We use Petaflops now. That's a thousand trillion FLOPS. Or a quadrillion FLOPS. You could also say a thousand teraflops." He smiled. "This new Chinese supercomputer was reported to have achieved a speed of 2.57 Petaflops."

"Do you have any particular point to make with all that?" Colt asked.

Blake leaned forward. "You and Linda asked for this information, didn't you?"

Colt grunted and then asked, "Do you think Russia or China will use the new computers to try to hack into our Federal Reserve System?"

"Someone already is trying to do that. It might be them," Blake said. "We know for sure multiple attempts have been made over the last two weeks."

"So do you have any recommendations for us as far as looking for any particular aspects of all the computer stuff?" Linda asked.

"Not specifically at this time, we'll see how things

develop," Blake said. He glanced at Colt. "Now you and Linda have been updated on the latest aspects of the current situation involving finance and computers that might have some relevance to your upcoming mission."

Colt exhaled slowly. "Yeah, and we probably know as much as we want to know about all that right now." He glanced at Linda.

"I can agree with Colt's statement." Linda gave a slight grin as she shook her head. "My brain is about saturated with the behind-the scenes financial details."

A brief silence ensued.

"We're in an odd position," Blake said. "We need to help the Federal Reserve, but we must be leery of the owners, the descendants who are still carrying on the work of their fathers. We know for sure the families of many of the original owners are still in place and they're all very secretive."

"Linda and I appreciate the information," Colt replied. "It could turn out to be really useful to be more aware of the different aspects we're going to be dealing with, and the financial aspects are certainly part of the picture."

Linda gave a slow nod.

"One thing we've learned from the intercepted phone calls is that we're facing a lot of new threats," Blake said. "We all need to give this huge challenge our best effort to succeed in preventing a catastrophe for the United States."

Knowing Blake's statement was accurate, Colt felt determination swell within him to do all he could to eliminate this latest threat to the continued existence of the United States.

Chapter 12

On his private island near the western shore of Finland, Ivan Titov sat in his office and fished an expensive Cuban cigar out of a container on his desk. He had just learned of the 7.7 magnitude earthquake in the vicinity of Jamaica. He wondered if that might delay their moving plans for a bit.

He took a deep breath and tried to relax.

Leaning slightly forward, Ivan flicked his lighter and held the flame to the end of his cigar. He savored a long puff and then stared out the window at the pouring rain.

His phone rang at that moment.

Ivan could see it was a call from the Kremlin. He quickly reached for the phone and answered. After a brief conversation, he disconnected and again stared out the window.

Despite the weather, things were looking better on many aspects of the project now. For one thing, there would be no delay in setting up their new headquarters in Jamaica. He puffed slowly on his cigar while he waited for Sergei Nikitin to enter the room.

When Sergei walked through the doorway, Ivan noted a slight look of irritation on his partner's face.

After Sergei hung up his wet coat, Ivan stood and waved him toward one of the chairs at the round conference table near his desk.

"Is everything going okay?" Ivan asked.

Sergei shook his head as he pulled the heavily padded chair away from the table and sat down.

"What's wrong?" Ivan took a long slow puff on his cigar and plopped down in an empty chair across from Sergei.

"We have some unexpected problems," Sergei said.

Ivan didn't comment. He took another puff on his cigar and waited for Sergei to continue.

"Have you heard about the earthquake?" Sergei asked.

"Yeah and I've received reports that we sustained no damage to any of our new facilities that have just been built."

Sergei waved a hand back and forth. "This was a big quake, and it might be a new trend."

"I doubt it. This is the first one since 1993 and the one before that was in 1907."

"Did you do that research?"

Ivan narrowed his eyes and took a puff on his cigar. "No, the information came with the report I just received."

"Well, I did a little research myself and found out Jamaica is in a geologically active zone. Things could be changing."

"They've been in a geologically active zone for centuries," Ivan said, "and you just heard the frequency of quakes over the last one hundred plus years. Even though there were a couple of aftershocks, our experts in Moscow don't expect us to have any more problems with earthquakes in Jamaica for at least twenty-five more years." He chuckled. "I think we'll have time to launch the missiles and bring down the United States."

"And you mentioned all of our facilities there are okay, right?"

"Right, our experts at the site checked everything multiple times before they issued their report."

Sergei gave a dismissive wave. "Guess I can't argue with that logic."

Ivan took a long puff on his cigar.

Sergei looked around the room. "I need some hot coffee."

Ivan motioned toward a side table by the window. "Help yourself." He stood and followed Sergei.

"When do we plan to go to Jamaica?" Sergei asked, as he grabbed a large mug off the table and filled it with coffee.

"Tomorrow," Ivan said. "The Kremlin assured me we won't need to delay. Everything is all set up."

"Including the quantum computer?"

"Yes and the first three Poseidon Missiles will arrive shortly after we get there. We'll need to supervise their setup."

"Our work crew is there?"

"They will be tomorrow."

After the two men were seated again, Sergei leaned forward. "After we get down there, what are our priorities?"

Ivan flashed a big smile. "We'll have Denis inspect our new computers and put them to good use right away. He can start doing some hacking into certain key banking systems. We'll get everyone organized, and then we'll have our experts work on improving the guidance systems for the missiles."

"Using the quantum computer?"

"Yes and I've already hired the man to head up our new hi-tech activity."

"Who?"

"Maxim Solomon," Ivan said in a confident tone. "You might know about him."

"Not yet," Sergei replied. "What's his specialty?"

Ivan leaned forward and explained.

"How soon after we get to Jamaica do we need to produce the results?"

"I don't have a written schedule from the Kremlin yet,

but they told me we'll need to make an impact on the United States within the first week we're there."

Sergei exhaled sharply and spilled coffee on the table. "Even with Maxim's expertise and everyone else's expertise, this is going to be a big challenge for us."

"I think we'll do okay," Ivan said. "You'll see. Are you ready to get started?"

Sergei narrowed his eyes. "I guess I'm as ready as I'll ever be."

"Our private plane is fueled and ready to go. We'll plan to be in Jamaica before the end of the day tomorrow. Denis Andreev and Maxim Solomon will already be there waiting for us."

"Is the quantum computer ready to use?"

"Maxim will lead the team that will test it and make sure it's functioning correctly."

Sergei gave a slow nod.

"By the way, we're going to execute one of our backup plans tonight in Tampa," Ivan said. "We'll try to get a nuke through the port there."

"What kind of nuke?"

"Tsar Bomba, 50-megatons"

"What if we lose it?"

"That won't be a huge problem. We have several of them and it's our oldest one. It's a risk worth taking."

"If we get it through, what are we going to do with it?"

"Move it to a strategic location in the United States where it can do the most damage right now and detonate it."

Chapter 13

The next morning Colt and Linda sat with Harlan and Jim at the round conference table in Harlan's office.

"Let's take a moment to relax before we start this meeting," Harlan said, as he took a sip from a large mug filled to the brim with hot coffee. He gestured toward the coffee service on a counter behind him. "Grab a mug. We have a lot to discuss and a lot to think about."

Colt and Linda both stood and walked to the counter. Each picked up a mug and filled it.

Just like Harlan, Jim already had a full mug.

After taking a slow drink of coffee, Harlan looked at Colt. "I've had several long conversations with Charles Andrews, the CIA Director, and he told me he's dealing with a lot of new threats. He wants you to command the taskforce he's putting together. You'll lead the team in the field and deal with a lot of diverse subjects, computer issues, financial issues, nuclear bombs, various hi-tech missiles, and, of course, assassins. He seems to have a high opinion of you. "

"That's a wide range of issues you mentioned," Colt said.

Harlan narrowed his eyes. "Well, are you game or not?"

Colt hesitated for a moment and then nodded.

Harlan and Jim each gave a thumbs-up and turned toward Linda.

"Am I on the taskforce?" Linda asked.

"Yes," Harlan said. "As usual, you'll help Colt in the field. You'll need to stay with him step by step."

Linda gave a slight smile. "I can do that."

"Boswic has a big role to play in the upcoming mission. We want to do our part to help eliminate at least some of the huge threats Charles referenced," Jim said. "Blake will work closely with you and provide a lot of research and analysis. As usual, he'll also work closely with all the intelligence agencies."

Harlan looked directly at Linda. "I don't think Boswic could offer any better support to the FBI and CIA than we have since our inception. Your work with Colt has contributed a lot toward that."

Linda smiled and didn't comment.

Harlan took a sip of coffee and stared over his cup at Colt and Linda. "Any questions?"

"Are we going to try to eliminate the threat from the Poseidon Missiles?" Colt asked.

"That will be our highest priority," Harlan said. "Charles mentioned NSA had intercepted several phone calls where Jamaica and the Russian and Chinese embassies there were mentioned a lot."

"Does that mean Jamaica is a possible launch site for the missiles?" Linda asked.

Harlan nodded slowly.

Linda narrowed her eyes. "It seems like our Military would be taking the lead on this."

"It might come to that, but Jim and I attended a high-level meeting with the CIA and FBI where that was explained." Harlan gestured to Jim.

"Our Armed Forces will get involved if we fail, but the President wants to try an all-civilian approach first," Jim said. "The President knows what Russia and China are doing through all our good intelligence work, and he wants to avoid another world war if possible."

"So, he thinks our new taskforce will be capable of resolving this?" Colt asked.

Jim shrugged. "He obviously wants to give it a try."

"Resolving that wide a range of issues is going to be quite a challenge," Linda said.

Harlan leaned forward. "You and Colt have already proven capable of resolving this level of threats and we stayed out of World War III. I think the President wants to give you another shot at it. Getting involved in projects like this is what we're in business for." Harlan wrinkled his brow. "However, this one is starting out a little more dangerous than usual. Earlier, NSA picked up bits and pieces of multiple phone conversations coming from those islands just off the western shore of Finland into various locations in the United States. Assassins were mentioned, assassins to knock off the Americans."

"And those Americans are us?" Colt asked while making a sweeping gesture which included both him and Linda.

Harlan nodded. "You in particular."

There was a brief silence.

"The CIA taskforce was also mentioned in the intercepted calls, but we don't yet know any details about what was discussed," Harlan said.

"You indicated NSA didn't get any complete conversations, right?" Jim asked.

"I was informed all those calls were expertly encrypted." Harlan gave a slight shrug. "NSA reminded me those guys are well funded, oil money, drug money, among other things. They can afford advanced technology as well as expert help. We were fortunate to extract as much information as we did."

"I'm glad CIA agents and FBI agents are both on the

taskforce. Working together, we'll get everything sorted out," Jim said. "Maybe we'll succeed in shutting down a lot of threats before they get started."

Harlan rubbed his chin. "It looks like we're going to be dealing with one hell of a combination of countries, people, and issues. China poses a different dimension than we've had before. We know they're working closely with the Russians to bring us down and right now they're letting the Russians take the lead."

"Why are they helping the Russians?" Linda asked.

"Profits," Harlan said. "It's all about profits, using big money to produce more big money. The Russians want to regain their status as a major world power and China wants to become the world's top economic power."

"And they both are up to more than profits." Jim stared at Colt and Linda. "They both want to destroy us."

"That's certainly part of the equation," Harlan said. He scanned the faces around the table. "After they accomplish their mutual goal of destroying us, I guess they'll fight it out among themselves. They both can't be number one in the world."

A brief silence ensued.

Harlan leaned forward. "Now we need to get to some immediate business. One of the calls NSA intercepted was from Moscow into the Washington DC area, likely to some moles who apparently think they have a completely secure line. But NSA can break into it." He looked at Colt. "You've been targeted for elimination at the Port of Tampa tonight."

"Why am I going to the port?" Colt asked. "And how do our enemies know about that."

Harlan looked directly at Colt. "A nuke is scheduled to arrive on a ship from Moscow. A lot of drugs will also be coming in. You and Linda have been successful in this scenario before and both the FBI and CIA want you to take care of this situation again," Harlan said. "To answer your other question, our enemies apparently have some moles in our intelligence agencies."

Colt figured the threat matrix presented to Grant Winston, the local FBI chief, everyday was becoming more ominous by the hour. He knew Grant maintained close coordination with the CIA concerning all the events Boswic was expected to be involved with.

Harlan rubbed his chin slowly and looked at Jim. "Go ahead and lead this discussion. You've just discussed all the details with Grant."

Jim pointed toward a large screen on the wall that displayed various satellite images of the Port of Tampa. He used a laser pointer to highlight an area and then glanced at Colt and Linda.

"Here's where you'll enter the port," Jim said. "You'll follow the same procedure as you did a few months ago. Mack Thompson will be with you. He's flying down from Washington."

Colt loved working with Mack, the CIA's top field agent. He knew Linda shared his opinion. The three of them made a great team.

"We know there will be assassins waiting for you to show up, but we don't know what their exact plan is," Jim said. "NSA is still trying to decrypt all the intercepted calls."

Harlan nodded. "Grant told me a couple of times he was anxiously awaiting the next update. He hopes we'll get a lot more details on every aspect of what we're dealing with."

"How do they know we've discovered there's an incoming nuke and how do they know we'll be the ones who'll show up to intercept it?" Linda asked.

"They're making assumptions, I'm sure," Harlan said. "The experts in Moscow know we've found out before and they know who our most expert team is. I'm sure they're doing a lot of planning for all the measures they're going to take to safeguard the nuke."

Jim nodded. "Their experts in the Kremlin know a lot about us and they've proven to be smart people." He went on to explain more details about their strategy tonight.

"When is Mack going to be here?" Colt asked.

Harlan glanced at his watch. "He should be landing about now. Grant's going to pick him up and come over here."

"Do we need to know more about the type of nuke we're trying to intercept?" Linda asked.

Harlan gestured to Jim. "It's time for Blake to join us."

After Jim made a phone call, Blake popped into the room.

Harlan gave a quick summary of the situation.

"So, Grant and Mack are coming over in a few minutes?" Blake asked.

"That's the plan," Harlan said. "We'll discuss all the relevant details."

Harlan narrowed his eyes and focused on Colt and Linda. "The assassins will probably be smarter this time and some of them might have a personal grudge now. The more you know about every damned aspect of this, the safer you'll be."

"We'll be careful, really careful," Colt said. He and Linda both gave a thumbs-up signal.

Harlan grunted and then turned toward Blake. "Give us some details about the nuke."

"According to the intelligence I received, they're shipping in their largest nuke. They've named it Tsar Bomba," Blake said. "It was originally intended to be a 100-megaton bomb but it was scaled back to 50-megatons. With the nuclear warhead, it weighs 2, 275 tons. It's a 3-stage bomb that's 1,570 times as powerful as the two combined we dropped on Japan."

Blake went on to give more details.

"They won't want to lose it," Colt said. "They're going to do a lot to protect it tonight."

Harlan narrowed his eyes. "They don't want to be too conspicuous. Maybe they won't do too much."

Jim nodded.

A brief silence ensued.

Jim looked back at Blake. "Anything new on the big picture from all the research and analysis you've just completed?"

"Quite a bit," Blake said. "Nick and I have received a lot of new Intel, and we've been comparing notes every few hours," Blake said. "The Russians have a new initiative they've named The Poseidon Initiative."

"That has to involve launching the Poseidon Missile," Colt said.

"Yes, multiple Poseidon Missiles to be exact," Blake said. "I suspect Titov and Nikitin are involved in all of this, but I don't think they're masterminding anything. They're both billionaires and they're smart, but there appears to be a higher intellectual layer running the overall operation."

Blake started to say more just as Grant and Mack were escorted into the room.

Chapter 14

After arriving in Jamaica, Ivan Titov sat at a large conference room table in the Russian Embassy and glanced out a window at the ocean scene near Kingston. He admired the view for a moment and then looked at Sergei Nikitin, Denis Andreev, and Maxim Solomon who sat across from him.

"Our new underground headquarters is almost finished," Ivan said. "The tunnels have been dug, and the remaining work is nearing completion." He looked at Denis. "We have plenty of funding to put in all the latest innovations we want, right?"

Denis nodded. "That's correct. All the advanced missile launching structures utilizing the latest technology will be installed and we can make a wide range of adjustments if we want to."

Ivan nodded slowly as he scanned the faces around the table.

"We have another issue to deal with. Something else just came up," Ivan said.

"Does this have anything to do with Randall?" Maxim asked.

"You're our computer specialist. Why are you concerned about Randall?" Ivan asked.

Maxim gave a slight shrug. "He screwed everything up the Kremlin was trying to do before and all the computer work involved was impacted."

Ivan reached toward his cigar box. He opened the lid and retrieved one of his classic Cuban cigars. "I've been informed Randall's not directly involved with what's going on down here at this exact moment." He took the wrapping off his cigar and looked at Maxim. "But he probably will be."

"And that's why I'm concerned." Maxim leaned forward and flashed a big grin. "Is this something Stephan needs to take care of?"

"Maybe," Ivan said as he reached for his lighter and clicked it on. Positioning the flame over the end of the cigar, he took some big puffs. "I've heard Randall is going to lead a new CIA taskforce that's being setup to combat the latest threats," Ivan said. "I'm pretty sure he'll be at the Port of Tampa tonight to try to intercept the nuke the Kremlin is shipping in."

Sergei looked at Ivan. "You hear about that from one of our moles?"

"Yeah, on our way down here," Ivan said.

"Do you think the taskforce will come to Jamaica?" Denis asked.

"We don't know yet, too early to tell," Ivan said. "The moles will keep us informed."

Maxim leaned forward. "If they do come here, we can't let them shut us down like they've done before."

"Don't worry about it." Ivan puffed steadily on his cigar and looked calmly at the three men sitting across the table from him. "We won't let them impact what we're doing in Jamaica. With China being our partner on this project we now have more support than we've ever had before."

There was a brief silence.

"Do you know yet when the missiles will be delivered?" Sergei asked with a hint of concern in his voice.

"They were supposed to have already arrived." Ivan shrugged. "Of course, I called and inquired about that. I was told there was a slight delay in the funding for the activity, and the problem has been corrected."

Everyone looked at Denis.

"The Kremlin had a concern about how hidden the funding for the missile delivery would be," Denis said. "I changed some things around on how the World Bank provides the funds to the World Trade Organization. Everything is okay now. The missiles are headed to our location."

Ivan kept his gaze focused on Denis. "We need to spend a lot of money going forward. Are all the other aspects of our funding in place?"

Denis gave a thumbs-up. "I don't anticipate any further problems."

"Good," Ivan said. "We don't need any additional issues we have to resolve. We have enough as it is." He took another puff from his cigar and scanned the faces around the table. "There's one other thing we need to discuss right now."

Sergei raised an eyebrow.

"When I called the Kremlin to inquire about the funding, they informed me the Chinese want to be more active in what we're doing here in Jamaica," Ivan said.

No one commented. Each man across from Ivan narrowed his eyes and waited for him to continue.

"They supplied a large amount of funding for developing the Poseidon Missile and they're supplying most of our funding for going forward on all of our active projects to bring the United States down," Ivan said, "so I guess they have a right to be more directly involved in what we're doing here."

"Get to the point. What do you want to tell us?" Maxim

asked.

"Three of their people are going to join us here in Jamaica in the next few days." Ivan took a long puff from his cigar. "They are Bing Yaw, a Chinese military leader, Chen Wan, a Chinese weapons specialist, and Ho Cham, their top assassin."

"Exactly what are they going to do?" Sergei asked.

"That's not fully clear yet," Ivan said. "I asked a lot of questions, and I didn't get many definite answers. I was told the Kremlin was working closely with all the top Chinese officials and we would be getting specific instructions as things developed."

"Any guesses?" Maxim asked.

"I think the Chinese Government wants to have firsthand knowledge of exactly what we do step by step so they can offer support in needed areas to ensure we succeed," Ivan said. "It's logical they would have some of their key people here with us. Our success against the United States is their success."

"They're sending their top assassin here. Are they expecting us to be attacked?" Denis asked.

"I'm told they don't want to take any chances." Ivan shrugged. "We've done our best to keep everything secretive, but it'll be good to have some extra support if the Americans find out what we're doing."

Sergei nodded slowly.

"If the Americans discover what we're doing and send a taskforce down here, do you think Randall will be a big factor this time?" Maxim asked.

"Most likely," Ivan said, "he certainly gave us a lot of headaches on many of our earlier projects. But to cause us any big problems, he'll have to penetrate our underground facility and we're well protected."

There was a brief silence.

Sergei looked thoughtfully at Denis "Are you still going to move some gold bullion down here to supplement our funding needs?"

Denis nodded. "It's good to have backup plans for certain contingencies if something goes wrong with the usual funding."

"Right," Ivan said. "It's critical the hoard of people who'll be working down here get paid on time. Having gold on site will help us get the support we need from the local banks."

"When does the Kremlin expect me to have the quantum computer ready to tap into the Federal Reserve System?" Maxim asked.

Ivan started to answer just as the phone in front of him rang. It was his secure line. He checked the caller ID and looked at Sergei and Maxim. "I think we're about to know more about the subject the two of you just referenced."

"Using the quantum computer to facilitate having some gold removed from the Federal Reserve Bank in New York?" Maxim asked.

"I'm guessing that's it. I requested more details from the Kremlin about that a few hours ago," Ivan said, as he picked up the phone.

After he finished his conversation and disconnected, Ivan regarded Maxim carefully and said, "The Kremlin wants you to proceed as fast as possible on having the quantum computer in top working condition. They want the work down here to start as soon as the scientists arrive, and they want all the backup plans to be in place to ensure everyone is paid on time. Our bosses in Moscow will tolerate no delays in launching the missiles on schedule."

"Did they mention anything else they're doing right now?" Sergei asked.

"Yeah," Ivan said. "They've never wanted to rely on just one project to satisfy all of their objectives."

Denis grunted. "Or as the Americans say, they don't want to put all their eggs in one basket."

Maxim gave a short laugh as he waited for Ivan to

provide some details.

"We have a lot of conventional nukes. Our experts on warfare want to position some of them in strategic locations in the United States," Ivan said. "That's another one of the backup plans the Kremlin always wants to have."

"Our main strategists, the chess masters?" Sergei asked.

"Probably," Ivan said. "They're always involved with major aspects of the planning."

"Do they have any nukes on the way?" Maxim asked.

"A Tsar Bomba is being shipped into the Port of Tampa tonight," Ivan said. I guess that will be followed by a lot of our more conventional nukes going into other ports."

"Randall is there in Tampa." Denis narrowed his eyes. "Is the Kremlin worried about our nuke being intercepted?"

"They're interested in knocking Randall off before he can lead the taskforce down here," Ivan said. "We have the most people and the most contacts in Tampa, and we haven't yet established the help we need in any other port. They're positioning some top assassins at the Port of Tampa to protect the Tsar Bomba and knock Randall off at the same time."

"We've tried this before, but Randall and his team not only survived, but they also intercepted the previous nukes we've shipped. Is the Kremlin doing anything different this time?" Denis asked.

"If Randall shows up, he'll get some surprises," Ivan said. "The Tsar Bomba is in a better container than the other nukes. Even though it's larger, it will be a lot harder to detect."

Chapter 15

After Mack and Grant entered the conference room at Boswic, Colt watched the two men ease into two empty chairs at the table.

"The CIA has compiled new intelligence," Mack said. "There's one hell of a lot going on. Ivan Titov and Sergei Nikitin are in Kingston, Jamaica now, and we think that's going to be the launch site for the Poseidon Missiles." Mack leaned forward and gave more details about what the CIA now knew about The Poseidon Initiative.

"What happened to using La Orchila north of Caracas?" Colt asked.

"Too many coral reefs and some other disadvantages," Mack said. "Kingston's the spot. They're setting up there now."

"And we learned all this from intercepted phone calls?" Harlan asked.

"Most of it," Mack said. "The rest was from adding two plus two. Paul and Nick reviewed all their thinking with me just before I left McLean to come down here."

"Is the nuke coming in tonight part of the strategy for The Poseidon Initiative?" Jim asked.

"We don't think so," Mack said. "It looks like that's something separate cooked up by the chess masters in Moscow. It could be some kind of backup strategy devised by the hoard of strategists at the Kremlin."

"So, the chess masters are still deeply involved in the strategy developed by the Kremlin?" Linda asked.

Mack nodded. "I'm told that's the case. They've been heavily involved in the strategy and the tactics from the beginning of all this."

"That's consistent with what I've heard from Paul and Nick," Blake said. He glanced at Mack. "But I just talked with them earlier this morning and they didn't mention the latest information you're giving us."

All the Boswic employees at the table looked curiously at Mack.

"Paul, Nick, and I were briefed by NSA just before I left," Mack said. "Since I was coming down here, they decided it was unnecessary to call you back to bring you up to date."

Blake nodded.

"The Russians probably want to get the Tsar Bomba into a strategic location somewhere around here." Colt looked at Mack. "You could be right; it's likely part of a backup plan the chess masters have developed."

Mack gave a short laugh. "That's definitely the way the analysts in the CIA have it figured."

"This whole thing is probably Russia's and China's joint initiative to bring the United States down," Harlan said, "and The Poseidon Initiative is a major part of it."

"Does anyone know if Titov and Nikitin are actually running The Poseidon Initiative?" Linda asked.

"We're not absolutely sure yet, but that's our best guess," Mack said. "We think that's why they're in Jamaica."

Harlan leaned toward Mack. "Among the other things, we need to keep trying to follow the money."

"Right," Mack said. "We'll keep working on that no matter how well they cover their tracks."

Harlan grunted. "China is probably involved in all aspects of this, the technology, the weapons, the money, the planning, and the execution."

Everyone nodded.

Colt knew things were going to escalate, that was a no-brainer. He was glad they were having an opportunity to be better informed about what and who they were dealing with.

Chapter 16

That night at the Port of Tampa, Colt, Linda, and Mack watched the big crane being moved into position as the large ship from Nicaragua docked.

NSA had intercepted some calls from Moscow into the Russian spy base in Nicaragua. Enough details of the Russia conversations had been decrypted for the CIA to have good knowledge of the plan for the nuke.

Grant had elected to stay in the control center and monitor the activity.

Along with Linda and Mack, Colt pointed his binoculars toward the lighted area along the docks. Groups of tough-looking men formed the various crews, and no obvious inspectors were on the scene. He trained his binoculars on the large bulk cargo vessel, same situation—tough-looking crew and no inspectors.

After watching the activity for another minute, Colt fished his secure satellite phone out of a pocket and punched a digit.

"They're almost finished. No inspectors," Colt whispered.

"As usual someone got paid off at the port here," Grant said. "Can the three of you get closer without being detected?"

"Yes."

"Do it. Get close enough to check the containers."

"Executing," Colt said. He disconnected and motioned to the other two. They eased toward the docks.

In a couple of minutes, Colt stopped in a dark area behind a large stack of metal containers.

Mack and Linda moved further to the right.

After removing a small high-tech device from a pocket, Colt turned it on and pointed it toward a large odd-looking container.

No reading.

Colt studied the large metal container for a moment and then moved closer to it.

This had to be the container for the nuke. It was different than any he had ever seen and it was larger than the other containers.

After moving to within five feet of the odd container, he pointed the device again. It showed a positive reading.

Colt punched a digit on his phone. Grant answered.

"We found the nuke. Judging by the size of the container, it probably holds the Tsar Bomba we were expecting," Colt said.

"A logical deduction."

Colt gave the exact location of the large container.

"Time for you three to get the hell out of there," Grant said. "I'll send in the SWAT team, careful on your way out, probably some assassins in the area have been expecting you to show up."

"Roger." Colt disconnected and signaled Linda and Mack. The three huddled in the darkest place they could find.

"Grant ordered us to leave immediately," Colt said. "We'll stay low and move fast back toward the Hummer."

Linda and Mack nodded.

Colt adopted a low crouch and moved toward the exit. Linda followed about five yards behind. Mack stayed about five yards behind Linda.

While constantly scanning his surroundings, Colt selected the darkest areas on the path toward their destination.

"There's some movement about thirty yards up to our right," Linda whispered into her tactical microphone.

Colt saw the movement and the protruding rifle pointed his way. After making a quick adjustment, Colt fired three times in less than a second.

The dark figure dropped.

A rifle clanged on the concrete.

Colt, Linda, and Mack each stopped and carefully checked the area. No other threats were evident at the moment.

Telling Mack and Linda to hold their positions, Colt cautiously moved in the dim light toward the barely distinguishable prone figure.

After picking up the SIG 550, Colt inspected the corpse. Three bullets in the chest, no body armor, definitely dead, Russian features.

Colt grabbed his secure satellite phone and punched a digit. "Just ran into a sniper. He's dead, area looks clear for the moment. Sniper looks Russian."

"I'll inform the team coming in," Grant said. "They'll clean up. At least you made their job a little easier, one less sniper."

Colt grunted. "No surprise the Russians had some assassins out here. I'm sure the clean-up team will be prepared for a lot more."

"Right," Grant said, "and they have full body armor, automatic weapons, and other special equipment. They'll handle the heavy lifting. Now the three of you get out of there as quickly as you can. Stay alert."

"Roger." Colt disconnected and signaled Mack and Linda to move.

Linda glanced at the SIG 550 Colt held and the dead assassin. She gave a thumbs-up.

Colt returned the gesture. Linda made a good partner, he thought. That could become more and more valuable as their work continued. The overall situation was becoming more complex by the day.

The Russians were obviously using all their assets in the western hemisphere. The ship coming from Nicaragua with the nuclear bomb was an indication of that, Colt thought. The Russians probably had multiple backup plans that would have to be addressed. At least they had good backup from the CIA, FBI, and other intelligence services.

Within another ten minutes, the three warriors moved through an exit and got to their parked Hummer.

After they scanned the area carefully and boarded the Hummer, Linda said, "Guess we handled this okay tonight. I think we did a pretty good job being the advance party for the SWAT team and setting things up for them to seize the incoming bomb."

"Speaking of the bomb," Colt looked at Mack, "have you given much thought to the fact the Tsar Bomba has an explosive power 1,570 times the combined bombs we dropped on Japan?"

"That's hard to comprehend," Mack said. "I hope nothing goes wrong with anyone trying to deactivate it. We certainly don't want it going off in the United States."

Colt and Linda both nodded as Colt drove the Hummer onto a main road and sped away from the Port of Tampa.

"I think we've passed our test tonight," Mack said. "I'm sure our bosses wanted to test us a bit more right now and see how well we can perform our assignments before we go on to bigger things in Jamaica."

"They probably wanted to make sure we haven't accumulated any rush in the last two months," Linda replied.

"Yeah, that's probably part of their thinking," Mack said. "Guess the overall strategy is still based on the President not wanting to take a chance on starting World War III. Too much offense from our Military right now could trigger a nuclear war with the Russians and Chinese."

Colt nodded. "I think we're ready for our next mission. We've shown we're prepared to move on to bigger things right away."

"Like eliminating the Poseidon Missile threat," Linda said. "That looks like it's going to be our biggest challenge ever."

Chapter 17

Early the next morning in Jamaica, Sergei grabbed his secure satellite phone and punched a button. He needed to check on several things. A look of determination flashed across his face as he heard Ivan answer.

"You hear what happened at the port last night?" Sergei asked.

"Not yet."

"Randall eliminated another one of our best assassins and the Americans got the nuke."

"When did you find out?"

"A few minutes ago," Sergei said. "I called one of our moles in the CIA. He had just received the news."

Ivan didn't comment.

"The mole also told me a new taskforce will be coming our way," Sergei said.

"Down here to Jamaica?"

"That's what he heard, and he also heard Randall will lead the taskforce."

"Do the Americans know about The Poseidon Initiative?"

"The mole thinks they know about some of it."

"When will the taskforce come down here?"

"Our mole thinks the mission is going to start soon,

within the next day or two."

"Does our mole know the specific location they're coming to?"

"He knows an area around Kingston is the designated target. He thinks that's because of our embassy being there."

"Will the mole be able to keep us informed on the progress of this new taskforce?" Ivan asked.

"I think so," Sergei said. "He's doing a lot of internal maneuvering to be in a position to do that."

"You're managing our group of assassins now. I saw where you brought Stephan Zak down here. Are you planning on him confronting Randall?"

"I'm sure he'll want to. He hates Randall with a passion. Their encounter in the Boswic parking lot whetted his appetite."

"I'm sure the taskforce will be heavily armed."

"Of course they will. Why are you bringing that up?"

"No particular reason, just thinking."

"I'll give Stephan a call and get his opinion on a few things," Sergei said. "I wanted to call you first and make sure you were up to date."

"Go ahead and call Stephan. We'll sync up on everything before the day is over."

"Talk to you later then." Sergei disconnected and punched in another number.

*****

In a newly developed hidden marina ten miles from the middle of Kingston, Stephan grabbed his vibrating phone and answered.

"Heard from our moles recently?" Sergei asked.

"Yeah, a few minutes ago," Stephan said. "I know Randall will be leading a taskforce that will be coming here. I'm looking forward to kicking some ass when they arrive."

"They'll be well armed."

"We'll be ready."

"Are all your men with you?"

"Yep."

"Do you have a plan?"

"Not yet, we'll work one out."

"I've been thinking about a few things in that regard."

"Such as?"

"You want to eliminate them as quickly as possible, of course."

"Do you have anything specific in mind?" Stephan asked.

"We need to get together and work that out."

"How soon?"

"I want to inspect the new marina, and I'll be there later this morning. I need to meet with Ivan first."

"Tell him I want every possible chance to eliminate Randall. I hate that bastard."

"I'm sure you'll get your chance. I'll see you in a bit."

After hearing Sergei disconnect, Stephan gazed out at the water and clinched a fist.

He hoped Sergei could help construct a brilliant plan. He had always wanted to be on the winning side and that hadn't changed.

Stephan glanced back at the water. A lot of thoughts were rushing into his brain.

The main thought was to get revenge against Randall and he was ready for action.

*****

An hour later, Ivan sat in his underground headquarters and stared across the round conference table in his office at Sergei.

"What's the latest on our plan to hack into the Federal Reserve System?" Sergei asked.

"Maxim and Denis both tell me all the details have been

worked out," Ivan said. "I'm more convinced than ever they can handle it. We can use the extra funding to increase our fortifications down here and we should get a lot of help from Chinese experts as well as from our own Russian experts."

Sergei nodded slowly. "We have a lot on our plate. Do you think we can handle all this at the same time?"

"That's what they pay us for." Ivan gave a slight shrug. "There's no reason to let the quantum computer sit around idle. We need it to control all the aspects of the advanced guidance systems for the Poseidon Missiles. We might as well put it to good use while we're waiting to launch."

"Even with a lot of expert help, trying to do too much worries me. I'm still concerned about our involvement with the additional nuclear bombs the Kremlin wants to ship into various ports in the United States."

"Let's get Denis and Maxim in here," Ivan said. "The four of us need to take some time to completely sync up. We shouldn't do any guesswork. We can't let things get screwed up."

Sergei narrowed his eyes. "That's what I've been trying to tell you."

Ivan reached for his phone.

After Ivan disconnected, Denis and Maxim appeared in less than five minutes.

Each settled into a chair at the round conference table which had seating for six.

"We have a lot to do in a short period of time," Ivan said. "We have to make sure we stay tightly coordinated." He looked at Maxim. "Let me know immediately when the missiles are here."

"The ship arrived an hour ago. They're being unloaded and moved toward the storage facility in the launch area as we speak." Maxim leaned forward, elbows on table. "I didn't know you wanted to be kept informed of every little detail."

"Should you be down there watching what's going on?" Ivan asked.

"I normally would be, but some of my top scientist have already arrived," Maxim said, "I trust them to take care of all the details for storing the missiles at the launch site."

"Another important detail I didn't know about." Ivan shook his head slowly. "That's why we need to have this meeting. All of us must keep track of every significant detail about what's going on as things progress. That's the only way we can all make the correct tactical decisions as things evolve."

Maxim and Denis each gave a slow nod.

"Are you expecting everything to get real complicated right away down here?" Denis asked.

"That's a definite possibility," Ivan said. "We know a taskforce is coming and Colt Randall will be leading it. He was a major factor in shutting down the last big Russian project a few months ago."

Sergei's gaze took in both Maxim and Denis. "We weren't directly involved in that. But the people who were involved took Randall too lightly and didn't prepare as well as they should have. We can't make that same mistake."

Maxim and Denis both nodded and didn't comment.

Denis looked at Maxim. "I have all the details available on how we need to handle the funding." He paused. "When do you think you'll have the quantum computer ready to tackle that?"

"The rest of my scientists should arrive this afternoon," Maxim said. "As soon as they're settled, I'll have a meeting with them and discuss all the relevant details. The quantum computer is in place and able to function. I think we should be ready to go by tomorrow morning."

Denis scanned the faces around the table. "Should we all plan to meet and discuss the details tomorrow morning?"

"Let's make it tomorrow afternoon," Maxim said. "Some of the scientists have had a long trip. I need to give them a chance to adjust to their surroundings down here. We'll have to work out the specifics of who will concentrate on the missile guidance systems and who will concentrate on hacking into the Federal Reserve System."

"Okay, we know the general situation for that." Ivan looked at Sergei. "You're coordinating all our defense preparations. When will the Chinese arrive?"

Sergei glanced at his watch. "They should have already landed at the airport. I have a group waiting there to bring them directly here."

"So, we should be able to discuss things with them within the hour?" Ivan asked.

Sergei nodded.

With his gaze focusing on both Ivan and Sergei, Denis leaned forward. "I understand there are three of them, right?"

"Bing Yaw, a Chinese military leader, Chen Wan, a Chinese weapons specialist, and Ho Cham, one of their top assassins should be joining us shortly," Sergei said. "Yaw and Wan will coordinate directly with Ivan. Cham will coordinate directly with me."

Denis turned toward Ivan. "Will they have any responsibility for the financing?"

"China will continue to provide funds, but they'll have no direct influence on how you set it up," Ivan said. "You'll continue to manage the money flow like you've been doing."

Denis gave a short nod and smiled.

"When the Chinese contingent arrives, we'll review all the basics and make sure we're all on the same page before we continue with The Poseidon Initiative," Ivan said. "The most important thing is to launch the missiles as soon as possible."

Denis looked at Ivan. "So, you and Bing Yaw will run the overall operation here?"

"I'll still be the one in charge, but I'm sure Yaw will offer a lot of advice," Ivan said. "Yaw will concentrate on the overall military aspects of the project, but I'll make all the final decisions."

"I understand Chen Wan will be responsible for the

missile guidance systems working correctly and will work closely with you and Bing Yaw." Sergei leaned toward Ivan. "I also understand Wan is an expert on the guidance systems in every way."

"That he is," Ivan said. He regarded Sergei carefully. "Another thing to keep in mind, Cham has the reputation for being China's top assassin and should enhance your defense substantially. From the start, he'll report directly to you, and I'll depend on you to make all the correct decisions in that regard."

Sergei narrowed his eyes and nodded.

Ivan looked at Maxim. "Be prepared to spend many hours with Wan. I want you to know as much about the missile guidance systems as he does."

Maxim gave a thumbs-up. "We'll make sure all the missiles hit their targets in the United States."

Chapter 18

Early the next morning at CIA Headquarters in McLean, Virginia, Charles Andrews (the CIA Director) sat at the round conference table in his office and met with some of his key agents.

Paul Collins (head of the Terrorist Threat Investigation Unit at the CIA), Nick Wallace (a CIA technology specialist reporting to Paul Collins), and Mack Thomson (the top CIA field agent) all waited for Charles to start the meeting.

Charles looked at Nick. "Do you think everyone down in Tampa is prepared for the next step?"

"I have a conversation with Grant at least twice a day. He assures me the FBI agents down there are fully prepared to continue to support our needs," Nick said. "He also assures me he stays in close contact with Boswic and they're ready to move forward on the taskforce as soon as we finalize the plan."

Charles gave a slow nod. "I know the President wants to get all the latest intelligence information before we put the finishing touches on our plan and arrive in Jamaica. NRO has a lot of surveillance satellites focused on the area and NSA is trying to pick up some relevant phone conversations. We'll try to make sure we know what we're doing before we go down there."

"While we're waiting for the latest details, do you have any new information we can discuss?" Paul asked.

Charles pointed toward a scene from Jamaica displayed on a wall monitor in his office. "That industrial development is new. It's an extension of the dock area, a combination of storage and manufacturing facilities. You might notice the warehouse in the foreground that looks brand new."

"Any idea what's in the warehouse right now?" Paul gestured toward the monitor.

"No," Charles said. "We're hoping to find that out when we get the next intelligence information. That's critical information we need to finalize our planning."

Nick punched Mack on the shoulder. "You'd better be ready for almost anything when you go down there."

"From the beginning of all this, I've been ready for almost anything," Mack said. "I'm sure everyone on the taskforce will be well prepared for a wide range of possibilities."

Everyone looked at the large monitor and studied the latest time-sequenced satellite reconnaissance photos from the NRO covering a wide area around Kingston, Jamaica.

"Lot of loose ends, you agree?" Paul looked at Charles and gestured toward the pictures on the monitor.

"That's why we need to send a taskforce down there," Charles said. "There are some things you have to do close up and personal."

Paul gave a short laugh. "Yeah, and I think we're preparing to cover this situation from every angle."

"Even more than I previously thought," Charles said. "The President told me this morning he wanted to be kept fully informed and would require briefings from us twice a day."

"Does Grant have these photos down in Tampa yet?" Nick asked, gesturing toward the monitor.

"He should have received them at the same time we

did." Charles reached for the speaker phone on the table and punched a digit.

Grant answered.

After a brief opening discussion, Charles asked, "Have you had a chance to study the photos?"

"Thoroughly," Grant said, "and I've just finished discussing them with everyone at Boswic."

"Any new thoughts?" Charles asked.

"Colt is anxious to lead the taskforce down there as soon as we can go," Grant said. "I got the impression Linda was anxious to go with him."

Nick and Mack each held an arm in the air, giving a thumbs-up signal.

"Looks like we have some anxious people up here too," Charles said. "We'll try to complete the final preparations this afternoon and be ready to go tomorrow. You can be prepared to make any necessary adjustments down there."

"And you'll have the plan finalized this afternoon?" Grant asked.

"Yes," Charles said.

"I'll make several adjustments immediately and be prepared to make some more as the mission gets underway," Grant said. He gave Charles a quick explanation.

"What's the status of the nuclear bomb you intercepted last night?" Charles asked.

"We've finished our initial inspection," Grant said. "It looks like it indeed has an explosive power of 50-megatons. It could have done a lot of damage to a large area."

"That fits with the Russian plan we've been watching unfold," Charles replied. "Are you shipping it out for further study?"

"Yes."

"Sending it by truck?"

"A special convoy is all set up, all the necessary precautions."

"Good, keep me posted." After a little more discussion

Charles disconnected and looked at Paul.

"The bomb that we intercepted at the port in Tampa was indeed the Tsar Bomba, 50-megatons of nuclear power," Charles said. "A lot of our intelligence experts think the Russians are increasing the warhead on the Poseidon Missile to 50-megatons."

"What are our experts basing their opinion on?"

"Multiple calls NSA has intercepted."

Paul narrowed his eyes. "It looks like Russia has made more progress than we thought. I've heard a lot of rumors about their wanting to create tidal waves to flood our coastal cities. A 50-megaton explosion will certainly add a lot to their chances of accomplishing that objective."

"Everything you just mentioned appears to be true and it's now evident China is helping them."

A brief silence ensued.

"Having Colt lead the task team is a good thing," Paul said. "I requested a detailed copy of his entire military record, and I found something I didn't know. He had a lot of experience with nuclear weapons when he was in Delta Force, and he was trained to dismantle them."

Charles nodded. "I knew about that. He might need to use that skill again in Jamaica. I hope he's not too rusty."

Chapter 19

That afternoon at Boswic, Colt and Linda spent several hours with Blake going over technical aspects of the upcoming situation. Blake brought them up to date on his latest discussions with other specialists.

"So, you still think the game of chess serves as the metaphor for the ongoing strategy we're facing?" Colt asked.

Blake nodded. "Everyone agrees we're dealing with the thinking of three chess masters working in the Kremlin. China is directly involved, but they're apparently allowing Russia to do all the strategic planning."

"Chess analogies might be useful in developing strategies, but they're not so useful in executing them. I think poker expertise can be a big help when you're in the field and having to make quick decisions," Colt replied. "In chess, the pieces are always in plain sight on the board. When you're playing poker, you don't know what the opposing hands are. You must deal with a lot of incomplete information, like we'll probably have in multiple situations down there in Jamaica."

"I agree," Blake said, "but using chess strategy helps us anticipate the plan the Russians have set up. If we can anticipate their strategy, we can adjust our tactics accordingly."

"What's your opinion of what we'll need to do first in Jamaica?" Colt asked.

"I'm guessing you'll need to find the exact launch site for the Poseidon Missiles." Blake pointed toward the large computer screen on the wall. "I've been studying a lot of construction activity near Kingston, but I haven't been able to determine conclusively from the surveillance photos where the exact site is. The construction equipment is spread over a wide area. I'm thinking all the CIA and FBI analysts have the same problem." He looked directly at Colt. "The taskforce will have to do that job on the ground."

Colt nodded and waited for Blake to continue.

"The ongoing construction we're seeing in the satellite photos is officially part of a joint project the Russian Embassy and the Chinese Embassy have established to improve the area," Blake said. "They have the funding for all the activity routed through the World Bank and wrapped around an official agreement by both nations."

"The Russians have been pursuing various means of gaining supremacy on the world stage for a long time and they've added some new twists," Colt replied. "The Kremlin obviously wants to take more aggressive action this time and still be in a position to deny any responsibility for that action."

"That seems to be the case," Blake said.

Colt glanced at his watch. "It's time for our scheduled meeting with Harlan and Jim."

"They've probably received some more information about tomorrow and we can firm up all the latest details for the taskforce mission," Blake said.

Colt nodded as he stood and moved toward the door.

Linda and Blake followed.

When Colt walked into the designated conference room for the meeting, he found more attendees than he had expected.

Grant sat at the large table with Harlan and Jim. Paul Collins, head of the Terrorist Threat Investigation Unit at the CIA, also sat at the table.

"We're fortunate Paul could fly down and join us," Harlan said, "much better than a phone conversation. He brought a lot of material we can use including some new information related to the big picture. We'll cover some of that before we discuss the details for our upcoming mission to Jamaica."

Paul scanned the faces around the table. "One of our intelligence agencies found some polymorphic spyware in the Federal Reserve System that could only have been produced by a quantum computer."

"How do we know that?" Blake asked.

"It's a long story and I don't have Nick here right now to explain the technical details," Paul said. "I don't think we should spend time on that anyway. The important thing is that it looks like the Chinese and Russians actually have a functioning quantum computer and are using it."

"Does this relate to what we'll be doing in Jamaica?" Colt asked.

Paul nodded. "We think they have one there and you might run across it in one of the structures you inspect, you need to know what to do."

"Such as?" Linda asked. She gave Paul a curious look.

"Not shoot holes in the quantum computer for one thing. We need to confiscate a working one." Paul gestured toward the wall-mounted monitor. "Watch the screen." He pushed a key on the laptop in front of him and the screen on the wall displayed a strange image.

"This screen shows an image of an unusual computer bug," Paul said. "It's a virus that can morph into millions of digital signatures to avoid detection."

"Any damage to the Federal Reserve System?" Jim asked.

"None have been detected yet," Paul said. "We've lost no money and I suspect this one was just a test. We think we got all of it, but we can't be sure. We could have missed some of the morphed parts."

"So exactly what should we do if we find a computer in one of the warehouses?" Colt asked.

"Let us know and we'll send the necessary specialists to inspect everything as soon as the area is safe," Paul said. "They'll take the necessary action relative to the computer."

"Do we have any clues as to the origination of the virus?" Linda asked.

"I won't go into all the technical details, but NSA experts think it came from a site in the Caribbean, probably Jamaica," Paul said.

"Is the new defensive shield our experts devised to protect against intrusion from quantum computers working?" Grant asked.

"Very well in the lab," Paul said. He scanned the faces around the table. "Let's hope it works well in actual situations."

"Is it ready to implement as part of the protection for the Federal Reserve System?" Blake asked.

"I think so," Paul said. "I think NSA is ready to install the shield and I know they have the needed permission."

"And all our experts have finished their latest research?" Blake asked.

"More testing will be needed." A brief smile flickered across Paul's face. He looked at Colt and Linda. "I've recommended we get both of you involved in this as much as possible while we go forward. You both have the IQ, and I think your opinions on certain things will be valuable."

"What's your logic on that?" Linda asked.

"You won't be inhibited by our previous thinking on the subject," Paul said. "You'll have fresh viewpoints." He looked at Blake. "Speaking of fresh viewpoints, have you studied those new regression theorems Nick sent you?"

"A little," Blake said. "It's easy to get lost. Nick's more of an expert on the mathematics of all this than I am."

"I know he just finished research involving Brownian motion of the oscillator involving random forces and Gaussian operators in various equations." Paul looked up from some notes on a sheet of paper in front of him and smiled. "I didn't understand much of what he was saying, but he assured me he would get together with you later to review his findings on all the relevant aspects of this."

"Good," Blake said. "I have some knowledge of the subject matter you mentioned."

Harlan shook his head slowly. "Most of us don't need to get into that crap, especially now. Blake and Nick can just give us the recommendations they can agree to."

Paul laughed. So did everyone else.

"Do you think the Russian chess masters developed the theorems Nick sent to us?" Blake asked.

"Yes, we know they're involved in a lot of aspects of this situation." Paul said. "Between the FBI and CIA, we've compiled quite a fact book on this. We'll go over any necessary technical details at a more appropriate time."

"Why would they have a quantum computer in Jamaica?" Colt asked. "It seems they would keep it in a more secure location."

"They're probably going to use it to fine tune the guidance systems for the Poseidon Missiles," Paul said. "Having it on site will be an advantage in several ways. That's also a good location to launch their cyber attacks from, so that probably is the origin of this current virus in the Federal Reserve System we've just referenced."

Colt grunted. "So, if our taskforce can prevent the quantum computer from operating down there, we're going to solve a lot of different problems."

"Right," Paul said. "We'll eliminate a lot of new threats to our monetary system and hamper the guidance system for the missiles."

"Why do we need to know all this extra stuff in order to do our job?" Harlan asked.

"Just hang on for a few more minutes," Paul said, "and you'll see how a lot of different things will come together."

Colt rubbed his chin. "And this new knowledge is going to be useful to us when we get to Jamaica?"

"Yes," Paul said. "Before you get down there a lot of additional things will become clear. You'll be able to function better by having the additional knowledge."

Colt glanced at Linda. She gave a slight shrug. Neither made a comment.

"The Chinese, of course, are the prime suspects for developing the computer bug," Paul said, "but we haven't yet been able to nail that down. There are a lot of false trails. Whoever created this latest sequence of events definitely knows what they're doing."

Blake gave Paul a thoughtful look. "And you're sure we have a defensive shield working properly in the lab?"

"As sure as I can be at this stage," Paul said. "I'm told our experts are ready to install it in our Federal Reserve System as early as tomorrow."

"Can you package it in a manner where we could test it here at Boswic?" Blake asked.

"I think so, if you feel you need to study it closely," Paul said.

"How soon can you send it over?" Blake asked.

Paul fished his mobile phone out of a pocket and punched a digit. After a short conversation, he disconnected and said, "We can begin installing it at Boswic around noon tomorrow."

Blake gave a thumbs-up. "We'll be ready."

"How big a group do you have working on this computer stuff?" Linda asked, giving Paul a curious glance.

"Fifteen people," Paul said. "Due to budget considerations, some are graduate students, but don't worry, they've been checked out thoroughly. I don't think we have any Russian or Chinese sympathizers in this group."

Colt narrowed his eyes but made no comment.

"After I get back to my office, I want to concentrate on verifying the origin of the detected network bug." Paul looked at Blake. "What do you recommend as my best first step to do this?"

"Talk to Nick and get him to do the initial analysis," Blake said. "I think he could make some headway by using various forms of regression analysis. He could try some nonparametric regression which would allow the regression function to lie in a specified set of functions which were infinite-dimensional."

Paul grunted. "Would you go over all this with Nick?"

"Of course," Blake said, "as soon as this meeting is over. He knows a lot more about what I just mentioned than I do. And of course, he should direct that group of fifteen analysts you mentioned to do some more research that's directly related to the problem you just mentioned."

Paul nodded.

"I hope you won't expect Linda and me to give an intelligent opinion on that sort of stuff." Colt's glance took in both Paul and Blake.

"After we come to a conclusion, we might want your opinions on our general logic," Paul said. "We won't expect you to form an opinion on our use of any of the heavy math."

Colt gave a slow nod. "I guess Linda and I can both comment on the general direction you're taking."

"This is all bullshit to me," Harlan said. "I don't want to hear any more discussions about mathematical details."

Jim gave a slight grin and didn't comment.

Linda started to say something just as Paul's phone rang.

"It's Charles," Paul said, glancing at the caller ID which displayed the name of the CIA Director. He answered.

After a short conversation, Paul disconnected and looked at Colt. "Charles just talked with NSA again. We have some new challenges."

"What's up?" Colt asked.

Paul leaned forward and explained.

"So, Charles thinks it's critical we get to Jamaica as soon as possible?" Colt asked.

"That's what he recommends," Paul said. "He suggested we wrap this briefing up as fast as possible. We can't afford to wait any longer. From what we can determine from the satellite images, the Russians and Chinese are moving faster than we expected."

Harlan narrowed his eyes. "We know these bastards all want to bring us down as soon as they can and they're probably aware we're sending a taskforce to Jamaica. It's no surprise they're moving things along at a much faster pace."

Paul nodded. "And that's why I just brought up all the technical stuff. We can't let Russian and Chinese scientists outthink us in any of the various areas we're getting into. We must at least keep up with them. Our scientists will stay heavily involved and maybe we can even get one step in front."

"I can agree with your objective," Harlan said, "even if I don't want to hear much about all this mathematical crap."

Jim, Colt, and Linda all gave a knowing smile.

Blake showed no expression.

Paul stood. "Well, let's get moving. It now looks like we have no time to spare."

Chapter 20

In a large conference room in his new headquarters in Jamaica, Ivan grabbed a mug and filled it with the hot liquid from the fresh pot of coffee he had just brewed. Even in the Caribbean, he liked his coffee hot. The excellent air conditioning in his new facility helped, of course.

Ivan savored the aroma for a moment before he took a sip. He knew his next actions would be critical to the success of The Poseidon Initiative.

Moscow made all the big strategic decisions, but he had the responsibility of developing all the tactical details and insuring everything happened correctly. In a couple of hours, they would meet with the Chinese contingent and begin putting all the specifics together to successfully complete their mission.

The United States must be defeated, Ivan thought. China had just failed in their attempt to bring down the United States with germ warfare, now it was up to him to succeed with the Poseidon missiles.

Ivan took a slow sip of coffee and then grunted. There was a lot to consider.

Everything was ready for him and his group to begin developing all the specific tactics for the big initiative. Even though he received the broad strategy from Moscow he knew he was solely responsible for the execution.

So far he had uncovered no glitches in the elaborate plan to drain billions of dollars from the Federal Reserve System and then destroy significant areas in the United States with the Poseidon Missiles.

Ivan took a long slow drink of coffee and stared at a picture of the Marriner S. Eccles Federal Reserve Board Building in Washington DC.

Marriner S. Eccles had been Chairman of the Federal Reserve in times past. Franklin Delano Roosevelt had dedicated the building on October 20, 1937.

The American law enforcement and the people in charge of the current American financial structure would get what they deserved, Ivan thought.

After taking another long slow drink of coffee, he glanced at two different lists of the twelve Federal Reserve Districts. There were twenty-four Federal Reserve Branch banks on one list and twenty-five on another list. That was okay. Taking advantage of some inconsistencies was part of his plan. Detroit, Michigan was shown on both lists as a branch of the Chicago District. Des Moines, Iowa was shown as a branch of the Chicago District on one list and not on the other. Ivan shrugged.

Gaining enormous wealth was his main goal and he didn't want to be totally dependent on Russia gaining more power to do that. If they took over the world, fine. He felt he would be in a favored position. If not, then he would at least be super wealthy and he would find a safe hideaway before it was too late.

Ivan looked toward the doorway as Sergei, Maxim, and Denis entered the room. He waited for them to settle into three of the empty chairs.

"Are the Chinese here yet?" Maxim asked.

"They're getting settled into their accommodations." Ivan returned Maxim's stare. "Bing Yaw, a military leader, and Chen Wan, a weapons specialist, will join us shortly. Ho Cham, the assassin who came with them, will join us a little later," Ivan said. "Wan will begin his discussions with you on fine-tuning the guidance systems on the Poseidon Missiles."

Maxim nodded.

"We won't get into all the details here in the conference room, will we?" Denis asked.

Ivan gave a short laugh and said, "Just enough so we'll all know the big picture about what's involved."

Denis gave a thumbs-up.

Ivan scanned the faces around the table. "Moscow wants us to move as fast as possible. They've discovered the Americans know we're down here."

"Do the Americans know what we're doing?" Maxim asked.

"Moscow thinks they know some of it," Ivan said. "That's why they're emphasizing speed is of the essence."

"Do we plan to put any additional defensive measures in place?" Denis asked.

"Of course," Ivan said. "Moscow is supplying some of our newest and fastest small attack boats to patrol the waters around us. Using them will help us ward off any surprise attacks from the ocean or at least enable us to be more aware of what's going on out there."

Denis gave a slow nod.

"Moscow is also sending some of the best Russian assassins to boost our security process." Ivan glanced at his watch. "They should all be arriving within the hour. Oleg Rowan, our leading weapons specialist, will be with them. He'll join us in our strategy discussions and planning."

"Does he have any computer knowledge?" Maxim asked.

"Of course," Ivan said. "Computers are weapons also. He'll also work with you and Denis on some aspects of the computer hacking."

Maxim started to comment but stopped as Bing Yaw and Chen Wan were escorted into the room and immediately settled into two of the empty chairs at the table.

"We're here to help destroy the Americans," Yaw said with narrowed eyes. His grin stretched wide on his face.

Wan leaned forward. "I'm here to ensure the Poseidon Missiles hit their precise targets in the United States. I helped make improvements to the primary guidance system used in each missile and I'll work on any necessary fine-tuning issues."

"Do you think we still have some fine-tuning issues?" Ivan asked.

Wan nodded. "There are always lingering issues with anything this complex. We have a group of engineers in China who are still running a lot of tests. They aren't yet satisfied with every detail in the results they're getting."

"Our top Russian engineers originally developed the guidance system," Maxim said, "and thoroughly tested it. I was personally involved in a lot of the development and most of the testing."

Wan pursed his lips and gave a slow nod. "Then we should make a good team." He displayed a wide grin.

Maxim didn't comment.

Yaw leaned forward and stared at Ivan. "I'll make certain we do the necessary damage to America. My bosses sent me here to ensure that it happens. I'm one of China's leading military experts and I'm really good at my job."

"You and your bosses failed on your germ warfare attempt a few years ago," Ivan said. "You failed to really do any permanent damage to the United States. I hope you can do better than that this time." He leaned toward Yaw and returned his stare.

"There were some unfortunate accidents that ruined our plan." Yaw narrowed his eyes. "We plan to succeed in bringing America down this time. Again, that's why I'm here."

Ivan regarded Yaw carefully for a few moments and then gave a slow nod. "Okay, we'll go ahead and start developing the details for how we're going to conduct our upcoming offensive and we need to make sure we get things right." He scanned the faces around the table "The Russian team should have executed better in the Bahamas. Moscow doesn't want any screw ups this time."

Chapter 21

At Boswic, Jim stopped in the hallway and looked into Harlan's office. Harlan was in his usual spot.

"Got a moment?" Jim asked.

After Harlan motioned him in, Jim took a seat in front of Harlan's desk and said, "Just wanted to talk some things over."

"You worried about something?"

"I'm worried about a lot of things," Jim said. "I just felt the need to talk to someone."

Harlan narrowed his eyes and asked, "What's on your mind?"

"This overall threat we're addressing is getting more complex by the minute. Blake just went over some more things with me, and he covered a lot of technical details."

"You're referring to all this computer stuff that I'm depending on you and Blake to keep up with?"

"That and other things," Jim said. "He knows a little about the guidance systems for missiles. The Russian Poseidon Missiles are rumored to have the most sophisticated technology available."

"So?"

"The missiles will have no trouble hitting strategic spots in our country along any of our coastlines."

"Even the Pacific Coast?"

"The Russians have a big spy base in Nicaragua and they'll be able to launch from Nicaragua's Pacific Coast," Jim said. "However, due to the sophisticated guidance system, Blake tells me they can also hit our Pacific Coast even if they launch from Jamaica."

"How can they do that?"

"Blake thinks the guidance system on the Poseidon Missiles will make them capable of maneuvering through the Panama Canal."

"The canal has different levels because the Atlantic Ocean and Pacific Ocean aren't on the same level. Ships going through the canal must wait while the corrective actions are taken to allow them to go from one ocean to the other."

Jim grunted. "I know all that." He gestured with both palms up. "What I'm trying to tell you is that Blake thinks the sophisticated guidance systems on the missiles can deal with all the complications."

"How?"

"The water depth must be deep enough to handle the big ships going through. The missiles will have guidance systems smart enough to allow them to hover for long periods along the bottom and go through as the ships are going through."

Harlan rubbed his chin for a few moments and didn't comment.

"So, the Russians can hit our West Coast from Jamaica if they choose to or they can hit it from Nicaragua," Jim said. "And don't overlook the fact they can also hit our East Coast from Nicaragua."

Harlan shook his head slowly. "I guess we can't consider any of our cities or strategic locations close to any of our coastlines to be safe from the attack of a Poseidon Missile."

"Do you have any recommendations?" Jim asked.

"Someone needs to talk to the President again and get more support for what we're doing. It looks like we will definitely need more military support."

Jim nodded.

"I'll give Ken and Charles each a call and talk it over with them," Harlan said. "I'm sure they'll see the logic about needing more military support." He reached for his phone.

After completing conversations where Ken and Charles each took his call as a priority, Harlan looked back at Jim.

"They both agree we need more military support, and they both think the President will carefully consider providing more," Harlan said.

"When do you think we'll hear something back?"

"Probably real soon."

"I hope so. Colt and Linda are taking our corporate jet up to Andrews this afternoon. They're leaving for Jamaica from there with the rest of the taskforce."

Harlan gave a slow nod just as his phone rang. He answered and listened for about a minute.

"When will they be available?" Harlan asked into the phone.

Harlan continued to listen. In another minute, Harlan said thanks and then disconnected.

"Are we getting more support?" Jim asked.

"Yes we are," Harlan said. "We're getting a couple of SEALIONs and a couple of Mark VI patrol boats complete with pilots on loan from the USS Truman."

"How soon?" Jim asked.

"They'll be in Jamaica before Colt and the taskforce get down there," Harlan said. "We're getting both the most recent generation of Navy patrol boats and the latest stealth boats for transporting SEAL teams. Charles gave me a lot of details." Harlan checked the notes he had made. "The 90-foot SEALION III was designed to be heavily armed and to transport ten-man SEAL teams in shallow water at high speeds. They can reach speeds of around 80 knots. That's over 90 miles per hour. The Mark VI only reaches a speed of 40 miles per hour, but it's heavily armed, carries a crew of ten, and will be perfect for scouting the shoreline around the island."

Jim nodded.

"The USS Truman will remain in the area for a while. There's no way the President wants any of those Poseidon Missiles to get launched and hit any of their targets."

"With the President not wanting to risk starting World War III, the Truman is going to be rather conspicuous sitting out there, isn't it?"

Harlan gave a short laugh. "Actually, this is a brilliant plan. The Truman is almost always in the general area while completing its routine missions. This time it will stay a little closer to Jamaica as it makes its rounds. Our taskforce will still do the initial fighting."

Jim leaned forward. "And our taskforce still consists of only Colt, Linda, FBI agents, and CIA agents?"

"Right," Harlan said. "Whichever set of boats they use at any given time, Colt, Linda and eight FBI agents will be in one boat. Mack Thomson and nine other CIA agents will be in the other boat. Colt will command the taskforce. The pilots will stay with the boats and plan to do no fighting except in self defense."

Jim gave a slow nod. "I like it. We have the best of both worlds. We'll earn our money and, along with the FBI and CIA, do all the initial fighting, but we have tremendous backup if we get into big trouble and need it."

Chapter 22

Colt and Linda walked toward the private hangar that housed the Boswic corporate jet at Tampa International airport. The jet sat in front of the hangar and looked ready for takeoff.

Linda flashed a look of concern. "I have a bad feeling."

"About what?"

"Not sure, but I have a good sixth sense."

They stopped and scanned the area closely. Colt noted Linda appeared calm, but alert and ready. That reinforced his feeling they were a good team.

Within a few seconds, two people came around a corner at the back of the hangar and walked toward them. Colt noticed the two Russian-looking men had expressions of recognition as they approached.

Colt and Linda stood ready to take any necessary action.

The two men stopped about ten feet away. They both stared at Colt and remained silent.

"You seem to know who we are," Colt said.

The man directly in front of Colt grinned and jiggled the fingers on his right hand.

Both men wore blazers over casual shirts with open collars. Colt could see a bulge under each one's left arm.

The man directly in front of Colt flashed an acid grin and spoke in a menacing heavily accented voice. "You've been messing around with the wrong people for a long time and that needs to stop."

"And who are those people?" Colt kept his gaze on both men.

Linda stayed silent.

The man in front of Colt narrowed his eyes. "We never reveal our clients. That's unprofessional."

"And we don't like answering questions from dummies," the man directly in front of Linda said.

Respecting Linda's ability, Colt didn't worry about the man in front of her. He kept his attention glued on the one directly in front of him.

"Ok Randall," the man in front of Colt said. "Yeah, we know who you are and why you're here. Your time on earth has come to an end." His eyes flashed as he reached inside his coat. A pistol came into view. He was quick, but not quick enough.

With a fluid motion, Colt brushed back his coat with his right hand and moved the pistol from the holster toward the back of his right hip. Executing a quick forward snap, he aimed and pulled the trigger of his Glock 19. The man in front of him went down.

Hearing another bang to his right, Colt glanced toward the other man. He was motionless on the ground. Linda had taken care of her part of the confrontation.

They stepped forward to examine the bodies.

It was obvious the two men were dead.

Colt fished his secure satellite phone from a pocket and hit a button.

"Are you calling Grant?" Linda asked.

"Yeah, he'll mop up and take care of anything that needs attention," Colt said. "You call Jim and give our report."

Linda punched a digit on her phone.

After both finished their phone conversations, Linda

turned toward Colt. "Good job partner." She grinned.

Colt returned the grin. "Looks like you're handling the emotional side of this well."

"I was involved in many situations in the Marines a lot more gruesome," Linda said. "We just got in a little more practice before we get to Jamaica. That's not all bad."

Colt gave a thumbs-up.

Linda punched Colt on the shoulder. "My sixth sense wasn't so bad, right?"

"Right," Colt said.

They both laughed.

It was good to stay loose, Colt thought. The two Russians deserved what they got. He was glad Linda could retain her sense of humor.

Colt started to say more just as Grant arrived with a couple of FBI agents.

Bill Abbot, the local police chief, also arrived with five policemen. Two were carrying body bags.

The policemen went about their duties while Bill and Grant walked over to where Colt and Linda were standing.

Grant narrowed his eyes. "They apparently knew your schedule and wanted to eliminate you before you went to Jamaica."

"I'm glad they both had big egos," Colt said, "at least they wanted to confront us instead of ambush us."

Linda gave a slow nod.

"The Kremlin obviously doesn't want you to get down to Jamaica and put a stop to what they and the Chinese are doing," Grant said.

"Their moles are doing a good job spying on us," Colt replied. "We'll need to try harder to stay one step ahead of them."

"We'll keep a closer eye on a lot of things as we go forward. The CIA will continue to provide a lot of support," Grant said. He glanced at Bill. "I want you in all the future meetings we have with them."

Bill looked at Grant and asked, "Do you have much Intel my men and I can start brushing up on?"

"I'll send you a ton of information as soon as I get back to my office," Grant said. "The CIA has already told me they want you on the team down here. Things are moving faster than we originally thought. I'll check with Ken and make sure he approves of everything I plan to send you."

"I have a top-secret clearance." Bill looked directly at Grant. "I hope he approves of my receiving all the Intel."

"It's likely he will. We have more than the underwater missiles to worry about," Grant said. "The Russians have been test firing a lot of their cruise missiles. They're in violation of a treaty they signed back in 1987 during the Reagan Administration."

"Yeah, Reagan and Gorbachev both signed it." Colt gave a slight shrug and looked at Grant "Have any of the intelligence agencies figured out how the Russians plan to use the cruise missiles?"

"Not specifically," Grant said, "but it looks like the Russians are preparing to mount a serious offensive."

Linda narrowed her eyes. "We for sure need to shut them down in Jamaica as quickly as we can."

Damned right," Grant said. "Looks like we've wrapped up here, Bill and I will let you get on with your trip."

Colt and Linda watched everyone leave and again walked toward the Boswic corporate jet.

"Too bad everyone left," Linda said. "I have that feeling again."

"Of imminent danger?"

"Right."

Colt and Linda stopped and scanned the area.

A huge man emerged from behind the hangar and charged toward them. He didn't seem to be armed.

"He looks Chinese," Colt said. "I've never seen such a mass of muscle, but I've heard about some of these types."

"Maybe he kills people with his bare hands," Linda

muttered. "He looks like he could kill people pretty easily. We should both open up with our Glocks and shoot him before he gets to us. He might be tough, but I doubt he can withstand a barrage of high caliber bullets."

"Give me a chance to see what I can do. We'll probably run into more of his type in Jamaica. I need the practice." Colt gestured at Linda and then focused on the bull-like figure.

"I'll shoot him if you get in trouble," Linda said. "He's not only huge, but he looks agile. In spite of your exceptional expertise, he might be more than you can handle."

"Just give me a chance. I need a test like this." Colt charged toward the approaching figure.

The bull acted like he knew who Colt was. He grinned and charged forward, attacking with a flying double-kick aimed at Colt's chest.

So, this monster is indeed agile, Colt thought while moving fluidly to one side.

The bull-like monster flew by, missing completely, but he expertly landed on his feet and quickly began turning to attack again.

Before the monster could complete his turn, Colt sprinted toward him and landed a vicious kick behind his left knee. Colt put all of his strength and most of his 225 pounds of weight into the kick, but it didn't bring the monster down.

The blow Colt delivered only caused the monster to stumble slightly.

Colt quickly moved closer to give the villain another kick.

But the monster didn't react as Colt expected. With surprising quickness, he regained his balance and launched a kick toward Colt's right kneecap.

Colt slid to his left with lightning speed, avoiding much of the blow. However, the partial impact still inflicted some damage.

The monster's grin widened.

Colt stepped backwards and flexed his right knee, trying to relieve the pain.

The monster glared at Colt. His blow had been delivered with enormous strength, and he was looking more confident.

Colt noted Linda had moved closer.

She was standing to his right with her Glock 19 pointed at the monster.

Colt could see concern on Linda's face as her finger tightened on the trigger.

"Hold off a moment," Colt said. "We still have a chance to get some information. I think I can cope with him. Don't forget I'm a well-trained warrior in this type of hand-to-hand combat and, as a Delta Force operative, I had plenty of experience in fights with a lot of huge talented men."

The monster seemed to understand what Colt said as the grin still dominated his face. Colt figured it made sense for him to be trained in the English language if he was assigned to operations in this country.

Colt noted the monster didn't seem to be concerned about Linda pointing a pistol at him. Maybe he thought his mass of muscle would act something like a coat of armor or maybe he didn't think Linda would fire until Colt had lost the fight. Colt figured it was a combination of these two things, and the monster had a plan to deal with Linda in the last few seconds as he was disposing of his first opponent.

The monster let out a huge growl and charged directly at Colt.

Colt darted toward the left and put all his strength into a vicious punch, one that would instantly drop any normal human.

Seeming unaffected, the monster stopped and continued grinning.

Colt stayed on the offensive.

The monster demonstrated more of his expertise and blocked Colt's straight punch toward his breastbone.

Colt tried several kicks that also met blocks.

This isn't looking good, Colt thought.

As Colt struggled to find an opening, he realized he had more of a challenge than he was expecting. This guy was different than anyone he had ever fought before.

The only good thing was that Colt constantly avoided direct contact from the blows of the monster Chinaman, mostly automatically while he prepared to launch his next blow.

Colt knew his strength training from lifting heavy weights and his agility training was paying some dividends right now on defense, but he needed to find some effective offense.

The Chinaman stood still and continued to grin, obviously showing no respect for Colt's ability to do any damage to him.

With his adrenalin surging, Colt moved toward the grinning monster.

The monster unleashed straight punches, chops, and kicks. Colt dodged all of them.

Colt knew he was doing okay, but he also knew he had to do more than okay to win. His goal of getting a prisoner wasn't looking very probable at the moment. Maybe he should ask Linda to go ahead and shoot?

After giving his latest thought a few seconds to sink in, Colt decided to continue to fight for a little longer. He was at least holding his own against this monster, which gave him some satisfaction.

The monster stopped and glared at Colt. He didn't appear quite as confident as he had a few minutes ago. He glanced at Linda and then looked back at Colt.

Watching the bull-like monster closely, Colt stood ready for anything, especially another charge.

The monster seemed to shift his strategy. He adopted a defensive stance and waited. He obviously wanted Colt to mount an offensive.

Colt decided he would oblige him. He knew he had the

skills to at least hold his own. He had already demonstrated that.

After moving forward, Colt tried to find an opening. He wanted to deliver a finishing blow, but he quickly found out he concentrated too much on the offense and not enough on the defense.

The monster landed a glancing blow to Colt's shoulder as he closed in on him. It was delivered with such force that it upset Colt's balance.

Colt struggled to regain his center.

The monster took advantage and delivered a kick to Colt's left hip. The blow's force sent Colt backwards.

Feeling excruciating pain and trying without success to regain his balance, Colt landed on his rear about ten feet away.

After Colt rolled on the pavement and struggled to stand, the monster growled and charged toward him.

Colt heard a series of shots. He saw the monster slow down and stagger to his left.

Turning slightly, Colt saw Linda was still pointing her Glock19 at the bull-like monster.

The monster dropped to one knee and then struggled to his feet. He uttered a huge growl and rushed toward Linda

Linda fired more shots in quick succession.

Good thing the magazine holds 15 rounds, Colt thought. He also drew his Glock and fired.

A lot more shots dominated the situation.

Five yards away from Linda, the monster dropped to the pavement, thrashed around a few times, and then lay still.

"I gave you your chance, but this had gone on long enough." Linda stared at Colt. "You're good, but not good enough to handle this guy. Bastard must be close to seven feet tall and weigh over 400 pounds. I would have shot him earlier, but you were doing okay for a while."

"Big guy all right, surprisingly agile too," Colt said. "Guess he was a little tougher than I expected, but I needed to try. We'll probably see more like him down in Jamaica. We know China has invested heavily in what Russia is planning to do."

Linda nodded and gave Colt a concerned look. "Are you going to be okay?"

Colt pressed various places on and around his left hip. The general area was still throbbing.

"Nothing seems broken, muscles and tendons seem okay too," Colt said. "I'll be okay, pain's already subsiding."

Linda gave a thumbs-up.

Colt gulped in some air while he walked over to the downed bull-like monster and felt for a pulse. There was none. The monster had now been eliminated, and Colt punched a digit on his phone.

He heard Bill answer.

"You left a little too soon." Colt gave a quick explanation.

"I'll have a crew there in less than a minute. We always keep some men at the airport to handle emergencies," Bill said. "Grant's in my patrol car with me. We were going to have a strategy meeting back at my office and talk things over. I'll turn around and activate the sirens. We'll be there in a couple of minutes."

Within the next minute, a swarm of uniformed policemen flooded the area and went to work.

"Guess the noise at the airport kept the gunshots from being obvious," one policeman said. "It's good we don't need to do any crowd control."

Colt and Linda nodded but didn't comment.

About a minute later, Bill and Grant appeared.

Grant pointed at the monster. "The bastard is a huge hunk of solid muscle and obviously well trained in the martial arts. China probably has a lot of them in their stockpile of assassins."

Everyone scanned the area again. Even with all the policemen around, this wasn't the time to go off alert.

Linda glanced at Colt. “Actually, you did well. Don’t lose your confidence. This fight was a huge challenge, and you hung in there for a long time.”

“Thanks”, Colt said. “If we run into another one like him, we know what to expect.”

“Yeah, shoot him immediately if he shows up. We know what we’re dealing with now.” Grant looked directly at Colt. “No more hand-to-hand combat with monsters.”

Colt and Linda each gave a thumbs-up.

Chapter 23

Ivan Titov looked across the large table in his main conference room. The room was hi-tech and designed exclusively for his new headquarters in Jamaica. All his team were there for discussion. He needed to review their plan for executing The Poseidon Initiative.

Leaning toward Yaw, Ivan asked in Russian, "Have you and your team completed your studies of the Russian language?"

Yaw shrugged and gave Ivan a blank look.

Speaking in English, Ivan asked the same question again.

Yaw displayed a big grin and said, "I guess you can tell we still have some work to do on using your language."

A brief silence ensued.

"We'll conduct all our meetings in English. We're all fluent in that language," Ivan said. "Trying to mix Russian and Chinese can result in some big mistakes."

Everyone nodded.

Ivan scanned the faces of the men sitting around the table. "Okay, who wants to get us started?"

"I think it's premature to mount a major initiative

instantly," Yaw said. "We still have some fine-tuning to do with the technology we're supplying. We need to make sure everything is working perfectly in all circumstances."

"I agree with Yaw," Denis said. "We need some more testing on the quantum computer to ensure we can hack into the Federal Reserve System without being detected."

Sergei looked directly at Yaw. "Has the testing been completed for the missile guidance systems?"

Yaw gestured to Wan.

"A lot of that has been completed for a long time." Wan's gaze took in both Ivan and Sergei. "Remember we were testing your Poseidon Missiles in China for a couple of years."

Ivan leaned forward. "How much testing do you have left to do?"

Wan shrugged. "I'll be able to determine that after our scientists have done more inspection."

After glancing at his vibrating phone on the table, Ivan picked it up and answered. He listened for several minutes without comment.

"When did all this happen?" Ivan asked into the phone.

"An hour ago, at the Tampa International Airport," the Pentagon mole at the other end of the line said.

"So, Randall is on his way down here?"

"Yes, the latest combined effort by the Kremlin and China to eliminate him has failed, but there are a lot more assassins available and they'll keep trying."

"China will also continue to supply assassins to the Kremlin?"

"Yes, all types," the mole said.

"Are there more monsters like the one who just got eliminated?"

"Yes, that type and others with superior weapons skills," the mole said. "If necessary, the Kremlin will send many expert snipers down to join you."

Ivan looked across the table at Ho Cham and chuckled.

"Good, we're already off to a good start. I have an expert Chinese assassin sitting across the table from me right now."

"Ho Cham?"

"You know about him?"

"He's supposed to be the best China has. The Kremlin informed me earlier China was planning to loan him to us."

"We'll put him to good use," Ivan said. "A couple of expert Russian assassins will be here to assist us too. We'll make sure Randall is eliminated as quickly as possible after he gets to Jamaica."

"Speaking of Randall, there's something else I need to tell you," The mole replied. "Randall will be getting some help from the United States Navy. They're furnishing a couple of their newest SEALIONs and a couple of their Mark VI patrol boats for him to use to scout the Jamaica coastline."

"What's a SEALION?"

"A navy craft that can hold ten warriors and go 90 miles an hour on the water," the mole said. "Randall and his taskforce will have two of them to use for assaults. I'm sure he'll use the Mark VI patrol boats to go all around Jamaica and look for any new structures built close to the water."

"Like the facility we built to launch the underwater missiles?"

"Precisely," the mole said.

"We'll work on making it as undetectable as possible."

"That would be a good idea. You might do the same for any warehouses you'll be using."

"We'll do that also," Ivan said. "Do you have any more advice right now?"

"That's all I have at the moment. We shouldn't stay on the call very long. I'll be back in touch when necessary."

Ivan heard the mole disconnect and noticed everyone around the table was staring at him.

"I just got some interesting information," Ivan said. He leaned forward and explained.

"We have some hi-tech boats too," Wan said. "They're better than any of the American boats and better than any of your Russian boats too. I'll make sure we have one shipped to us."

"Don't we need more than one?" Oleg asked.

Wan gave a short laugh. "This one has a lot of weapons and it's faster than the SEALIONs. I think one is all we need."

Ivan gave a slow nod and then asked. "How soon will we get it?"

"Tonight," Yaw said. "I'll have one of our military cargo jets fly it over. Wan and I both anticipated we might need one."

Yaw glanced at Wan and then punched some digits on his phone. After a short conversation, he disconnected.

"The plane carrying the boat will be on the way here in a few minutes," Yaw said.

Ivan gave a thumbs-up.

"We should concentrate on eliminating Randall and his taskforce as soon as they get here," Maxim said. "Wan and I need sufficient time to run some final tests and ensure the software is foolproof in the Poseidon Missiles."

Wan nodded. "The routes they need to take will be super complex. They'll need to avoid detection and hit their exact targets too."

"How long do you think that will take you?" Ivan asked.

"After our bosses decide on the exact targets, a couple of days at least," Wan said.

Sergei narrowed his eyes. "We might not have that much time."

"We will if we eliminate Randall and his group before they can give us any trouble," Ivan said.

"I agree," Yaw said. "China has spent a hundred billion dollars to construct our facilities here in Jamaica. We must make sure we succeed."

"Russia has spent a lot too." Denis leaned toward

Maxim. "We must get some of that back by hacking into the Federal Reserve System with our quantum computer."

"Maxim and I must first concentrate on the guidance systems for the missiles," Wan said. "After the missiles have been launched, we can concentrate on getting the money."

Ivan grunted. "Depending on the designated targets, you might not have much time. If the missiles blow the hell out of any key infrastructure supporting the American money flow, you might not be able to get any money."

"We'll work it out," Wan said. "Maxim and I can go fast on the hacking setup. It's not as complicated as fine tuning the missile guidance systems to get the missiles to exactly the right spot at exactly the right time to detonate."

Denis shrugged. "Whenever we do it, I just hope we can get a lot of our money back before the American Federal Reserve System is disabled."

Wan gave Denis a long stare. "We'll all make sure we have time to do that. Don't worry about it. Just concentrate on your work."

Denis didn't comment.

Ivan scanned the faces around the table and then leaned forward. "Okay, let's firm up our plans. Our first priority is to eliminate Randall and his taskforce when they arrive tomorrow."

"Did the mole know what time they're arriving?" Sergei asked.

"He thinks around noon," Ivan said, "and according to the phone conversation we intercepted, they're going to use the Mark VI patrol boats immediately and make a full sweep around the island."

"Looking for anything specific?" Yaw asked.

"We aren't sure," Ivan said, "but I'm certain it's to make a note of anything that looks suspicious. We're right on the water, but everything is underground. We've built in a good area where the missile launching facility is fifty feet below the surface and our headquarters is twenty feet below the surface. I don't think they'll be able to detect we're here."

"Don't we have a lot of ventilation pipes sticking up from the ground?" Denis asked.

"They're all camouflaged to look like patches of sea oats," Ivan said.

Denis gave a slow nod.

"Well, who has a good idea on how to eliminate Randall and his crew?" Ivan asked.

"We have a lot of options," Yaw said, "My first choice is to use the firepower on our super fast stealth boat to destroy his patrol boats when Randall is inspecting our shoreline." He stared at Ivan.

Ivan looked around the table. "Anyone have any objections to that being our first initiative?"

"Sounds good to me," Sergei said.

Everyone else nodded.

Ivan's glance took in both Yaw and Wan. "Are either of you experts on how to operate the boat?"

Yaw gestured toward Cham. "He is. All our top assassins are trained on how to use it. The name of the boat we're receiving is the Sea Ghost."

"Okay," Ivan said. "We'll plan on Cham being on board along with two of my top assassins who will join us tomorrow morning." He glanced at the Chinese contingent. "Their names are Stephan Zak and Ludvig Glinka. You may have heard of them."

"Zak and I have worked together before," Cham said. "I'll look forward to working with him again and I'll look forward to meeting Glinka."

Ivan leaned forward and smiled. "I'd like Stephan Zak to be in charge of the boat. You can give him any necessary technical instructions."

Yaw and Wan didn't comment. They both looked at Cham.

"I'm fine with that," Cham said.

"Then that will be our plan. You can help familiarize

both Stephan and Ludvig with the Sea Ghost tomorrow morning," Ivan replied. "I'll call our mole back later and see if he can get more details about Randall's schedule involving the Mark VI patrol boats and the SEALIONs."

Chapter 24

Relaxing as much as he could, Grant glanced out the window of his office and took a long slow sip of coffee while he waited for Steve Lockett to arrive from Washington and the Boswic leadership group to come over for a coordination meeting. There was a lot to discuss.

It was becoming increasingly obvious a brilliant strategy was driving the enemy plans. The Kremlin was staying in the background, but Grant knew they were spearheading another initiative to bring down the United States and gain dominance in the world.

Grant knew China was also involved but at the moment he didn't have the details as to what extent. He savored a swallow of coffee just as a call came through on his secure line. He glanced at the caller ID and answered.

"Got new information from RAND," Ken said, "just finished sending it to Steve. I'm sending it to you right now. Steve just landed and he's on his way from the airport."

"Good. I'll make sure Harlan has all the new data."

"I sent him a full report an hour ago. He has all the information I'm sending you."

"Harlan's coming over with Jim and Blake for a

scheduled meeting a few minutes from now, sounds like we'll have a lot to discuss."

"The new data from RAND should add some spice to your discussion. They've provided some new detailed analysis on what Russia and China are doing."

"How accurate do you think RAND's information is?" Grant asked.

"It's backed up by data from several intelligence agencies," Ken said. "The CIA also provided a lot of new information. Everything has been rechecked by experts at NSA. We're certain both Russia and China have new surveillance satellites in orbit."

"Do you know how many?"

"Three satellites we know of," Ken said, "You'll need to alert Randall he's going to be watched. Also encourage him to ask for help when he thinks he needs some."

"I'll give him the details as soon as he lands in Jamaica and urge him to not take any extreme risks."

"Do you think you and Colt have the same definition of extreme risks?" Ken asked.

"Probably not," Grant said. He gave a short laugh. "But I'll make sure he knows we can quickly send more help when he makes the request."

"I'll keep you posted on any new developments."

Ken disconnected just as Harlan, Jim, and Blake were ushered into Grant's spacious office.

"Steve should be here in a few minutes." Grant gestured toward the coffee pot. "Help yourself if you want some. You'll probably need it."

"Are we going to discuss all the new details Ken sent us?" Harlan asked.

"Yeah, we need to get moving on developing solutions" Grant said. He leaned forward. "The Russians and Chinese have at least three new surveillance satellites in orbit. Everything our taskforce does out in the open will be under observation."

"We have surveillance satellites too. Have we learned any more about what the enemy is doing in Jamaica?" Harlan asked.

"Most of what the Russians and Chinese have built recently has been underground," Grant said. "We know the general locations, however. Most of the construction equipment had to be on the surface, but it was scattered over a wide area. Steve will give us an update when he gets here. He's completed a lot of analysis."

Harlan gestured toward Blake. "He's done a lot of analysis too. Between the two of them, we should learn a few more things that can do us a lot of good down there."

At that point Steve walked into the office and eased into a chair beside Grant at the round conference table with seating for six.

"Coffee?" Grant asked.

Steve grunted. "Thanks, but I had plenty on the flight down."

"Then let's get straight to business," Grant said. He glanced at Steve. "Give us your updates."

Steve opened a folder he had placed on the table and took a moment to organize the contents.

"There's evidence the Russians and Chinese have built some tunnels leading from their respective embassies to the new construction," Steve said. He went on to explain the details of how he had arrived at that conclusion.

"So, they'll probably be going and coming through their embassies instead of showing up around where all the construction equipment was located, right?" Jim asked.

"That's my conclusion," Steve said. "I've alerted all the people who control the satellites and all who analyze the data. They know what to stay alert for."

"Do you have it setup where they'll immediately keep us updated on what's going on?" Harlan asked.

A slight grin flickered across Steve's face. "Of course," he said. "They'll alert Grant and me, and we'll make sure you and Colt stay informed."

Harlan nodded.

Steve looked at Blake. "We've compared notes on a lot of information in the last few days. It will probably be a good idea to share a lot of it while we're all together here. Go ahead and start us off."

"Of course, our main concern is to keep Russia from launching any of the Chinese-enhanced Poseidon Missiles," Blake said. "They're likely more deadly than we originally thought. Besides killing a lot of people and destroying a lot of infrastructure, they could be super effective in disabling most of our critical functions, including our entire economy."

Blake scanned the faces around the table.

Everyone nodded slowly.

"They're nuclear-powered and they're designed to cross entire oceans to reach their targets," Blake said. "They can be launched from devices constructed on the ocean or they can be carried and launched by specially designed submarines."

Steve nodded. "And remember the missiles themselves can travel at depths far below what any submarine can reach, even our best nuclear subs."

"We aren't sure about the planned strength of the warhead," Blake said. "Some reports state it could be as much as 100 megatons."

Steve leaned forward. "Just to put that in perspective, the bomb we dropped on Hiroshima in World War II was 1.5 megatons and the one we dropped on Nagasaki was 2 megatons."

"Do you have any guesses as to what size warhead it actually carries right now?" Jim asked.

"The consensus from FBI and CIA analysts is around 5 megatons," Steve said. "Keep in mind that's over twice as powerful of the one we dropped on Nagasaki."

Harlan grunted. "We better make sure none of those

damned missiles ever get launched."

Grant looked at Harlan and gave a short laugh. "I'd say that's the understatement of the year."

"But it's the damned truth," Harlan said.

Everyone nodded.

"And that's why we're discussing this," Grant said. "We'll certainly do everything we can to prevent that. If our taskforce fails, I'm sure the President will immediately unleash our Military, especially our Navy."

A brief silence ensued.

"The best data we've collected indicates the missiles can travel underwater at a speed of 80 miles an hour," Steve said. "That's faster than our nuclear-powered attack submarines and their anti-ship missiles. The Poseidon Missiles can also travel at a depth of 3,280 feet. That's far lower than any of our submarines can go."

"The Russians call it their Tsunami Apocalypse Torpedo," Blake replied. "Since it's powered by a miniature nuclear reactor, it effectively has unlimited range."

"There's a possibility the Chinese have helped Russia improve the speed to exceed 200 miles per hour," Steve said. "They've added ramjet engines and have been able to create a bubble of gas for the missile to travel in. This reduces friction with the water."

"Do you know for sure if this is true?" Jim asked.

"We've seen several reports the Russians and Chinese been working on improving the speed of the missiles by doing this," Steve said, "but we don't know if they've perfected it yet."

Harlan narrowed his eyes and then pressed his right palm to his forehead. "We damned sure better succeed in Jamaica."

"I don't think we all could agree more on that," Grant said. He looked directly at Harlan. "We'll for sure give it our best effort."

Steve thumbed through the folder in front of him and

removed a single sheet of paper. He glanced at the paper for a moment and then scanned the faces of the people sitting around the table. "There's one more thing I should mention before we go to another subject."

"The United States did some testing relating to underwater nuclear explosions back in the 1940's and 50's," Steve said. "They named two of the projects Crossroads Baker and Hardtack I Wahoo. The bombs detonated were roughly the sizes of the ones dropped on Hiroshima and Nagasaki. The explosions ejected seawater more than a mile high and caused considerable damage around the area."

"Any details on the damage caused?" Harlan asked.

"Some old warships staged in the general area were vaporized," Steve said. "Others further away were tossed into the air for miles. All were heavily damaged with crushed or cracked hulls."

After a brief silence, Grant leaned forward. "Well, I guess we've heard enough about the threat we're facing. We know we must stop it. Let's agree on what we need to do to help Colt and the taskforce."

"When they arrive in Jamaica they're going to quickly board the two Mark VI patrol boats and scout the coastline all around the island, right?" Jim asked.

"Right," Grant said. "And we'll make them aware both Russian and Chinese surveillance satellites will be zeroed in on them."

"Do you think the enemy will try to stop them from scouting the coastline?" Harlan asked.

"Probably," Grant said. "And I'm sure Colt will plan to take evasive action as necessary."

"Do we have any information about what the enemy is preparing to do regarding that?" Jim asked.

Grant gestured to Steve.

"We know the Chinese have developed some small hi-tech boats themselves," Steve said. "From intercepted calls, we know they've shipped one called the Sea Ghost to

Jamaica."

Blake leaned forward. "That's an interesting name."

"It has some technological aspects that give it a lot of advanced stealth characteristics," Steve said.

"How advanced?" Jim asked.

"We don't know all the details yet, but it's likely our radar won't be able to detect it," Steve said.

"What about our surveillance satellites?" Harlan asked.

"There's a possibility it can disappear from sight for a short period of time," Steve said. "We aren't sure about that, but we've intercepted some calls where someone mentioned it has that capability."

Harlan slapped his forehead again with his right palm. "How can they be that advanced?"

"The Chinese seem to concentrate on developing hi-tech weapons more than we do," Steve said. "They certainly throw a lot more funding at it than we do."

Harlan leaned forward. "In spite of any advantages the Russians and Chinese might have, I hope Colt can go kick their damned asses down there in Jamaica and end this damned nightmare. I hope the President keeps the USS Truman on high alert. We'll probably end up needing some super strong help."

"I've expressed the same concern," Grant said, "and Ken has told me several times the President has constantly reassured him if the taskforce fails, the United States Military will use whatever force is necessary to eliminate the threat in Jamaica."

Chapter 25

The next morning along the south shoreline in Jamaica, two military boats entered the ocean around Kingston.

Colt and Linda rode with a pilot and eight FBI agents in the first Mark VI patrol boat. Mack Thomson rode with a pilot and nine other CIA agents in the second boat. They had just pulled away from a private marina owned by the US Embassy.

Under camouflage fatigues, each warrior wore a suit of tungsten disulfide-based nano-composite material, over five times stronger than steel. The short-sleeved armor suits (with improved ventilation for tropical areas) protected each person from neck to knee.

Colt, Linda, and each FBI agent carried a SIG 556 rifle and a Glock 19 pistol. The Glocks had 15 round magazines with 9mm ammunition. The SIGs had a short stock and two pistol grips. The magazine could hold 30 NATO 5.56mm rounds. Each rifle weighed 7.8 pounds, was 37 inches long, and could fire 900 rounds per minute.

Each CIA agent carried an M16A2 rifle, using NATO 5.56mm ammunition, and a Browning HP 9mm pistol. Each rifle magazine held 30 rounds, and each pistol magazine held

13 rounds.

Everyone had extra magazines for a sustained firefight, if necessary.

Sleek and low in the water, the Mark VI patrol boats ran along the coastline at 40 miles per hour almost silently.

The pilot glanced at Colt. "This craft is better than the older model, the Mark V. Haven't studied all the statistics yet, but I can tell a big difference." He swept a hand down the length of the boat. "The boat is 84.8 feet long and it can carry eight additional people in addition to a crew of ten. You probably noticed we have six mounted 50 caliber machine guns."

After nodding, Colt glanced at Linda. She held a device pointed at the Eastern shore of Jamaica. A small green light blinked on top of the device. It was designed to turn red if any nuclear material was detected within 500 yards and yellow if certain types of drugs were detected.

Colt didn't know how the device worked, but he had been assured it did. He glanced at the blinking green light and then scanned the area. No other boats were near them.

*****

Stephan Zak stood on the deck of the hi-tech boat provided by China. Glancing toward their lead engineer, he asked, "Are you sure this baby can outrun any American craft?"

"I'm positive," the engineer said. "We can go over 100 miles an hour without turning over."

"Have you tested that?"

"Not completely, but I've been over 8o and had no problems when I made some sharp turns."

Stephan nodded and checked his watch. He fished his secure satellite phone out of a pocket and punched a digit.

"We're ready to move out," Stephan spoke into his phone.

"Do a visual check of the ocean again. We don't have a

good satellite picture at the moment," Sergei said. "We know Randall and his team are probably out there by now. It's likely they're close to Kingston. Best to know exactly where they are and how many. When the satellites can zero in on the area again we'll monitor as best we can from here."

"I'll be back in touch in a few minutes." Stephan disconnected from his call, moved off the boat, and walked along the pier toward the south exit of the largely enclosed marina.

Stephan stopped at the far end of the pier. That vantage point would give him the best view of the ocean. He scanned the area around him.

Two boats about a mile away were coming in his direction. He raised his binoculars and studied them.

Stephan turned and ran back toward his docked boat as fast as he could.

While he was running, Stephan removed his secure satellite phone from a pocket and punched a button. When he heard Sergei's voice on the other end, he said, "Two Mark VI patrol boats are headed our way. It must be Randall and the American taskforce."

"You know what to do."

Stephan heard Sergei disconnect and returned his phone to a pocket. He ran harder.

As soon as he got inside the marina, Stephan yelled at his men. "Let's go right now, no time to waste." He sprinted to the boat and jumped aboard. "Go, we'll soon find out if the Sea Ghost lives up to its reputation."

The pilot responded. After pulling away from the dock, he steered to the left side of the channel leading to the ocean and headed toward the marina exit.

With all his men being highly trained professionals, Stephan knew it wasn't necessary to give a lecture on elementary items, but it would feel good. That was why he would do it, because it would feel good, damned good.

Stephan gave a two-minute lecture and let off a little

steam as the boat exited the marina.

The boat sat low in the water and used navigation equipment developed by top engineers. Due to their improved stealth design and camouflage-like coloring (designed for blending with the water), Stephan knew his boat was hard to detect. Having enormous funding offered huge advantages.

Stephan thought about the Sea Ghost having enough firepower to wreak havoc on the Mark VI patrol boats. He grinned. This was what he lived for.

If Colt Randall was on one of the boats coming toward him, Randall would get what he deserved.

*****

Paul Collins, head of the Terrorist Threat Investigation Unit, hurried into his boss's corner office at CIA headquarters.

"Mack just called. They're checking the Jamaica shoreline," Paul said.

"How much have they checked?" Charles asked.

"They're just starting," Paul said. "They're moving along at 40 miles per hour. Everything is in progress and going according to plan."

"Hopefully we can find the location of the missile launch site."

Paul nodded and then narrowed his eyes. "So far, our analysts haven't been able to tie everything completely together. The details we've uncovered have been too scattered. Some details point to the Russians being more involved down there and some point to the Chinese."

"There's no doubt they're both heavily involved in the overall situation," Charles said. "We need to get more clarity on exactly what's going on in Jamaica as quickly as possible. Maybe we'll tie some details together today."

*****

Ivan sat in the main conference room in their underground headquarters in Jamaica and scanned the faces around the table. Sergei, Oleg, Maxim, Denis, Yaw, Wan, and Cham were all present.

Yaw narrowed his eyes and looked at Ivan. "We should try to sink Randall's boats right now."

Ivan punched a button on his secure satellite phone. He heard Stephan answer.

"Are you out in the ocean yet?" Ivan asked.

"Yes," Stephan said, "and the two Mark VI boats are still coming in our direction."

"Have they spotted you?"

Stephan hesitated and then said, "It's unlikely. They haven't increased their speed to come after us."

Ivan grunted. "All the stealth characteristics must be working well."

Stephan didn't comment.

"The boats are probably carrying the taskforce we've been expecting and Colt Randall is probably on one of them."

"We'll eliminate him and the taskforce."

"Do you have the torpedoes ready to fire?"

"Yes," Stephan said, "both of them. We'll aim one at each boat."

Ivan asked, "What if you miss one of the boats?"

"We have a lot of options. We can go close in and try to sink them with machine guns, or we can outrun them if we choose to go back to the marina and reload the torpedoes."

"Are you worried the torpedoes might not launch properly?"

"I've considered the possibility."

After glancing at Yaw, Ivan asked, "Have the torpedoes been tested?"

"I'm not sure on this particular boat," Yaw said, "but I know they've been tested on a lot of other similar boats."

Ivan spoke back into the phone. “Don’t take any big chances. Keep all your options open.”

*****

After staring at the water for a moment, Stephan looked at the boat pilot. “Keep the speed at 5 knots and ease toward the oncoming boats.”

The pilot nodded.

Stephan continued to study the boats. “Be prepared to accelerate on command. Before they’re aware of us, we want to move close enough to launch the torpedoes.”

“Just give me the signal when you’re ready,” the pilot said. “Both torpedoes are ready to launch as soon as I press the respective buttons.”

*****

Colt peered out of the lead Mark VI patrol boat and focused his gaze on the long stretch of Jamaican shoreline. He expected some type of trouble, but none was obvious at the moment.

Linda gestured toward the shoreline. “See any kind of structure that looks like it could support launching a Poseidon Missile?”

“Not yet,” Colt said. “And I’m sure it won’t be obvious.”

“Are you looking for anything in particular?”

“Something on the shoreline that’s well camouflaged or an inlet of some kind that has some structures along the edge of the water.”

“If you see an inlet like that are you taking us in close to inspect?”

“Of course,” Colt said, but we’ll be very cautious. They could be expecting us and waiting in ambush.”

Linda pointed her device toward the shoreline and swept

it left and right. "We're less than 500 yards from shore. No detection of any illegal drugs yet. No nukes either."

"Keep trying," Colt said. "Too bad we don't have the capability to scan for a supercomputer."

*****

"Due to our stealth characteristics, I don't think they've spotted us yet, but we're still about a half mile away," Stephan said. "Hold steady and keep easing toward them. We want to get as close as we can before we fire the torpedoes. We want to maximize our chances for putting Randall and his taskforce out of action right away."

The pilot narrowed his eyes and seemed to concentrate on keeping their direction straight toward the middle of the two approaching boats and their speed at exactly 5 knots.

"We have a good plan, but we need to be careful," Stephan spoke into his tactical microphone. "To maximize our chances, we need to get real close before we launch the torpedoes. No loud noises."

"Yes sir," came multiple replies.

"How close do we need to get before we launch the torpedoes?" a crewman asked.

"I'm told their accuracy is best if you're within a quarter of a mile," Stephan said. He raised his binoculars and studied the two boats again. Something wasn't right.

He had great intuition and a hidden alarm was sounding deep down. He had to figure out what it was that was bothering him.

*****

At CIA headquarters in McLean, Paul thought more about his discussion with Charles and some additional research he had just completed. He decided there were several things Mack should be made aware of. He grabbed his secure satellite phone and punched a digit.

Mack answered.

"Got some new information you might need," Paul said. "Can you talk?"

"For a few seconds, we're all concentrating on inspecting the shoreline."

"The boat we heard about, the Sea Ghost, appears to be down there," Paul said. "A Navy Mark VI patrol boat reported an incident early this morning close to Kingston where an odd-looking boat suddenly appeared and then roared off at a high speed. Navy crew estimated it was up around 100 miles per hour."

"That doesn't sound possible."

"Maybe not, but this was a veteran crew. They also reported the boat had a stealth design and didn't leave much of a wake. It obviously has some advanced technology."

"Did they chase it?"

"Yeah," Paul said. "But since the maximum speed of the Mark VI is 40 miles per hour, they lost it pretty quickly."

"Yeah, we're all aware of our speed limitation."

Paul grunted. "I wanted to make you aware of the incident. If you have an encounter with the Sea Ghost, there's no need to chase it."

Mack hesitated a moment and then said, "Thanks for the information. I'll make Colt aware of this as soon as we disconnect."

"Good luck to all of you."

*****

As Colt scanned the area with his binoculars, he heard Mack's voice ring in his ear.

"Paul just phoned and warned we might encounter the Sea Ghost out here."

Colt listened to Mack's explanation and then said, "That's probably the boat I'm looking at right now. It's barely moving, but it's coming toward us."

"What does it look like?"

"It's about the size of our boats. It's well camouflaged and has a stealth design, probably why no one spotted it earlier."

"That has to be it."

Colt asked, "Did Paul have any information about any weapons it could be carrying?"

"No," Mack said. "Apparently none were obvious."

"We only have machine guns, but they might be armed with torpedoes. That would put us at a disadvantage."

"There's something I didn't mention that could help us out there," the pilot said. "We have a customized device on each boat that can release shrapnel into the water. Any torpedoes that home-in on metal will be diverted. If we can spot the torpedoes in time, we can release the shrapnel and accelerate out of the immediate area."

Linda looked at the pilot. "Have you been involved in any tests of this type of situation?"

"Yes," the pilot said, "quite a few." He broke into a wide grin. "The shrapnel works like a charm."

Colt spoke into his tactical microphone, "Keep scanning the area, but pay special attention to the camouflaged boat with the stealth design ahead. It's about a half mile away and coming slowly toward us."

"Should we alter course?" Mack asked.

"Not yet," Colt said, "but we should be ready to drop some shrapnel and accelerate out of here instantly if we notice any trails of torpedoes in the water. Keep a close eye on the area in front of the boat."

"Roger," came multiple replies.

*****

Stephan peered through his binoculars and watched the two oncoming boats. He felt sure they hadn't yet seen his craft.

They certainly hadn't reacted in any way.

It's time to get fully prepared, Stephan thought. He lowered his binoculars and turned toward the pilot. "Get ready to launch the torpedoes and then turn back toward the marina and kick this baby into high gear."

The pilot nodded. "Roger."

"On second thought, once we launch the torpedoes, plan to continue past the marina up the shoreline toward our base around Port Antonio. I've decided to get the hell out of this immediate area as soon as we can," Stephan said.

"You don't want to stay around and make sure there are no survivors?" the pilot asked.

"I have orders not to do that," Stephan said. "Someone else will do the cleanup. Ivan doesn't want to take any chances on this advanced craft suffering any damage." He looked at the pilot. "Keep it slow and steady. We're almost at the right spot to launch."

*****

Colt grabbed his vibrating satellite phone. He knew he wouldn't be getting a call unless it was important. He answered and listened to the new information from Grant.

"NSA just decrypted some more calls," Grant said. "An advanced boat carrying two torpedoes will be intercepting you."

"I think we're looking at that boat. It's less than a half mile away now," Colt replied. "Do you know what kind of torpedoes?"

"That information wasn't available. I just wanted to give you a heads-up on what to expect."

"Thanks," Colt said. "We've already considered that possibility and formed a plan. We'll stay alert and take proper care of things."

"Do you have any defense?"

"These boats have a device for dumping Shrapnel in the

water."

"Good and good luck." Grant disconnected.

*****

Stephan raised his binoculars and studied the two Mark VI patrol boats that were now about a quarter mile in front of him.

"When I give the signal, launch the torpedoes and kick it hard to the left," Stephan said to the pilot. "Get up to 100 miles an hour as fast as possible. We need to get to Port Antonio in one hell of a hurry."

"Roger." The pilot gave a thumbs-up and kept the boat straight ahead.

Stephan gave the signal.

The pilot pressed two buttons simultaneously to launch the torpedoes and then veered sharply to the left.

Their boat stayed steady in the water as they sped east at 100 miles per hour.

Grinning broadly, Stephan glanced at the pilot. "Give it full throttle. Let's get this baby over 100. I want to leave Randall and his taskforce in the distance before the torpedoes explode."

*****

Colt saw two small wakes form and move toward them at high speed. He waved his right hand and pointed toward the wakes. "Dump the shrapnel and move further out into the ocean as fast as we can go."

The pilots of the boats pressed the proper buttons and, within a few seconds, were moving at 40 miles an hour away from the Jamaica shoreline.

Along with everyone else on the boats except the pilots, Colt looked behind them toward the area where they had dumped the shrapnel.

Within a few more seconds, two large explosions and a mountain of seawater dominated their view.

*****

In the main conference room of his underground headquarters in Jamaica, Ivan, along with everyone else, watched the images on the large monitors spread across one of the walls.

"That didn't work out so well," Ivan said. "I'm glad I didn't ask Stephan to hang around."

Yaw shrugged. "His boat has the speed to leave Randall and his taskforce far behind if they pursued him."

"Dumping the shrapnel in the water was a surprise," Ivan said. "Randall might have had more surprises up his sleeve. It's safer for Stephan to get out of there and prepare for our next move. We'll still get Randall and we'll be smarter about it next time."

Yaw continued to shrug. "It seemed smart to make sure the torpedoes could home in on the nearest metal in the water. That made it more certain they would home in on the patrol boats even if they changed course."

Ivan narrowed his eyes. "That's what I'm talking about. We were surprised and I didn't want to take any more chances. For now, I suggest we give our full attention to what Stephan will do next."

Yaw narrowed his eyes and looked at Ivan. "He's going to our main warehouse at Port Antonio?"

Ivan nodded. "He can regroup there while we decide on our next move." He gestured toward one of the monitors. "The satellite images are good. We can keep tracking Randall and his taskforce as we work out our strategy."

*****

For a few seconds, Colt studied the many pieces of shrapnel

floating in the water about a quarter mile behind him. The plan had worked perfectly. He then raised his binoculars and studied the mystery boat that was fast disappearing toward the east.

"I don't know what speed that mystery boat can reach, but it's obviously a lot faster than our patrol boats," Colt said into his tactical microphone.

"I think NSA intercepted a call where someone mentioned it could go over 100 miles an hour," Mack replied. "It was developed by the Chinese. I guess that's not surprising since they put most of their money into developing advanced technology."

After a brief hesitation, Colt said, "We need to figure out what to do next. You give McLean a call and I'll check with Grant in Tampa."

"Roger."

Chapter 26

In the J. Edgar Hoover Building in Washington DC, Ken, Frank, and Steve sat around the large table in the main conference room.

"Did we lose the mystery boat?" Ken asked.

"Not completely," Steve said. "NRO tracked them into an area around Port Antonio. That's on the northeast coast about 60 miles from Kingston. Based on other evidence we have, we know they have some warehouses there."

Frank narrowed his eyes. "Are we going after them?"

"Yes," Ken said. "We know Ivan Titov is a smart guy and we figure he's following an overall strategy developed by the chess masters in the Kremlin. We need to concentrate on making smarter moves than he does."

Frank grunted and turned toward Steve. "You've been keeping up with the technical details. Are we looking at current satellite footage?"

"Yes," Steve said. "NRO is reanalyzing the entire area around Port Antonio." He gestured toward the monitors on the wall. "We're tied into their system."

Frank clinched a fist. "We need to take the offense and give these bastards what they deserve."

"NRO and NSA have made this their top priority," Ken said. "And just before this meeting, I was informed NSA was in the process of decrypting some new phone call intercepts. They've already discovered Titov has some warehouses at Port Antonio. NRO is in the process of pinpointing their locations. We'll be contacted as soon as any of them have more details. For us to make smarter moves than Ivan Titov all agencies need to coordinate even closer and we're all trying to do that."

"Should you give Charles a call?" Frank asked.

"I talked to him just before this meeting," Ken said. "He informed me about NSA. He's currently discussing things with his staff in McLean. We're going to compare notes again in a few minutes."

"Steve and I will call Grant and give him the latest information," Frank said. He's keeping Harlan Pierce and Jim Boxer at Boswic fully informed. We're all staying right on top of this thing. We're investigating every aspect of the developments as they happen." He pointed toward one of the monitors. "I think Randall and the taskforce should check those warehouses as their next task. They can make their scouting trip around the entire island later."

Ken nodded. "I think you're right. I'll inform Grant. I'll also recommend that to Charles when I call him. I expect him to agree with us."

Frank looked at Steve. "You okay with our plan?"

"Of course," Steve said, "but this thing could get out of hand in a hurry if they outsmart us and are able to launch the Poseidon Missiles. We shouldn't spend too much time at the warehouses."

Ken nodded and reached for his phone.

*****

At CIA headquarters in McLean, Director Charles Andrews disconnected from his phone call and looked across the large table in the main conference room at Paul and Nick.

Various live satellite images of Port Antonio in Jamaica were on all the large monitors lining the walls.

"You could probably tell by listening to my side of the conversation that was Ken who called," Charles said. "He recommends we take some action right away."

Nick pointed to one of the monitors. "I'm guessing he wants the taskforce to do a quick check of those warehouses."

Paul laughed. "A brilliant deduction, amazing you could figure that out."

Charles and Nick laughed too.

"Okay," Charles said. "It's good we're not too uptight. Now we need to make sure we plan correctly and get the taskforce into action at the warehouses as soon as possible. We'll recheck everything quickly and make sure they're fully prepared for all the possibilities."

*****

At Boswic in Tampa, Harlan stared across his desk at Jim. "I got the latest information from Grant, and I hope Colt can handle everything."

"You might be too concerned about Colt being in charge of the taskforce," Jim said. "He's already proven he can rise to the occasion when he needs to handle difficult tasks."

"This mission is over the top. It has almost limitless complications." Harlan stood and walked back to the round mahogany conference table in a corner of his spacious office. He plopped down in a well-padded chair.

Jim followed and eased into a chair across from Harlan.

"Colt being in charge puts all the pressure on Boswic to produce the desired results," Harlan said, "and this mission has too many complications. If those Poseidon Missiles get launched and if the United States continues to function, we're never going to get another project with the CIA or the

FBI."

"We're paid big bucks for Colt leading the taskforce and I'm confident Colt and Linda will handle things really well. They also have a great team of agents. Mack is one of the best fighters on the planet."

"So, you're not worried?" Harlan asked.

"About Colt performing well?"

"That's the main subject," Harlan said gruffly. He leaned toward Jim. "Colt might have a lot of talent, but he never had to endure all the rigorous tasks we had to handle in the Marines."

Jim flashed a brief look of irritation. "Some people think he had to handle even tougher tasks. Delta Force has a stellar reputation."

Harlan grunted and made no comment.

"Just giving you some feedback," Jim said. "Ken Johnson and Charles Andrews both think Colt has had the best training possible. Remember Colt also went through a couple of their most advanced training programs before they selected him as the taskforce leader on the previous mission."

"We should have pulled some strings and gotten him scheduled for advanced Marine training."

"Two years ago, he went through the Robin Sage exercise given by the Special Warfare Training Group. Don't forget they told us Colt was the best who had ever gone through there."

Harlan rolled his eyes. "Nothing is as tough as Marine training."

"You should be over your concern by now about Colt being cocky. Colt has performed well on all his previous missions and I'm sure he'll keep it up."

"I still think he's too cocky," Harlan said. "That bugs the hell out of me." He flicked a hand. "Just wait, his cockiness is going to lead to a big screw-up eventually. That will reflect badly on us and cause a problem in getting future business."

Jim leaned forward. "Are you telling me Ken and Charles can't judge character?"

"Ken and Charles don't work directly with Colt," Harlan said. "We do."

"They see him often enough and they know a lot about him."

"Maybe so," Harlan said. "But they could be missing something."

Jim gestured with both palms out. "Colt leading the taskforce is good for Boswic and Linda being a member of the taskforce is another endorsement for us."

Harlan stood, walked over to a pot of freshly brewed coffee, and filled a couple of ceramic mugs. He carried them back to the table and placed one in front of Jim. "I'll give this some more thought. Maybe I'll end up with a different opinion."

"If it makes you feel any better, I'll keep reminding Colt to keep his ego under control," Jim said. "Don't forget I've lectured him a few times in the past about that."

Harlan gave a slight nod as he glanced at his watch. "We should be getting another update from Grant real soon."

*****

After pulling his vibrating phone from a pocket, Stephan checked the Caller-ID. It was Sergei. He answered.

"What's your status?" Sergei asked.

"I'm in our main warehouse at Port Antonio," Stephan replied. "Are you able to see our location right now?"

"Yes, we have clear images of your location live on the monitors fed by our most advanced satellites. We have both broad and close-up views of the area," Sergei said.

"Is Randall's taskforce anywhere around?"

"Not yet, but we'll keep monitoring the area closely. We want to stay at least one move ahead of Randall and his taskforce."

Stephan gave a short laugh. "You're still using chess strategy?"

"Ivan and I don't care what kind of strategy it is as long as it works."

Stephan made no comment.

"The Chinese technology is useful. Our technical capability far surpasses the Americans now," Sergei said. "We have great weapons, great transportation assets, and we have the best communications and spy technology."

"Are you expecting Randall and his taskforce to show up here anytime soon?" Stephan asked.

"Yes, are you ready for them?"

"Of course," Stephan said. "I have many of our best assassins here and prepared for action. Ludvig Glinka is in the group. Some people believe he's better than I am."

"You're the best, but Glinka is damned good."

Stephan couldn't help but smile. He gave a thumbs-up to the men around him.

The men responded with the same gesture.

"I'll let you know as soon as Randall gets in the area," Sergei said.

"Roger."

When he heard Sergei disconnect, Stephan scanned the faces of the men around him and said, "Are you ready to give the Americans a lot more problems to deal with?"

The group responded with a loud cheer.

"I'll be notified if they come anywhere close to us," Stephan said. "There will only be 20 of them. Our job will be to eliminate every last one of the bastards as quickly as we can."

The group again responded with a loud cheer. Many of them shook their fists in the air.

Ludvig ambled over to Stephan. "I want first shot at eliminating Randall."

"I don't care who eliminates him as long as someone

does," Stephan said. "We'll see how things work out."

*****

Following instructions he had received from Grant, Colt directed both boats into a large marina at Port Antonio. Grant had assured him that everyone stateside was coordinated and that he, Grant, would be the person in direct contact with him and the one providing directions during this next part of the mission.

Colt left a pilot with each boat and led his team of twenty further inland away from the marina.

Mack and Linda walked alongside him.

"Do you have the directions for getting to the first warehouse?" Linda asked.

"General directions," Colt said. "The satellites are zeroed in on the exact spot, and some FBI and CIA analysts are doing a detailed inspection of the images they're receiving right now. Grant will keep us updated."

"Is Grant making the strategic decisions for the taskforce?" Linda asked.

"I don't know, but he's clearly the one giving us the decisions right now," Colt said.

"Paul told me everyone in the Washington area decided it was best to keep Grant fully up to date on all the available information and let him generally call the shots for what we do," Mack replied. "We'll still get calls from our various bosses, but Grant will make the necessary strategic decisions as we progress." He looked at Colt. "They, of course, still want you to make the tactical decisions."

Colt grinned. "Guess we're as organized as we can be for the moment. Let's hope we can execute as well as we need to and go kick some ass."

Mack and Linda returned the grin.

Colt was glad they could stay loose and not get too uptight. In his opinion, that was a key characteristic of true professionals.

Chapter 27

Grant looked out the window of his office in Tampa. Besides the current mission, he had a lot on his mind.

There was mounting evidence that supercomputers were involved in many aspects of what they were dealing with, and it was becoming increasingly obvious a brilliant strategy was driving things. The Kremlin was staying in the background, but Grant knew they were spearheading another initiative to bring down the United States and gain dominance in the world.

He was certain Russia would launch at least one of their Poseidon Missiles in the very near future and the launch site would be somewhere in Jamaica, probably near Kingston."

Grant knew China was also involved, but at the moment he didn't know to what extent. He savored a swallow of coffee just as a call came through on his secure line. He glanced at the caller ID and answered.

"Got new information from RAND," Ken said, "just finished discussing it with Frank and Steve."

Ken relayed the information and then asked, "Are you

keeping in close contact with Harlan?"

"Yes, I'll make sure he has all the new data."

"I've already sent him a full report. He has all the information you have. He should be able to discuss it when you call. Randall's the main reason we hired Boswic. Let's see how much progress he and his taskforce can make before we change any plans."

"How accurate do you think RAND's information is?" Grant asked.

"It's backed up by data from several other agencies," Ken said. "CIA also provided a lot of new information. Everything has been rechecked by experts at NSA."

"So, we're certain both Russian and Chinese surveillance satellites are zeroed in on our taskforce?"

"Three satellites we know of," Ken said, "We might have to change some of our plans. We don't want to fall into some traps. I'll keep you posted on any new developments."

After Ken disconnected, Grant punched a digit on his phone and heard Colt answer.

"You're still being watched closely, but the Russians and the Chinese aren't the only ones who have good satellite surveillance. We have a lot of new information," Grant said. He explained.

"So, we're now aware of at least three warehouses we need to search?" Colt asked.

"That's correct and there might be more," Grant said, "we'll keep you informed."

"Any clues as to what's in the warehouses?"

"Mostly drugs, we think. They've spent billions getting everything constructed down there in Jamaica. We know they've created a lot of super structures that all contain advanced technology. They're doing a lot of drug trafficking to replenish their funds."

"How do you know that?"

"NSA has intercepted a lot of calls, and they've been able to decrypt a lot of content from many of the conversations."

There was a brief pause.

"Okay, here are the latest details pertaining to your situation down there." Grant took a few minutes to explain.

*****

After getting the update from Grant, Colt led his team of twenty toward the first warehouse. Knowing they were under surveillance by multiple satellites, Colt made sure they kept the best possible cover as they proceeded.

In a few minutes, the team, using maximum stealth, entered the first warehouse and moved cautiously past filing cabinets and stacked boxes. Multiple shadows stretched across the expansive area.

As he prepared for action, Colt realized his confidence level might be too high. Jim's advice came to mind.

Knowing overconfidence was a potential weakness, Colt scanned the area with great caution as his team spread out across the hundred-yard-width of the giant warehouse and moved forward.

Everyone kept their tactical microphones activated and stayed in constant contact.

There, to his left, in the shadows. Colt spotted movement out of the corner of one eye, but too late.

A figure grabbed the barrel of his SIG 556 and jerked.

Colt released the rifle and stepped back, staying evenly balanced. He saw a knife flash in the dim light.

After taking another step back, Colt moved his Glock 19 from the holster with a fluid sliding motion. He executed a quick forward snap, aimed at his target, and pulled the trigger.

A muffled pop sounded.

The figure with the knife went down instantly. The knife clanged on the concrete floor. The smell of gunpowder hung in the air. The whole thing happened within a couple of seconds.

Colt dropped to a semi-crouch and kept his balance on both feet while scanning for more combatants. After seeing no more threats, he holstered his Glock and retrieved his SIG 556.

"One assassin eliminated," Colt said into his tactical microphone. He gave a quick explanation.

After conducting a thorough search, the taskforce found no other threats in the first warehouse. Colt left four men behind to guard the place and then moved outside toward the second warehouse.

Light rain fell from the now darkened noon sky as the combatants spread out and moved forward. Colt held his silenced SIG 556 rifle in ready position and scanned the area. He spotted a figure on a rooftop. The figure swung a rifle toward him.

Colt aimed and fired. The figure dropped.

After shooting five more combatants in various positions around the second warehouse, Colt stopped and took cover. He continued to scan the area around him. It looked all clear and he spoke into his tactical microphone and asked for a status report.

"I got four," Linda said.

Mack reported he had also eliminated four enemy combatants. The other agents reported eliminating eighteen other enemy combatants among them.

Colt grabbed his secure satellite phone. "I'll give Grant a status update and then we'll search inside the warehouse."

When he heard Grant answer, Colt gave his status report and then listened for a few moments. He disconnected and spoke into his tactical communications unit, "Grant thinks our intelligence agencies have discovered the location of the Poseidon Missiles. We might need to break off from the warehouses real soon and go back toward Kingston. It's critical we don't allow any of those missiles to be launched."

"Are we going to continue searching the warehouses for

right now?" Linda asked.

"Maybe, but we need to hold up and stay in good cover for a few minutes," Colt said. "Grant told me the group in Washington needs to analyze the latest data some more and make sure they don't send us on a wild goose chase. He thinks they'll make a decision in less than ten minutes. Unless they find some hard evidence of the location of their headquarters, I'm guessing they'll have us continue what we're doing here. Cutting off a big source of their funding from drug trafficking is important too."

There was a brief silence.

"Stay alert and as soon as Grant gets a decision, we'll either leave to go back to Kingston or we'll go inside this second warehouse," Colt said

He heard everyone answer in the affirmative.

Chapter 28

At CIA headquarters in McLean, six people gathered in a hi-tech conference room with a line of large monitors on each wall. Different images were on each monitor.

Charles Andrews, CIA Director, Paul Collins, head of the Terrorist Threat Investigation Unit, and Nick Wallace, Technology Specialist were there from the CIA.

Ken Johnson, FBI Director, Frank Hellman, head of the Special Investigation Unit for Domestic Threats, and Steve Lockett, Technology Specialist represented the FBI.

"Grant told me the taskforce is mopping up at the warehouses so far," Ken said. "I think the taskforce is cutting off a lot of funding from the illegal drug business to Titov and his henchmen in Jamaica and, if we're smart, we can make some significant headway in doing a lot of damage to this latest Russian Chinese partnership."

Charles nodded. "Maybe even bring it to a screeching halt. The calls NSA just decrypted had more details about drug trafficking, stealth boats, exploding their Poseidon Missiles in our oceans, and their latest computer hacking plans using their quantum computer and supercomputers. Most importantly, the information in the calls had some details relating to the location of the Poseidon Missiles. We need to review that information quickly and make sure we haven't missed anything important before we send Colt and the taskforce back toward Kingston."

"Yeah, they might have intentionally included some information to lead us into a trap," Ken said. "We know the Russian strategy for world domination is some weird combination of poker and chess tactics and they're still playing for high stakes."

"It still looks like the chess masters are developing the initial strategy, but the people executing, namely Ivan Titov, are employing the characteristics of professional poker players. They obviously have some flexibility," Charles replied. "We can't afford to waste any time, but we must be sure we have the correct data before we act. We have some quick decisions to make." He gestured to Paul.

"Based on their latest phone calls, it appears the strategists have added to their original plan," Paul said. "They're going to use more cyber warfare while giving certain tactical elements of their team a little more time to inflict some damage on us. We know they have a quantum computer, and we know they have some supercomputers."

Steve leaned forward. "We've determined the villains have at least four supercomputer sites: one in Moscow, two in Beijing, and one in Jamaica. Various hacking attempts have been coming from all four of these locations."

"Do you still think the supercomputer in Jamaica might be in one of the warehouses in Port Antonia?" Frank asked.

"Maybe, we haven't been able to pinpoint the exact location," Paul said. "It might be a good idea to see if the taskforce can find it before they leave for Kingston. Indications per the intercepted calls are the preparations will go on for a few more days before they're ready to launch the Poseidon Missiles."

"Ivan Titov has some connection to every threat we're concerned about." Charles scanned the faces around the table. "He owns one of the supercomputers, probably the one in Jamaica. He's handling the launch of the Poseidon

Missiles. He's been running the illegal drug trafficking activity. And he seems to be the primary decision maker for devising the tactics to knock off Colt and the taskforce."

A brief silence ensued.

"Has NSA been able to determine the exact location of the Poseidon Missiles?" Ken asked.

"No," Paul said, "but they haven't yet been able to decrypt all the content from the calls. They're still working on it."

*****

Ivan sat in the main conference room in their underground headquarters in Jamaica and scanned the faces around the table. Sergei, Oleg, Maxim, Denis, Yaw, Wan, and Cham were all present.

Ivan looked at Wan. "Moscow has just informed me a part needs to be updated in the guidance system of the Poseidon Missile and China is sending the new one. How soon will it get here?"

"Tomorrow around noon," Wan said. "Then it will take a day to install. We need to be careful and make sure it functions correctly so we must take time to do the necessary testing."

Sergei narrowed his eyes and focused directly on Wan. "Why was this new part necessary?"

"Yeah," Oleg said. "Our Poseidon Missiles have been through thousands of tests during their development. I was heavily involved with all the details on a lot of them."

Wan leaned forward. "Remember, China has always supplied most of the advanced technology." He shrugged. "Our newest innovation will improve the accuracy and effectiveness of the explosion and that's very important to both of our countries."

"When we first told the Kremlin about our newest innovation, Moscow gave us the approval to switch out the part," Yaw said. "Our new part will ensure the American targets suffer much more devastation than they would if we didn't replace the part."

"Have you had many phone conversations about the new part with Beijing?" Ivan asked.

"Four or five," Yaw said. "I wanted to make sure I knew all the details about how effective it will be."

Ivan banged his fist on the table. "Damned," he said. "The Americans probably know we'll be holding up the first launch for a while."

"Why would that make any difference?" Wan asked. "They don't know where to find us and there's no way they could know the location of our launch site. We've used the most advanced technology on the planet to build the perfect setup."

Ivan set his jaw as his gaze rested on the three Chinese. "One thing I've learned throughout the years is that you can't underestimate these devils. If there's a way they can get you they will."

Sergei nodded. "That's correct. We can't give them a lot more time to find us or the launch site." He looked directly at Wan. "Make sure you do your work as fast as possible."

"I always do that," Wan said, "but I'll need to be thorough. We must make sure it works properly. We want to maximize the amount of radioactive seawater that will be dumped on the target, and we've developed the perfect solution."

"Which is?" Oleg asked.

"The new part in the guidance system has a much better sensor to ensure detonation at exactly the right spot," Wan said. "It's able to probe ahead and measure depth and distance to the continental shelf. It triggers the explosion when the position of the missile will produce the maximum damage." He went on to explain in detail.

"Are we sure we can wait a few more days?" Denis asked.

"I've just finished a long discussion with one of our moles," Maxim said. "He told me the American taskforce will probably go through all our warehouses there in Port Antonio before they do anything else. The mole also told me the Americans think our supercomputer might be in one of them."

Everyone laughed.

"Did our mole know if the Americans have discovered the general location of our headquarters?" Ivan asked.

"The Americans suspect it's around Kingston, but, according to our mole, they don't know the exact location, and they aren't sure it's underground," Maxim said. "The mole thinks they're going to continue to search the warehouses right now."

Ivan gave a slow nod and looked at Sergei. "Let Stephan know to be prepared to eliminate Randall and his taskforce at the warehouses, so we'll have even less to worry about."

Sergei nodded and lifted his phone.

*****

In McLean, Charles picked up his vibrating phone and punched a button. He listened for a few moments and then disconnected.

"NSA just decrypted some more information, Ivan Titov is waiting for an updated piece of equipment for the Poseidon Missiles," Charles said. "It'll definitely be a few more days before any of the missiles have been refitted and are ready to launch."

"Has any additional information been uncovered about the location of their headquarters down there?" Frank asked.

"Not yet," Charles said. "But NSA is still decrypting more information from the intercepted calls, and we have over a hundred analysts still working hard on the tons of information we already have."

"Did NSA get any information about the reason for the

new part?" Ken asked.

"The Chinese think it will ensure detonation of each Poseidon Missile at just the right spot to produce maximum damage on the target," Charles said.

"We have to make sure the missiles are never launched." Paul clinched a fist. "We need to locate the missiles and then deactivate them."

Ken scanned the faces around the table. "Should we tell Colt to break off the mission at Port Antonio and return to Kingston?"

"We certainly can't let the Russians and Chinese launch any of the Poseidon Missiles," Paul said. "I'll vote for going back to Kingston right now and start looking for them. Colt and his group will add a new element to the search by being on the ground in the general area."

"Since we don't know where they are, that might take a long time and involve a lot of wasted effort," Steve said. "Maybe it would be smarter to allow NSA and NRO a little more time to come up with some good clues as to probable locations."

Nick looked at Paul. "You're my boss, but I think Steve has a good point." He shrugged. "The taskforce might find some information in one of the warehouses that would help, especially if they find a warehouse housing the supercomputer."

A discussion followed that lasted for about ten minutes.

"Okay," Charles said. "The consensus is to let Colt continue his mission in Port Antonio and I agree with that."

Ken reached for his phone. "I'll tell Grant to let Colt know to continue at the warehouses."

*****

Near Port Antonio, Colt disconnected from his phone call and spoke into his tactical communications unit, "We've been cleared to continue searching the warehouses. Let's go check this next one. It might not be that well defended inside."

Colt led his remaining team of sixteen warriors toward the back entrance of the second warehouse. They moved in single file and remained five yards apart.

After Mack used his tools to open a back door, the taskforce split into groups of two and spread out across the width of the huge warehouse, which looked to be over a hundred yards.

Each group of two moved up a different aisle toward the front of the warehouse, which appeared to be about fifty yards away.

A musty smell hung in the air. Colt figured it was from a large stash of drugs.

Colt and Linda continued moving toward the front of the warehouse. The floor in front of them was empty.

Speaking into his tactical microphone, Colt checked with the rest of the team. So far no one had encountered any resistance and the team back at the warehouse they had left reported all was still quiet.

"All the agents still with me keep moving up the aisles toward the front of the warehouse," Colt said. "We need to ensure any assassins in this place have been eliminated before we move on. We now know of two more warehouses we need to check."

When they reached the front of the warehouse, Colt left four of his men as guards and, led the remaining twelve members of the taskforce out the front entrance toward the third warehouse.

Chapter 29

Colt approached the third warehouse and noted it had two levels. He spoke into his tactical communications unit, "We'll apply the same tactics we just used to check out the first floor. Depending on what we find, we'll then decide how we want to check out the second level."

"Roger," came multiple replies.

As before, Colt moved toward the back entrance. The others in his team of twelve followed in single file and stayed about five yards apart.

Mack moved up beside Colt and grabbed a small kit from a vest pocket. He removed a pick. In a few seconds, the twelve warriors eased cautiously through the doorway and looked for cover inside the warehouse.

While crouching behind some large crates just inside the back door, they surveyed the huge room with a high ceiling and no windows. About a hundred stacks of wooden crates dominated the space.

A wide stairway was prevalent in a distant corner. A couple of elevators were visible along a side wall close to the stairway.

Colt instructed the twelve warriors to stay in their

twosomes and spread out. They all took cover behind wooden crates stacked in rows across the area, creating multiple aisles.

Forklifts and other pieces of equipment were scattered along the floor around the stacks of crates.

With his internal alarms going off, Colt moved toward a better vantage point to scout the area. Linda followed.

After peering around the corner of the row of stacked boxes, Colt pulled back quickly and whispered, “Movement up ahead.”

Linda also peered around the corner and then looked at Colt. “I see two people on a raised walkway in the direction of the elevators. I estimate they’re less than 50 yards away.”

After mulling over several options, Colt said, “Linda, target the one on the right and fire on my mark, three seconds.” Colt gave a hand signal and started to count. “One thousand, two thousand…” He aimed and fired.

Two soft pops sounded. One man fell to the floor, motionless.

“We got one, at least,” Colt said. He and Linda rushed out from behind the stack of crates and ran a zigzag path toward the downed enemy combatant.

Colt, alert for danger, kept his SIG 556 in ready position. He and Linda charged forward, taking full advantage of various pieces of equipment on the floor to maintain maximum cover.

After reaching the downed enemy combatant who had fallen in plain view, Colt saw the other one had fallen on the raised walkway. Each enemy combatant remained motionless and had an obvious head wound.

Colt stopped behind a forklift and continued to scan the area. “Another guy moving this way.”

“Don’t see him,” Linda whispered.

“He’s approaching from my right. Hold your position. Watch my back.”

“Roger.”

Colt maneuvered toward the approaching figure. He had only gotten occasional glimpses of the man, but that was enough to know he looked Russian.

Giving the situation a little more thought, Colt decided he wanted to maneuver around behind the approaching Russian. He veered off on a cross aisle and then circled back.

Trusting his instinct honed from years of training and experience, Colt guessed right. Peering around a corner of a stack of crates, he saw he was just behind his adversary. He stepped out from the corner and leveled his SIG 556 at the enemy combatant.

"One mistake and you're dead." Colt held his rifle steady.

The enemy combatant turned slowly toward Colt. He dropped his rifle and raised his hands in the air.

Staring hard at the man, Colt said, "Lose the pistol, left hand, two fingers. That's right. Now drop it and step away."

Colt whispered into his tactical microphone. "Linda, join me. I'm thirty yards to your left front. I have a captive."

"Moving," Linda whispered.

Within seconds, Linda appeared behind Colt. She immediately moved behind a crate and scanned the area.

When Colt glanced at Linda, the Russian moved with lightning speed and unleashed a karate-style kick powered by his entire body.

When his rifle went flying, Colt realized Linda couldn't help immediately because of their relative positions. He was too much in her field of fire.

After the Russian's foot connected with Colt's SIG 556, the Russian was momentarily off-balance. Colt quickly stepped forward and slammed a forceful Karate punch just under his adversary's lower right rib cage.

The punch obviously injured the Russian, but it didn't take him out of action.

Snarling, the Russian bolted toward Colt and unleashed a straight punch. Colt moved to his right.

The punch hit nothing but air.

Colt immediately countered with a punch of his own. He connected.

The Russian went down. Colt dove at him, but the Russian squirted away.

Gasping for breath, the Russian rolled toward his discarded rifle. He quickly grabbed it and swung the barrel toward Colt, who had sprung to his feet.

Reacting instinctively, Colt drew his Glock 19 from the holster on his right hip and fired twice.

When the 9mm slugs hit the enemy combatant, he dropped like a lead weight, his head in shambles. His AK-47 clanged on the concrete floor.

"Damn," Linda said.

Colt turned. Two enemy combatants about thirty yards away, more Russians, charged from his right.

They rushed toward him with rifles pointed and fired.

The bullets went wide. It was the only chance they got. Linda (aiming her SIG 556) and Colt (still holding the Glock 19) fired multiple times.

Both enemy combatants sagged to the ground and remained motionless. They were obviously dead.

Linda glanced at Colt. "Guess they thought they'd surprise us."

A slight grin flickered across Colt's face. "We aren't that easy to surprise."

Linda returned the grin.

Colt spoke into his tactical microphone, "Status in the third warehouse?"

The rest of the taskforce in the warehouse reported having successfully disposed of several dozen more of the enemy. They all reported being all the way down to the area around the stairway and elevators.

Even though he knew the Russians were planning to delay launching their missiles for a couple of days, Colt felt a high level of urgency to finish checking the warehouses as soon as they could.

"Everyone with me ready to check out the second level?" Colt asked.

"Roger," came several replies.

"I'll lead the way up the stairs," Colt said. "Follow in single file and maintain a safe distance behind the person in front."

Colt charged up the stairs to the second level. Linda stayed about five yards behind Colt. Mack ran up the stairs behind Linda. Everyone else followed.

After reaching the second level, everyone maintained their spacing and moved down a wide hallway. No enemy appeared to be around.

Colt tested the communications. "Everyone copy?"

Eleven voices echoed in the affirmative in Colt's ear.

"We need to stay alert for an ambush," Colt said. "There are a lot of hiding places."

"Roger," came multiple replies.

Observing this level was much like a modern office building, Colt thought as he walked down a carpeted hallway with many open doorways, still no one in sight.

Linda moved a little closer to Colt.

Momentarily, Linda said, "Voices." She pointed. The voices came from behind two large, closed steel doors.

"Hold up for a few moments," Colt spoke into his tactical microphone. "Linda and I have something we need to check."

At first Colt thought the people behind the doors were talking loudly; then, he noticed a small vent above the doors. He pointed toward the vent. Linda nodded.

"Plan to enter on the left side of the right door and prepare for anything; I'll see if it's locked," Colt said. As he approached the door, he saw Linda get into position to his left.

Grabbing the knob with his right hand, Colt held his SIG 556 in his left hand with a finger on the trigger. The door was unlocked. He eased it open.

Colt and Linda stormed through the doorway.

Two men at the table began drawing pistols. But their guns never made it to their intended positions. Colt and Linda each fired once. Both men were obviously dead before they hit the floor.

A third man at the table took advantage of the momentary distraction and dove behind a row of filing cabinets about five feet in front of the back wall.

With rifles pointed, Colt and Linda rushed behind the row of cabinets.

"An elevator," Linda said.

Colt decided not to use the elevator. Someone would probably be waiting for them at the other end. He spoke into his tactical microphone, "We've taken out two people in a firefight, but one person escaped in a one-person elevator, going down. Everyone stay alert and hold your positions. Linda and I will look around for a few more seconds and then we'll proceed".

*****

At the Tampa FBI Headquarters, Grant leaned back in his chair at the large conference table in the makeshift operations center. Steve and Blake sat beside him. Frank and Paul sat across the table.

"Should we check with Colt on what's happening?" Paul asked.

"Yeah, he won't answer if he has too much going on." Grant punched a digit on his phone. Colt answered.

"Can you talk?" Grant asked.

"Yes," Colt said. "We just finished searching the third warehouse. We killed a lot of Russian assassins but one escaped. None of the enemy seems to be left in this warehouse. We're ready to move on."

"I'll check the area around you again." Grant looked at

a set of new satellite images on the wall monitors. "I'm looking at some infrared images, and I think I can tell you where a lot more enemy is congregated." He gestured to the other four men with him and pointed to one of the new images.

A startled expression spread across Frank's face.

"That's a lot of people," Frank said.

Grant noted the other three also looked startled as he spoke back into his secure satellite phone, "A huge amount of people are in the next warehouse. We have some new images just in."

"What do you see?" Colt asked.

Steve punched Grant's arm before Grant answered and pointed at one of the images.

"We know a lot of people are in the warehouse from the infrared images. We also have an image from one of the regular satellite cameras that shows Stephan Zak going inside," Grant said.

"We'll be prepared for a large reception committee," Colt replied. "Keep us informed of any changes as we go forward."

"Will do," Grant said. "We'll recheck all the current images thoroughly and I'll be back in touch in a few minutes."

Colt left four warriors to secure the third warehouse and moved outside with the other members of his band of eight.

The trade winds were blowing softly, and the temperature was 75 degrees. Not bad conditions, Colt thought, too bad we're too busy to enjoy it.

At least all the gear felt comfortable enough and it looked like they were going to need all of it.

There obviously was a lot more work to do.

Chapter 30

Ivan sat in the main conference room in their underground headquarters in Jamaica and scanned the faces around the table. Sergei, Oleg, Maxim, Denis, Yaw, Wan, and Cham were all present.

"Randall and his taskforce have taken out three of our warehouses and eliminated a lot of our assassins." Sergei studied Ivan for a few moments. "Shouldn't we change our tactics and get more aggressive instead of playing defense so much?"

"Do you have something specific in mind?" Ivan asked.

Sergei looked at Yaw and asked, "You're our military expert. What's your thinking?"

"This isn't the only chance we'll have to damage the United States and support our future domination of the world," Yaw said. "I don't think it's critical to take any significant risks on trying to eliminate Randall right now. He'll never find us down here and we'll still be able to launch the Poseidon Missiles. I think we can afford to play defense."

Ivan nodded slowly and then looked at Denis. "How close are we to breaking into the Federal Reserve System?"

"Very close," Denis said, "but I don't think we need to be in a huge rush. We need to do some more probing to ensure we'll be completely successful. With proper use of the quantum computer, I think our probes into the American monetary supply can remain undetected."

"Do you think you have time to be as careful as you plan to be?" Sergei asked.

Denis leaned forward. "Our quantum computer is down here with us and shouldn't be at risk. I think we have plenty of time to ensure we make no mistakes when we hack into the American monetary system and take all their money. If we're careful, we should be undetected and they probably won't know immediately their money is gone."

Ivan laughed. "Those are the kind of things I like to hear."

Maxim nodded. "It's a good thing we didn't put the quantum computer in one of the warehouses."

"I never thought that was a serious option," Sergei said. "It was just something we considered when we were looking at all the possibilities."

Yaw leaned forward. "Don't forget one of our supercomputers is also here with us. It's been useful for sorting through all the various options the chess masters have devised for our tactics down here and for our overall tactics for dominating the world."

"I haven't yet checked on it. Which one did you put there in the computer room?" Maxim asked.

"We've been using a scaled-down version of the Sunway Taihulight," Yaw said. "The one we have in our National Supercomputing Center in Wuxi operates at a speed of 93.01 petaflops per second."

"What's a petaflop?" Ivan asked.

"A FLOP is a floating-point operation in a computer," Maxim said. "A petaflop represents a thousand trillion of them. In this case, we're talking about 93 thousand trillion operations in one second."

Sergei narrowed his eyes. "That sounds pretty fast. Why do we need a quantum computer?"

"Because a quantum computer uses a lot of atoms that can all function simultaneously," Maxim said. "It's a million times faster than the best supercomputer on the planet."

Ivan gave a short laugh. "That should certainly help us break into the Federal Reserve System."

"That's correct," Yaw said, "and the speed of our supercomputer has been more than enough to help us analyze all the options for our tactics."

Maxim looked at Yaw. "You told us about your supercomputer in Wuxi, but how fast is your scaled-down version here with us?"

Yaw shrugged. "I'm not a computer scientist like you are. "I've reviewed some statistics, but I've never seen any numbers on the one my bosses sent here. I just know it's been very helpful for analyzing all the various options for our tactics so we can pick the best combinations to use."

"We have a better chance of repelling Randall this time," Sergei said. "Stephan will be in the last warehouse, and he has better security around him than we had at the other warehouses."

Ivan nodded. "And Stephan is one hell of a fighter himself. He hates Randall and he's determined to take him out."

"Remember, even if Randall takes over the warehouse," Yaw said, "we shouldn't be impacted here. We'll have plenty of computer power remaining and we'll still be able to launch all our Poseidon Missiles once we get the new parts installed in the guidance systems."

"And the new parts are still on schedule to arrive tomorrow?" Maxim asked.

Yaw nodded.

Maxim gestured toward Oleg. "Good, we'll both be

ready to work with Wan to get them installed as quickly as possible."

"There's no reason to wait around any longer than we have to," Ivan said, "especially if Randall takes over our last warehouse. Even though we think we're totally safe down here in our underground chambers and tunnels, it's not smart to take any unnecessary chances. The sooner we launch the better."

"I think we all agree with that," Yaw said. "We'll all make sure we move as fast as we can. I just don't think there's any reason to suffer from a lot of anxiety and make mistakes by rushing things."

After studying the latest satellite displays on the monitors, Ivan reached for his secure satellite phone and punched a digit. He heard Stephan answer.

"Randall's taskforce is down to eight but they're still a lethal group and they're getting close to your warehouse," Ivan said.

"We can handle them."

"Are you fully prepared?"

"We have forty men inside waiting in ambush," Stephan said. "We'll let them all come inside and then we'll chop them up. This time, Randall won't survive."

Ivan laughed. "That's definitely something I wanted to hear."

"You can count on it," Stephan said.

Ivan laughed again, louder than before.

Chapter 31

Colt and the other seven warriors that were remaining in his current assault force stayed in single file with the usual spacing as they moved toward the fourth warehouse. The warriors moved on a rustic trail through an area dominated by shrubs and palm trees.

They soon moved past a small inland harbor with a few docked boats. There was little activity at the moment.

When he moved within eyesight of the last warehouse, Colt could see it was a large one-story modern building with brick walls.

As they approached the target, they found wooden crates stacked in multiple rows along about 50 yards of concrete slab just outside a large metal sliding door at the back.

The door was open.

Colt and the other warriors with him cautiously melted into the available shadows along the slab. With everyone being careful to maintain about five yards between each warrior, they stopped behind some large crates.

Shadows from other stacked crates stretched ominously around them, but no immediate threats were apparent.

Mack eased up beside Colt.

"Paul just informed me we have a Hawkeye in the vicinity," Mack whispered. "It's off the Truman that's currently sitting about twenty miles away out in the Caribbean."

"Know if the Hawkeye has infrared?" Colt asked.

Mack nodded. "The Hawkeye shows forty people inside this warehouse. They obviously are inviting us into a trap."

"We'll take the necessary precautions," Colt said.

Peering around the corner of the crates and holding his silenced SIG 556 in ready position, Colt waved everyone forward.

*****

Stephan spoke into his tactical communications unit. "Colt and his group are now inside. Don't be careless and don't react too quickly but prepare to take them out according to plan."

Multiple confident responses rang in Stephan's ear.

"Don't be overconfident. Remember, this Randall bastard is a fierce warrior," Stephan said as he kept his AK-74 in ready position and scanned the area. "We shouldn't underestimate the jerk no matter how anxious we are to get him out of our way. We must be extremely careful."

*****

While moving along a row of boxes, Colt carefully scanned the surrounding area. Linda followed, now about ten yards behind.

As he moved forward, Colt alertly turned his head from side to side. There, to his right, behind some boxes, he saw the figure out of the corner of his eye. The figure swung a rifle in his direction.

Colt aimed his SIG 556 and fired, got him.

Linda moved closer and gave him a thumbs-up.

After hearing more muffed pops from their sound-suppressed rifles while he moved forward, Colt got an update from several of his warriors. They had disposed of ten more.

"Anyone who sees Stephan Zak, report it," Mack whispered into his tactical communications unit. "The views from the satellites have confirmed he's in here. They recorded him coming in and he hasn't gone out."

"Roger," came several replies.

Colt heard several muffled pops coming over his communications unit.

"Two men carrying AK-74 rifles are down," Mack said. "Each man has multiple bullet holes in his chest, no body armor."

Using extreme caution, everyone continued slowly forward.

A faint metallic sound from the top of a stack of crates well in front of him got Colt's attention. It was just a faint sound, but it instantly triggered his internal alarms. His past experiences had honed instincts that he couldn't explain, but, nevertheless, they were there.

"Incoming!" Colt said into his tactical mike as he dove behind one of the many stacks of wooden crates.

Torrents of bullets buzzed all around, kicking up small chunks of concrete from the floor and creating an explosion of splinters.

"Anyone injured?" Colt asked.

"Okay here," came multiple replies.

Colt looked around and couldn't see Linda. She had stayed five yards behind him the whole time.

"Linda?" Colt asked.

"Yeah, I'm okay," Linda said. "Thanks for the warning."

"Well, we got at least some of the assassins to commit themselves." Mack hesitated for a moment. "Colt, how in the hell did you know they were getting ready to let lose?"

"I recognized the sound of a rifle barrel on metal railing and somehow felt a flood of bullets would be coming."

"Didn't hear the sound," Mack whispered.

"The sound was probably closest to me," Colt said. He glanced up. "We all should keep an eye on the ceiling. There's a lot of railing up there."

"Roger."

Colt continued to glance up for a few moments, nothing. He peered around the corner in the aisle, still nothing.

Waiting a moment and again peering around the corner of the stacked boxes, Colt saw a man slowly coming toward him.

The man was hugging the crates, staying in the shadows, holding his rifle in ready position.

Colt stepped into the aisle and fired instantly, his silenced SIG 556 only making a soft pop. The man went down.

"One more down in my territory," Colt whispered into his tactical microphone. He eased into the aisle and moved forward, hugging the sides of the crates. His left hand closed around the front grip on the barrel of his SIG 556, which he pointed in front of him, barrel upwards at a 45-degree angle. His right hand squeezed the pistol grip. His right index finger was snug on the trigger.

Linda stepped around the corner of a crate and back into the aisle. She again stayed about five yards behind Colt as she moved.

As Colt continued forward, his mind flashed back to the many training exercises simulating these same conditions.

Two men popped out into the aisle about fifty yards in front. He cut the first man down with one shot. Instantly training his rifle on the other man, he fired again—the man toppled backwards just as his companion had.

Neither enemy combatant had gotten off a shot.

"Two more down. All look like Russians so far," Colt whispered. "Looks like Ivan Titov loaded his defense with his countrymen. I expected to see a few Chinese."

"Yeah, the one I got over here was also Russian," Mack replied. "I'm still moving forward."

Except for an occasional slight scuffing noise from his boots on the concrete floor, Colt moved silently forward along a row of cube-shaped metal containers, each measuring about six feet on each side. He constantly scanned the area, keeping his SIG 556 rifle in ready position.

Colt stopped for a moment and coordinated with the other warriors. They had remained in pairs and there were eight aisles, so his plan was to go all the way to the end of the warehouse and move over to the other aisles on their way back to where they had started from.

"Good place for an ambush," Colt whispered.

"Damn right," Linda said. "We need to spread out a little more."

Now keeping about ten yards apart, Colt and Linda moved forward cautiously.

"My internal alarms are screaming," Colt whispered into his tactical microphone. "But where are the enemy combatants?" He scanned the area ahead but detected no threats.

Colt eased forward. A burst of gunfire sent his rifle clattering across the stone floor. His mind registered an impact to his chest. The body armor worked, but the breath was knocked out of him. He rolled on the floor and struggled to breathe.

Breathing was one thing and staying alive was another. Colt reached deep down, summoning extra energy, as he rolled behind the nearest metal container.

From cover, Colt scanned the area. Where did the shots come from?

More shots rang out and Colt noted the direction of fire

this time.

Still struggling to breathe, Colt felt his chest. It ached, but there was no penetration from the bullets. His vest was well padded, and he didn't think he had any broken ribs.

"You guys okay," Linda whispered.

Everyone answered in the affirmative, even Colt.

Colt rose to a position similar to a sprinter starting a race. He bolted out from behind the container, scooped up his rifle, and rushed toward another container further down the aisle.

Reaching the container, Colt flattened against it and tried to catch his breath. Within a few seconds, he began to breathe regularly again. There were many benefits to being in great physical condition.

Colt reached the end of the row and peered around the corner. He studied the area where the last group of shots had originated.

"Looks all clear in front of me at the moment, but I'm going to wait a minute or two before I continue," Colt said into his tactical microphone. "I took some big hits on my vest. It worked well, but I want to give my lungs a little more time to recover."

"Colt, I'm coming up to join you," Linda said into her microphone.

"Still looks all clear, but be quick," Colt replied.

Colt took some deep breaths and exhaled slowly while he peered around the corner of the container and assessed his options.

In a few seconds, Linda appeared beside him.

Taking another deep breath and exhaling slowly, Colt noted his lungs were still painful, but he felt a lot better. He continued to push around the chest area with his hands.

"You sure you're okay?" Linda asked.

Colt gave a short laugh and glanced at Linda. "Okay enough. Get ready to move forward again."

A few more shots rang out, but these were sound-suppressed shots. Colt figured they were from his taskforce members. He heard Mack's voice in his earpiece.

"Got three more of the bastards," Mack said. "My partner and I are still moving forward in our aisle."

Colt heard several other similar reports and then glanced at Linda. "Let's go. Give me a five-yard head start."

Linda nodded.

Colt moved back into the aisle and immediately saw two enemy combatants round the corner of a large container in front of him.

Their rifles were pointed in his direction.

Keeping his SIG 556 pointed forward, Colt cut the first man down with one shot.

The other man aimed his AK-47 rifle at Linda and started to squeeze the trigger. Linda fired first. The enemy warrior toppled backwards.

Colt noted the enemy warriors had a mix of AK-47 rifles and the newer AK-74 rifles. He didn't attach any particular significance to that.

"Linda, good reflexes," Colt whispered into his tactical microphone as he scanned the area and prepared for more action. "Everyone report status."

"The two of us are at the end of our aisle," Mack said. "It's clear around us. We're ready to move to the other side and go back to the other end of the building."

Colt received the same report from the other two teams and spoke into his tactical microphone, "Linda and I have the same situation. Let's go back to the other end of the warehouse along the four aisles we haven't inspected. Linda and I will again take the aisle along the side wall. The other three teams will keep their same order from the wall."

"Roger," came a chorus of voices.

Chapter 32

At Boswic in Tampa, Harlan looked across his desk at Jim.

"Two things are becoming increasingly clear: the President doesn't want to escalate this conflict by using the military and the Russian leaders are trying to preserve their deniability by keeping their distance," Harlan said.

"But we know two prominent Russian businessmen are very much involved in the conflict."

"Moscow can still deny the Kremlin has anything to do with that." Harlan said. "At least the President has the Military ready to step in if we don't get the job done. He seems to fully understand the urgency of preventing the firing of any Poseidon Missiles from Jamaica."

"And we seem to be doing okay with our current efforts. Colt and the taskforce are making some real progress and Colt deserves a lot of credit for that."

"Let's hope we can keep it up. Grant called me a few minutes ago and mentioned we need to get ready to deal with a different twist to this conflict."

"Did he give you the details?"

"It looks like the Chinese are more involved than we thought."

Jim leaned forward and asked, “In what way?”

“In just about every way possible,” Harlan said. “They’re supplying both manpower and technology. They’ve enhanced Moscow’s capability to hack into our Federal Reserve System, and they’ve improved the range and effectiveness of the Poseidon Missiles.”

“I understand the missiles are powered by a miniature nuclear reactor. I thought they had unlimited range to begin with.”

“They did in a general sense,” Harlan said, “but Grant told me they now have more precision to maneuver into places that previously would have been difficult for them to reach. They have a better system for detecting depth and better capability to stay on a very narrow path to get through obstacles.”

“Where’s Grant getting his information?”

“From several intelligence agencies and from RAND, Grant emphasized a lot of updated information has just been gathered by the NRO, NSA, and the CIA. He mentioned the intelligence agencies had shared all the information with RAND to get the benefit of the additional analysis from their leading experts on the various subject matter involved.”

“You mentioned the Chinese are involved in every possible way. Do you have some more details?”

“They’ve completely taken over the computer hacking effort into our Federal Reserve System.”

Jim narrowed his eyes. “I’m assuming we know most of this information from multiple phone conversations NSA managed to intercept.”

Harlan nodded. “The CIA, with help from the RAND Corporation, has confirmed the money flow supporting the project for launching Poseidon Missiles goes through the World Bank via the IMF. In this case, the WTO is also heavily involved. The money flow is well disguised, but we’re on to them now.”

Jim shook his head slowly. “I guess it makes sense for

the International Monetary Fund and the World Trade Organization to be the major participants in Russia and China circulating the money as inconspicuously as possible."

"Damned right," Harlan said, "the most prominent international financial institutions are the IMF, the World Bank, and the WTO. They can provide the best cover. Millions of confidential transactions go through their systems every minute."

"Do you know exactly how the WTO fits into this?" Jim asked.

Harlan grabbed his phone and punched a digit. He waited a few seconds before he spoke into it, "Come down to my office."

After Harlan disconnected, he looked at Jim and said, "Blake will be joining us in a minute. He can explain the details better than I can about how all the money flows down to Jamaica."

At that moment, Blake walked through the doorway and settled into the empty chair beside Jim.

Harlan gave a quick explanation to Blake and then asked, "You've had time to study all the information RAND sent us. Can you explain exactly what the WTO's role is in this?"

"Let me start by reminding you that the WTO negotiates international trade agreements and settles trade disputes," Blake said. "Money, of course, is always involved in the agreements and the disputes."

Harlan and Jim, obviously waiting for Blake to continue, didn't make any comments.

"The WTO can create a lot of confusion about what certain funds are really for. That's one way the WTO gets into the mix of the international financing," Blake said. "On certain projects, the various factions of the World Bank also mix in with the WTO to create more cover from public awareness. The details I'm going to give you are going to get a bit complicated. If I try to summarize too much, some of the meaning is going to be lost." Blake's gaze took in both the other men. "Be prepared."

Harlan and Jim both nodded and again made no comment.

"Remember the World Bank is composed of five different international organizations. They're referred to as agencies, IBRD, IDA, IFC, MIGA, and ICSID. They all can play a part in any specific flow of money, especially a large amount."

"Like the billions supporting The Poseidon Initiative?" Harlan asked.

Blake nodded.

Jim gestured to Blake. "Before you continue would you give us the full names of those five agencies you mentioned? You've probably explained this many times at Boswic, but Harlan and I have never heard the explanation."

Harlan grunted and said, "Yeah. Even if I've heard some of it before, I don't retain the specifics of all this financial crap in memory. Jim and I don't work with all the details everyday like you do."

Blake stood and walked to a white board on the wall. He grabbed a black marker and started writing as he spoke.

"IBRD stands for International Bank for Reconstruction and Development. IDA stands for International Development Association," Blake said. "Actually, when someone is referring to the World Bank, they're generally referring to those two agencies." He paused for a second. "IFC stands for International Finance Corporation, MIGA stands for Multilateral Investment Guarantee Agency, and ICSID stands for International Centre for Settlement of Investment Disputes."

Harlan and Jim remained silent until Blake finished writing.

Blake gestured toward the board and focused his gaze on both Harlan and Jim. "Does this help any?"

"A little," Harlan said. "At least I know reconstruction and development are major functions of the IBRD and both the Chinese Embassy and the Russian Embassy have just finished big infrastructure projects in Jamaica."

"I can see the potential for creating a lot of confusion," Jim replied. "And that would fit into what the Russians and Chinese would want to do to try to mask the financing for any major construction activity anywhere in the world."

Harlan shook his head slowly and stared at Blake.

Jim narrowed his eyes.

Both men remained silent as they waited for Blake to continue.

"We've known for a while the Russians and Chinese will use supercomputers and a quantum computer to support various aspects of the Poseidon Initiative," Blake said. "We still think only the quantum computer will be used to hack into our Federal Reserve System."

"Okay," Harlan said. "Jim and I know all that. We don't need to rehash it. Let's get to the point. What can we do to cut off the money flow supporting what China and Russia are doing in Jamaica?"

Blake shrugged. "On the surface, the way the Russians and Chinese have it set up is ingenious. It has too many twists and turns in it for us to unravel any time soon."

Harlan leaned back in his chair and stared at the ceiling for a few moments before he looked back at Blake. "Well at least you gave us more insight into the whole damned money situation involved with the Poseidon Initiative." He pursed his lips tightly and then continued. "Let's hope Colt and his taskforce can continue their success and put the Russians and Chinese out of business with regards to computer hacking and firing the missiles."

"One thing we've learned from the intercepted phone calls is we all need to give this new challenge our best effort to succeed in preventing a catastrophe for the United States," Blake said.

Harlan nodded slowly. "Colt must succeed. Any slipups down in Jamaica could result in a major disaster for the United States. If even one of our major cities is hit by a tidal wave of radioactive seawater we'll have several problems we might not recover from."

Chapter 33

Ivan sat in the main conference room in their underground headquarters in Jamaica and scanned the faces around the table. Sergei, Oleg, Maxim, Denis, Yaw, Wan, and Cham looked back at him.

"How many Poseidon Missiles will be arriving in the first shipment and what size warhead will they have?" Ivan asked as his intense gaze took in both Yaw and Wan.

"We have three in route from La Orchila Island," Yaw said. He glanced at his watch. "They should be arriving within two hours."

"And they all still have 2 megaton warheads?" Ivan asked.

"We upgraded them to 5 megatons," Yaw said, "and the two new ones we're constructing in China will have the 100 megaton warheads. They're a little larger, close to 80 feet long and 8 feet wide."

Sergei narrowed his eyes and leaned toward Ivan. "Should we wait on the larger ones?"

Ivan hesitated for a moment and then glanced at Yaw

and Wan. “When will the larger missiles be ready?”

Yaw and Wan exchanged glances. Yaw gestured for Wan to provide the answer.

Wan shrugged. “That’s impossible to determine right now. There are many technical issues to be resolved with the larger size. We have our best team of experts working on all the issues. I expect to get an updated progress report within the next few days.”

Ivan nodded slowly and made no comment.

Staring at Ivan, Sergei asked, “Well?”

“I think we can do enough damage with the 5 megaton ones,” Ivan said. “We’ll go ahead as planned. After all, we have three of them. If necessary, the chess masters can probably devise an excellent strategy for maximizing the effect of exploding them all together.”

Oleg leaned forward. “They already have. I discussed this very thing with them yesterday. They’re going to send me their updated plan tomorrow.”

“Did you ask them if they thought it was best to select three targets or to use them all on one target?” Ivan asked.

“They told me they’ve presented all the various options to the Kremlin, and they haven’t received a decision yet,” Oleg said. He looked directly at Ivan. “We should get the Kremlin’s decision tomorrow.”

Ivan grunted and then looked at his watch.

“We need an update on Stephan’s situation,” Ivan said. “If he can knock Randall off, that certainly would remove the urgency of needing to launch quickly. I talked to him ten minutes ago and he told me he thought Randall would be coming toward his side of the warehouse in a few more minutes.” He gestured to Sergei. “Give him a call.”

“Is he keeping his phone on vibrate?” Sergei asked.

Staring at Sergei, Ivan narrowed his eyes and wrinkled his brow. “Of course he is. That’s standard operating procedure for these types of situations.”

Sergei shrugged. “Just being extra careful, I don’t want

to take a chance of screwing things up."

Ivan grabbed his phone and punched in a number. "Never mind, I'll make the call. I have some specific things I need to ask him, anyway."

"Hello," Stephan's voice rang in Ivan's hear.

"You busy yet?"

"No, but I know Randall's getting close. One of my scouts just reported he's about fifty yards away and coming down my aisle."

"How many men do you have left?"

"Fourteen and we're well positioned. We shouldn't have any big problem. We know there are only eight of them."

"Good luck," Ivan said. "Give me a report as soon as you can."

"Roger."

Ivan disconnected and scanned the faces around him. "I think the odds are overwhelmingly in our favor. We should be able to eliminate Randall and a large part of his taskforce."

"I regret I'm not there to help," Cham said. "I'm better than any of the assassins you have in the warehouse."

Ivan hesitated a moment and then said, "If by some chance Stephan fails to eliminate Randall, you could end up getting a chance to do that here. It's unlikely Randall will survive the ambush and, if he does, it's unlikely he can find us down here." Ivan looked directly at Cham and chose his words carefully. "But if Randall does survive, that's why you're here. If he by some chance finds us, we expect you to be able to eliminate him."

Cham grinned. "You can count on that. I'm the best in the world, much better than Randall could ever hope to be."

Chapter 34

Colt and Linda moved slowly down the aisle. They had now moved out of the area of the large metal containers and back into an area of stacked wooden crates.

It was likely they were moving into an ambush, Colt thought, and they would need to react quickly. They would need to be lucky too. Maybe one of the assassins would make a mistake and give away their position in time for him and Linda to react first?

"Get lower," Colt glanced at Linda and whispered into his tactical mike as he crouched and moved toward a better vantage point along the aisle. He stopped and surveyed the situation.

Linda occupied a position on the other side of the aisle, about ten yards behind and to the right of Colt. She also stopped and studied her surroundings.

Within seconds, Colt whispered into his mike, "Some movement about fifty yards up ahead." He dropped flat on the concrete floor. "Two heads are showing above some wooden crates at the end of the aisle."

"Got them," Linda said.

"Target the one on the right. Three seconds." Colt gave a hand signal and started to count. "One thousand, two thousand…"

Two soft pops sounded.

One man fell out into the aisle, motionless. The other disappeared.

"Got one, at least, Linda and I will check," Colt

whispered into his tactical microphone. "The rest of you hold position." Colt signaled to Linda and moved forward while staying close to the crates on his left.

Both warriors moved cautiously toward the prone enemy combatant lying in the open.

When they reached the downed enemy combatant who had fallen in plain view, they saw the other one had fallen behind a crate, both were dead.

Colt and Linda immediately took cover behind a stack of wooden crates along a small connecting aisle. Colt peered around the corner of the crate he was behind and looked in the direction they had been moving.

"There's another guy moving this way ducking in and out of cover," Colt whispered. "I'll wait for him to get close and then I'll deal with him. We could still use a prisoner. Watch my back."

"Roger."

When the assassin got within ten yards, Colt stepped out from the corner and leveled his SIG 556 at the enemy combatant. "One mistake and you're dead."

After a stunned glance at Colt, the enemy combatant dropped his AK-74 and raised his hands as high as he could.

"Lose the pistol," Colt said. "Left hand, two fingers, that's right. Now drop it and step away."

Colt gestured for Linda to join him. "I've got the one I saw. Careful, there may be more."

Within seconds, Linda closed on Colt's position.

The assassin grinned and stood motionless.

Linda glanced at Colt. "Someone else is coming."

When Colt made the mistake of shifting his gaze to Linda for an instant, the assassin moved with lightning speed and unleashed a karate-style kick. Colt's rifle went flying.

The thought flashed in Colt's mind that all these enemy combatants were damned good fighters, hand-to-hand included. He knew they were the best money could buy.

Linda realized she couldn't help immediately because

of their relative positions. Colt was too much in her field of fire.

After his foot connected with Colt's rifle, the assassin tried to recover his balance. Colt stepped forward and slammed a forceful Karate punch just under the assassin's lower right rib cage.

The assassin went down.

Colt dove at him, but the assassin squirted away and rolled toward his discarded AK-74.

The assassin bounced to his feet and expertly scooped up his rifle.

Linda fired multiple times.

When hit with the high caliber slugs the assassin dropped straight down and his AK-74 clanged on the concrete. He was obviously dead.

Colt gave a thumbs-up and sprinted toward the felled assassin.

Linda followed.

They immediately took cover behind some stacked crates along a connecting aisle and scanned the area.

Colt could hear more muffled pops on several other aisles around him.

As soon as the shots stopped, Colt spoke into his tactical microphone, "Status report."

"My partner and I just knocked off five assassins along our aisle," Mack said. "Looks all clear at the moment, we're still moving forward."

Colt got a similar report from the other two teams.

"We should have them pretty well cleaned out in here," Mack said. "Our satellites would have spotted any reinforcements coming in."

"Has anyone seen any sign of Stephan Zak?" Colt asked.

All replies came back negative.

"Let's keep going all the way to the end of the warehouse and then we'll consult with Grant and decide what to do," Colt said.

"Roger," came multiple replies.

Colt motioned to Linda and continued forward. There were only about twenty yards to go before reaching the entrance where they had started.

Moving cautiously and staying prepared for an instant reaction, Colt eased forward. He scanned the area ahead of him carefully as he progressed toward the forward wall of the warehouse. Things seemed to be going well until he heard a loud voice behind him.

"You think you're good but you're not nearly as good as you think you are, not nearly as smart either."

Colt and Linda started to turn.

"Freeze or you die instantly," Stephan said.

Colt and Linda complied with the command.

"Drop the rifles now and don't say anything into your tactical mikes or to each other or you die immediately!" Stephan said. "I'll instantly understand anything you say. I speak perfect English."

Colt knew he had no choice. He remained silent and his SIG 556 fell straight to the floor.

Linda followed Colt's example.

"Now you can turn slowly toward me," Stephan said.

Colt turned slowly and noted Stephan was in perfect position and had a smirk on his face.

The guy was as good as his reputation, all right, Colt thought. He noted Stephan stood behind a crate that rose to just above his waist and his AK-74 was pointed at a space about halfway between him and Linda.

"Reach up slowly and turn off your tactical mikes," Stephan said. "Don't make any wrong moves or you die. I know exactly how they work."

Colt and Linda complied.

Stephan stared at Colt. "You screwed up. I prepared this crate I'm standing behind perfectly. I cut small holes in it so I could hear and breathe easily. I heard you go by and then I silently pushed open a side panel I had made into a small door." He flashed a big grin. "And here we are. I've outsmarted you."

"You don't have a sound suppressor on your rifle," Colt said. "When you shoot us the rest of my team will be after you in an instant."

"Yeah, but both of you have sound suppressors on all of your weapons," Stephan said. "I'll use one of yours." He continued to grin. "I don't have orders to not shoot you this time. It's the opposite." His grin expanded.

Colt and Linda didn't comment.

"Now slide your rifles this way," Stephan said. "Slide them easily along the concrete floor."

Colt glanced at Linda and didn't move. He definitely wasn't going to slide his SIG 556 toward Stephan Zak.

A brief silence ensued.

Colt knew he had screwed up, but was it really his fault? Maybe it was, maybe it wasn't? It wasn't reasonable to stop and check every crate to see if someone was hiding inside. Colt exhaled slowly. He and Linda could have spread out more though. Stephan Zak had outsmarted him this time.

Stephan narrowed his eyes and pointed his AK-74 directly at Colt. "Okay, smart ass. I'm not going to waste any time and play any games with you." He raised his rifle slightly and tightened his finger on the trigger.

"Hold it." Linda looked directly at Stephan. "Don't shoot him. I'll slide mine to you." She slowly took a step toward her rifle and placed her right foot behind it. Being careful to not make any sudden movements, she eased the rifle in Stephan's direction.

"Keep going," Stephan said. "I need it closer."

Linda took another slow step and repeated the process.

"Okay that's close enough," Stephan said. "Now slowly return to your original position. Remember, any unnecessary moves by either one of you and both of you die instantly."

Colt saw Stephan lift his AK-47 slightly and point it

directly at him. Stephan again tightened his finger on the trigger for emphasis.

Linda carefully eased back to her original position.

Stephan flashed a triumphant grin as he kept his AK-74 pointed directly at Colt. He stepped out from the crate and used his left foot to rake the SIG 556 toward him. While keeping his rifle pointed at Colt, he squatted quickly and grabbed Linda's rifle.

Colt's eyes narrowed. "I guess you think you're pretty smart?"

"Smarter than you, at least," Stephan said. "I'm going to enjoy watching an egotistical jerk like you die. And you're going to die slowly." He stood and placed the SIG 556 on top of the crate, the end of the barrel pointed toward Colt and Linda.

"Even if you kill us, you won't make it out of here alive," Colt said. "Somebody will get you."

"I'll deal with the others later." Stephan flashed a huge grin and waved his AK-74 back and forth between Colt and Linda. "I have some things to tell you before you die a slow death. I'm going to enjoy seeing your reaction."

Colt and Linda remained silent.

Stephan looked directly at Colt. "You're an overrated egotistical fool and you deserve to die. I'm proud to be the one to eliminate you. In fact, I think I would enjoy eliminating you with your own weapon more than with your partner's weapon." He gestured toward the SIG 556 on top of the crate.

Colt began to feel there was some hope creeping into the picture. Stephan was displaying a huge amount of ego himself and probably wasn't going to be as careful as he should be.

While keeping his AK-74 in his right hand pointed at Colt, Stephan grabbed Linda's rifle off the top of the crate with his left hand. He quickly pointed the SIG 556 at Colt and lowered his AK-74 to the crate. "Okay Randall, I now have a sound suppressed weapon pointed at you. Any unnecessary movement and you're dead. There'll be minimal noise from the shot."

Colt made no comment. As he waited for the expected instructions from Stephan, he began to mull over his options.

After glaring triumphantly at Colt, Stephan said, "All right Randall, let's see if you're smart enough to follow some simple instructions. You're probably not, but we'll see." He laughed at his own humor.

Colt evaluated his chances of unsnapping the strap over his Glock and being able to draw quickly enough to beat Stephan firing the bullet that would be coming his way. At the moment, it looked like Stephan was too much on ready to allow him enough time.

"All right, Randall," Stephan said. "Let's get started. Do like Linda just did, very slowly take some steps toward your rifle until you can touch it with your feet."

Colt followed instructions while Stephan narrowed his eyes and watched him like a hawk.

"This isn't going to do me any good to cooperate with you," Colt said. "It makes no difference to me what rifle you shoot me with."

Stephan grunted. "I'll let you live a little longer if you cooperate." He shrugged. "Maybe you'll figure out a way to survive, although that's not likely for a dumbass like you."

Colt didn't comment.

"Now lift your right foot slowly and nudge your rifle toward me," Stephan said.

Stephan's eyes were still narrowed, and his grin was still intact.

"Follow my instructions perfectly now or you'll die within the next second." Stephan kept the SIG 556 in his hand aimed at Colt as he tightened his finger on the trigger."

Colt again followed instructions.

Stephan kept Linda's rifle pointed at Colt as he squatted and grabbed Colt's rifle off the floor. He stood. An even larger grin stretched across his face as he pointed Colt's rifle at Colt and placed Linda's rifle beside his AK-74 on top of the crate. "Okay Randall, you can see I know how to get things done."

Colt remained silent, but his mind was racing. Surely he didn't need to put up with this crap from Stephan. Surely he would find a way to take the offense, if only the strap wasn't over his Glock.

Stephan aimed the SIG 556 halfway between Colt and Linda. "Get closer together."

Colt and Linda followed instructions. Colt was glad Stephan seemed overconfident. Maybe they could irritate him a little without being shot. He glanced at Linda and noted she seemed to understand. It was good to have a smart partner.

"How did you get involved with what's going on here in Jamaica?" Linda asked.

Stephan gave a slight shrug. "That has no relevance to what I'm doing right now. Besides that's none of your business."

"Do you work for the Kremlin?" Linda asked.

"Again, that's none of your business," Stephan snapped. He pointed the barrel of the SIG 556 at Linda. "One more smart-ass question and you'll die on the spot."

"Okay, sorry," Linda said. "But I'm wondering about something that relates directly to you. I'd really like to know the answer before I die."

"And die you will," Stephan said with a big laugh. He stared at Linda. He seemed to be thinking.

He's curious, Colt thought.

"Okay, what do you want to know?" Stephan asked. He pushed the SIG 556 slightly more toward Linda.

"You're so much better than we are," Linda said slowly. "What did you do to get so good?"

Colt noted that Stephan brightened. He enjoys talking about himself, Colt thought. Linda has a brilliant idea. Now

I need to do my part.

Linda moved her left hand slowly to her face.

"Hold it right there." Stephan pointed the SIG 556 directly at her. "No more movement."

"My face is really itching. It's driving me crazy," Linda said. "I have to scratch it."

"No, I can't let you do that," Stephan said. He narrowed his eyes and stared at Linda. "You have to stay perfectly still."

"We're going to die anyway," Linda said.

Stephan laughed. "You're smarter than I thought." He extended the SIG 556 toward her. "You'll go first." His finger tightened on the trigger.

When Linda had first started her distraction routine, Colt had very slowly moved his right hand closer to his holster. Now he unsnapped the strap over his Glock and removed it from the holster in less than a second.

Colt pointed his Glock 19 at Stephan and instantly fired multiple times at his chest.

Stephan dropped his rifle, twisted, staggered to the side of the crate, and dropped to the concrete floor. He thrashed around a moment and then lay perfectly still.

Colt prepared to fire at Stephan's head in case he was wearing a bulletproof vest.

A lot of blood began to cover the floor around Stephan, so Colt decided he didn't need to fire any more. It was obvious Stephan wasn't wearing a bullet proof vest. He walked over to check Stephan's pulse. There was none.

Colt glanced at Linda. "I fired at his chest for two reasons. One is that I didn't want to take a chance on missing and two, with my pistol moving upward from the holster, it was quicker to acquire the target."

Linda nodded.

"Even if he were wearing a vest, I also figured the full metal jacket hollow point 9mm bullet would have enough impact to prevent him from pulling the trigger," Colt said.

"Exactly the logic I would have used," Linda muttered as she and Colt quickly retrieved their rifles and scanned the immediate area.

No more threats were evident.

Colt reached up and switched on his tactical microphone. "Mack, are you there?"

"What the hell happened?" Mack asked. "We've been giving you and Linda progress reports and received no answer. We were about ready to come over and check on both of you."

Colt quickly explained.

"Great job," Mack said. "Are you at the end of your aisle?"

"Yes," Colt replied. "We're now right against the front wall."

"Okay, we should be all finished here," Mack said. "The rest of us eliminated four more assassins while you and Linda were delayed a bit. I think we've now eliminated the whole damned bunch."

"I'll call Grant and give him a full report. The Navy has a crew on the Reagan that's on standby to provide cleanup operations around here. Grant will alert them," Colt replied. "Our taskforce will return to our boats and continue our mission after the Navy crew arrives."

Chapter 35

The next morning in McLean, Charles drummed his fingers on the large table in the main conference room at CIA headquarters. He and Paul both looked at several wall-mounted monitors.

Multiple satellite photographs of several areas in Jamaica were displayed. A broad area around Port Antonio was displayed as was a broad area around Kingston.

Paul wrinkled his brow. "Did you study all the latest information from NSA, and the NRO?"

"Yeah, there's a lot more to think about now," Charles said. "It looks like the Kremlin is calling the Poseidon Missile their Tsunami Apocalypse Torpedo. There's no longer any doubt about what they have in mind for how they're going to use it."

Paul gave a short laugh. "I don't think there ever was any doubt, but the latest name we've heard certainly confirms what we've been thinking.".

"So, it still looks like they're going to make their first attack on the United States from Jamaica. I hope Randall and the taskforce can accomplish their mission and prevent any of the missiles from being launched."

Paul gestured toward the satellite picture on one of the monitors. "The consensus of all our analysts and all the analysts at NSA is the missile launch is going to be from an underground area connecting to the ocean somewhere close to Kingston."

"And they still think entrances to the underground area

are built into both the Russian Embassy and the Chinese Embassy?"

"That's what they're telling me."

Charles nodded slowly and then said, "Surely they have at least one more way of getting in. They wouldn't want to take the chance of our shutting down both embassies for some reason."

"Knowing how the Chinese operate, they probably built at least one backup entrance somewhere and have never told the Russians."

Charles laughed. "Yeah, I certainly wouldn't argue with that."

After a brief silence, Paul asked. "Did you get any updates just before our meeting about the next step for the taskforce?"

"You've been to all the briefings I've been to." Charles took a quick peek at his watch. "Based on what we heard last, I would expect to get another update real soon. The taskforce is all finished in Port Antonia and they're back in Kingston. Navy personnel from the Truman have secured the warehouses."

Paul narrowed his eyes. "Grant is still the one responsible for keeping in close contact with Randall, right?"

"He's the only one I've gotten status reports from," Charles said. "Why are you asking this?"

"I keep thinking we're missing something."

"Such as?"

Paul gave a slight shrug.

Charles studied the expression on Paul's face for a moment. "Okay, surely you have some idea about what's bothering you?"

"I can't put my finger on it yet."

"We know the taskforce is back in the Kingston area," Charles said. "They should be looking for the launch site for the Poseidon Missiles now."

Paul gestured toward a couple of monitors on the wall displaying live satellite footage. “Maybe we can find a way to help them some in their search.”

“We have a lot of analysts working on that,” Charles said. “You and I need to concentrate on the big picture and make sure we’re not missing anything.” He leaned toward Paul. “Something along the lines of what you were trying to identify just a moment ago. I’m told the analysts at NSA have now been through every detail, so have our analysts. We should be able to figure out what’s going on. I doubt we’ve missed anything.”

“However, I don’t think we can ever rule out more surprises,” Paul said. “I think that’s the main thing bothering me.”

“Trying to avoid the next surprise?”

Paul gave a slow nod. “I think that’s the best way to put it.”

Charles narrowed his eyes and didn’t comment.

“From the beginning, China has stayed in the background. The Russians are still trying to stay in the background, and both countries are throwing more firepower into this than we expected. Many different aspects of this could accelerate at any moment.” Paul leaned forward. “You think the President should reconsider using the military for more than just support and backup?”

Charles rubbed his chin. “I think it’s best to let the taskforce continue to handle this. Using the military could be overkill at this juncture. Grant is fully capable of making the right calls and Colt is fully capable of making the correct on-the-spot tactical decisions.”

Paul gave Charles a sober look. “But, we still have a lot of unanswered questions. We know the chess masters in the Kremlin are hard at work, but I think this is more of a poker game we’re in. We don’t know exactly what cards they’re holding and that’s another thing bothering me. I guess that goes along with wanting to avoid more surprises.”

Charles nodded. “And this poker game has intensified. The bets have been raised.”

“The Russians and Chinese have too many options. Since their apocalypse torpedo is powered by a miniature nuclear reactor it has unlimited range. It can destroy any of our key facilities on any of our coasts.”

“Should we call Nick in here to review all the relevant technology again with us?” Charles asked.

“He’s busy trying to analyze more of the information we got on the intercepted phone calls,” Paul said. “I told him I especially wanted him to find out more about their timing to use their quantum computer to hack into our Federal Reserve System.”

“The computers they’re using weren’t in any of the warehouses we searched in Port Antonio. It’s not likely they’re in the embassies. They must be in their underground facilities around Kingston.”

Paul grunted. “And that puts the emphasis back on finding the location of the underground facilities and figuring out how to get into them.”

Charles lifted his phone. “I’ll call Grant and get a status report. Colt and the taskforce need to succeed on that really quickly or we’ll going to have a lot of big problems in a lot of ways.”

Chapter 36

In the main conference room of the J Edgar Hoover Building in Washington DC, Ken Johnson, the FBI Director, sat at the long table and studied several rows of monitors along two walls. After a few moments, he glanced at Frank Hellman (head of the Special Investigation Unit for Domestic Threats), and technology specialist Steve Locket.

Ken's gaze rested on the monitors again and then he leaned toward Steve. "You've been working closely with the CIA analysts, right?"

"Yes sir, Nick Wallace in particular," Steve said.

"And you think they've found the launch site for the Poseidon Missiles?" Ken asked.

"Yes sir," Steve said. "It's real close to Kingston."

"Does Grant have all the latest information?" Ken asked.

"I've given him every bit of data I have," Steve said. "And I told him I think we're close to finding an entrance into the site. It's not very far from the Russian and Chinese embassies."

"Did Grant confirm he's still coordinating closely with Colt?" Ken asked.

"Yes sir," Steve said. "He told me they just had a conversation ten minutes before we talked." Steve glanced at his watch. "The taskforce should have all the intelligence data we've accumulated, and they should be expecting Grant to call back shortly with the location of at least one secret entrance to the missile launch site."

Ken nodded slowly.

Frank looked directly at Steve. "And you still believe the group of analysts you've been working with is going to find one of these entrances within the next few minutes?"

"Yes sir," Steve said. "They had a lot of clues about the location, and they were working on it when our meeting here began."

"What confidence level do you have it will be in the next few minutes?" Ken narrowed his eyes.

"99.5%," Steve said with a grin. "Not much in this world is absolutely certain until it actually happens."

"It's logical the Russian moles we've been coping with are keeping the Kremlin fully informed about everything that's going on," Frank replied. "They'll probably let Ivan Titov know Colt and the taskforce could be arriving at his underground base within a short period of time."

Ken nodded. "I think we can be sure of that, and I think we can be sure the Chinese leaders are getting a full briefing too." He looked at Steve. "How many analysts have you been working with?"

"Over a hundred," Steve said.

Ken laughed. "Yep, I'm 100% sure the information got out to some moles. Colt and the taskforce need to give this their best effort in every way. We damned well better succeed down there in Jamaica. Time might be running out before they launch their Tsunami Apocalypse Torpedoes."

Chapter 37

In the main conference room in his underground headquarters in Jamaica, Ivan disconnected from his phone call and scanned the faces around the table. Sergei, Oleg, Maxim, Denis, Yaw, Wan, and Cham were all present.

"Randall and his taskforce might be showing up somewhere around us in an hour or so," Ivan said. "I just got tipped off by Moscow."

"Are you referring to their showing up here in the Kingston area?" Sergei asked.

Ivan pointed at the table and moved his forefinger rapidly straight up and down. "I'm referring to right here in the underground area." He pursed his lips and stared at Sergei. "And don't overlook the two secret entrances that were built. They might have found one of them through satellite surveillance."

"It's unlikely that could happen." Yaw looked directly at Ivan. "When we did the construction we took special care to construct the entrances in areas with a lot of cover from satellite view. We were very careful."

"That's good and I hope you're right," Ivan said, "but we'd better be prepared anyway. We'd better alert all our people down here and make sure they're prepared to fight off an attack."

An evil grin spread across Cham's massive face. "I'll welcome some action. Randall won't get past me. Neither will any other members of his taskforce."

"During our construction we also installed an excellent warning system," Wan said. "Anyone entering any of the underground areas without having keyed the proper access code will set off multiple alarms."

Sergei leaned toward Wan. "I know you did that, but I didn't listen carefully to all the details. Tell me again exactly what we'll hear."

"Loud sirens will go off in multiple locations down here," Wan said. "You can be confident everyone in the underground tunnels will hear them." He pointed toward a small round fixture on the wall. "We'll get a beeping sound and flashing lights in here."

Sergei nodded slowly and made no comment.

"Okay let's get back to business." Ivan looked at Wan. "How soon will the three missiles be updated with the new part?"

"I just checked on that before we started this meeting," Wan said. "They're ahead of schedule. We should be ready to launch within four hours."

Yaw looked directly at Ivan. "Don't forget, our new part will ensure the American targets suffer much more devastation than they would if we didn't replace the part."

Ivan set his jaw as his gaze rested on the three Chinese sitting at the table. "One thing I've learned during the last year is that you can't underestimate Randall. You can't overlook any possibility. If there's any way he can get you he will."

"We're fully prepared to repel Randall and his taskforce if that proves to be necessary," Yaw said. "If he somehow gets down here, we'll make sure he won't succeed in stopping us."

Ivan narrowed his eyes and looked across the table at

Wan. "Once we launch the missiles they're virtually unstoppable at the speed and depth they'll travel, right?"

Wan nodded. "They'll be using our latest version of the supercavitating technology used by your current high-speed torpedoes. They'll use underwater ramjets rather than propellers and travel inside a bubble of gas to reduce friction. We expect them to achieve speeds in excess of 200 miles per hour."

Ivan looked at Oleg. "Did you find this in your testing?"

"That was an innovation the Chinese added after we finished our testing in Russia," Oleg said.

Wan flashed a huge grin. "That's an advantage of having us partnering with you. We've added a lot of advanced technology to everything we're doing." Wan made a sweeping gesture. "That includes everything we've set up down here to facilitate our bringing down the United States."

Ivan nodded and then his gaze rested on Denis and Maxim. "Are we ready to hack into the Federal Reserve System at just the right moment?"

"We're sitting on ready," Denis said. "By using the quantum computer, Maxim and I have probed all the financial safeguards the Americans have. We've developed solutions to bypass every one of them."

Ivan looked directly at Maxim. "You're our computer specialist. Do you agree?"

Maxim gave a slight shrug. "I'm not a financial expert like Denis, but we're ready as far as I can tell."

Yaw looked directly at Ivan and flashed a huge grin. "You're lucky we're helping you out."

Ivan narrowed his eyes. "And you're lucky our scientists developed the Poseidon Missiles in the first place and planned all this. Also, our chess masters in Moscow have done an excellent job developing our strategy."

Yaw gave a slight shrug. "It's been a good team effort from the very start. It's good we're on the same team. If Randall shows up, he'll get a lot of surprises. The alarms will go off, and our defenses will kick in. Our numerous assassins will go into action. We're all well prepared to repel any invasion of our headquarters."

"We have to at least be a delaying factor until our missiles are launched and our computer hacking has been completed," Ivan said. He looked intensely at the Chinese contingent. "Make sure you have backup plans in place."

Yaw flashed another big grin. "We have everything set up properly. You can rely on us."

Chapter 38

In McLean, Virginia, the group from Boswic, along with the delegation from the FBI followed some CIA agents to the doorway of a large conference room.

CIA Director, Charles Andrews, waited at the table, along with his head of the Terrorist Threat Investigation Unit, Paul Collins. Nick Wallace, their top analyst, also waited there.

Ken Johnson, Frank Hellman, and Steve Locket represented the FBI. Harlan Pierce, Jim Boxer, and Blake Morgan represented Boswic.

The CIA group stood and greeted everyone. After pleasantries were exchanged, everyone settled into a chair.

"Ken and I left the Whitehouse a couple of hours ago," Charles said. "The President sends his thanks for our bravery and accomplishments so far and emphasized we need to finish the job as soon as possible. He reassured us he has substantial military assets in position to provide any necessary backup."

No one commented, but most gave a slow nod.

"We already know the Russians want to bring us down so they can become the world's leading military power. And we know China has the same idea, but they're even more ambitious. They also want to be the world's leading economic power," Charles said. "They both think that's their rightful place on the world stage."

"They should realize they can't both achieve all their goals," Harlan said. "Something needs to give. Only one of them can be the dominate world power."

"They have one mutual goal though: to bring us down," Charles replied. "We're in the way for both of them and we have to be eliminated as the leading world military power and as the leading world economic power. So, they're working together for the time being."

"China better be careful on that," Harlan said. "If they destroy our economy, they destroy their own economy, at least for a while."

Paul nodded. "I don't think they're thinking about that at the moment. Both countries are obsessed with getting us out of their way. I think they've decided they'll figure out solutions to all the other problems later."

Charles gave a short grunt. "Yeah, I think that's correct and that brings us back to deciding what we're going to do right now to make sure they never have to decide how to divide up the spoils."

Ken gestured toward Steve and Nick. "We probably need to get their latest analysis about the strategy being used before we get into a detailed discussion about what our next step needs to be."

"I think the Russians are using probabilistic mathematics to determine the optimum strategy for world domination by predicting our most probable actions before and after they launch their attack," Steve said. "They want to keep us off balance and then destroy any ability we have left to resist their takeover. All our experts at the FBI are convinced the Russians have a complicated plan that's been in motion for years. And we think the chess masters who've been part of this are still developing the next steps."

Harlan gave Steve a quizzical look. “So, you think we’re playing chess?”

“Chess has a relationship to all of this. It’s tied to game theory,” Steve said. “In fact, there’s a good analogy here. After ten moves in chess, a tree-diagram of options has around 170 million branches. That’s why we haven’t figured out all the details yet.”

Harlan glanced at Ken. “Is that the way you see it?”

Ken nodded. “They want to keep us stirred up and grasping at shadows. I think China is working right along with them on executing this strategy. The Russians have been trying to create panic and prolonged uncertainty for a long time. They want to destabilize our culture, and China is now aiding and abetting all the Russian strategy in this regard. In fact, we’re certain China is providing almost all the funding for what they’re doing right now in Jamaica.”

Charles made a sweeping gesture toward Nick, Blake, and Steve. “Do any of you analysts have anything more you want to say about this before we move forward in our discussion?”

“I agree neither China nor Russia seems to be worried at the moment about how they’re going to divide up the spoils,” Nick said. “They’ve teamed up really well to try to take us out. That’s their focus and that’s their clear goal at the moment.”

“We know Russia has supplied the initial weapons and China has supplied supercomputers and a lot of other advanced technology,” Blake replied. “They’ve indeed teamed up really well to try to bring us down.”

“There is a lot of information about the size of the warhead on the Poseidon Missiles,” Steve said. “Some data lists it as 100 megatons. It looks like the missile is large enough to accommodate a warhead of that size, but my guess is its closer to 5 megatons. I think 100 megatons is Russian propaganda.”

Charles nodded. “I tend to agree. However, we need to

remember that one and a half megatons is the size of the bomb we dropped on Hiroshima and two megatons is the size of the bomb we dropped on Nagasaki. Each of them did a tremendous amount of damage. Colt and the taskforce need to finish the job quickly down in Jamaica. There's no way we can allow any Poseidon Missiles to be launched. We know if any of them ever get on their way they're going to be almost impossible to stop." He started to say more when someone walked into the conference room and handed him a piece of paper.

"Sorry for the interruption sir, but I felt sure you would want this information as soon as possible," the agent said as he turned and left the room.

After studying the paper for a few moments, Charles said, "We think we've located one of the entrances to the underwater launch site in Jamaica. That same complex probably also contains Ivan Titov's underground headquarters down there."

"Do you have the precise location?" Ken asked.

"Yes," Charles said, "and not only the precise location but also the process to use for gaining entrance."

"Isn't the entrance hidden from satellite view?" Frank asked.

"Yes, but the Russians and Chinese aren't as smart as they think they are." Charles looked back at the paper. "After we thought we had identified the location, we kept watch over the area for a while. Later we were able to move one of our satellites with infrared capability into the correct position to record all the motions the people entering went through."

Everyone gave their own version of a cheer.

"Great." Ken looked directly at Charles. "Is the procedure a complicated process?"

Charles looked back at the paper and studied it for a few moments. "I would define it as such, but I think the members of the taskforce can figure out precisely what to do when they get to the site. I don't think it will take them long to figure out how to get inside."

Ken punched a button on his secure satellite phone. "I'll tell Grant to let Colt and the taskforce know so they can get started immediately."

Chapter 39

When the taskforce arrived at their target close to Kingston, Colt called a halt and dispersed seventeen members of his group around the area.

In a few moments, Colt, Linda, and Mack moved forward. They soon peered out from thick foliage at what appeared to be a wall of solid rock.

Colt studied the infrared photography he'd received on a transmission from Grant.

"Got it figured out?" Mack asked.

"Pretty much," Colt said. He pointed to a section on the rock cliff. "We need to get closer to that area."

Colt selected a position and put his feet on a couple of discolored spots on the rocky ledge while putting each hand in respective small indentions immediately above him in the rock wall.

As Colt watched part of the rock open, he knew his process of studying the satellite photos and some special infrared shots had borne fruit. An opening, about 12 feet high and 20 feet wide, appeared in front of the threesome, the same opening they had seen in the infrared photos.

"I'll be damned," Colt muttered. "It actually works." He then spoke into his tactical microphone and issued orders.

He left ten of the agents outside, posting them in key areas for added security. He waved Linda and Mack forward. He asked the other seven taskforce members to wait five minutes and follow.

"Is the door going to stay open?" Linda gave Colt a quick glance.

"Most likely, I don't expect any time limit," Colt said. "I think we'll have to go through a similar routine somewhere inside here to close it."

They used extreme caution as they continued forward, keeping about five yards distance between each of them.

The slightly rounded modern-looking tunnel was about twenty feet high and fifteen feet wide. Some type of grey stone blocks dominated the architecture. The tunnel continued straight ahead as far as they could see, and the entire area looked empty.

"No sign of anyone," Colt said.

"Could be a trap," Linda whispered. "They could have a lot of built-in hiding places inside the walls."

Colt whispered into his microphone, "You next seven come on in. We've had no contact yet but use extreme caution."

"Roger," came a chorus of voices.

In a couple of minutes, Colt noted a gradually sloped stone ramp appeared on the right side of the tunnel. It looked like it was about six feet wide.

The tunnel they were in maintained its width and height. With the appearance of the ramp, the distance between the walls expanded to about sixteen feet.

When they got closer to the ramp, Colt noted it went through an arched opening and continued upward.

They walked up the stone ramp. After they walked under the arch they noticed there was another level. A stone ledge extended for about 50 yards.

Colt whispered into his microphone, "Linda, Mack, and I have gone up a stone ramp to another level. It's about 15 feet higher than the previous level. The three of us will explore it. The seven of you keep going straight when you get to it."

"Roger."

Colt glanced at Linda and Mack. "I see about five medal doors along the wall to our right."

"One has a white vertical strip, about an inch or so wide," Linda said. "It must be a marker for something. I suggest we try to get in."

Colt looked at Mack and whispered, "Get your toolkit ready."

Keeping their weapons in ready position and continuing to scan the area, they arrived at the door with the white strip without incident. As expected, the door was locked. The white strip was a thin piece of plastic molding. It seemed to have no purpose other than to be a marker.

Mack grabbed a small kit from a vest pocket and removed a pick. In a few seconds the three of them eased through the doorway and looked for cover. The door stayed open.

Colt scanned the large chamber. Rows of stacked wooden crates extended before them.

The three warriors crouched behind the nearest crate and surveyed the situation. A pungent smell hung in the air; Colt couldn't quite identify it. He scanned the surroundings again. The chamber had a high ceiling and at least one other open doorway.

About a hundred rows of stacked wooden crates dominated the space. Forklifts and other pieces of equipment were scattered along the solid-rock floor beside the stacks of crates. Midway down the chamber, a large door was open. A wide stairway was conspicuous in a distant corner. What looked like a bank of elevators was along a sidewall close to the stairway.

Colt spoke into his tactical microphone, "Linda, use a zigzag pattern. Follow ten yards behind me. Mack, you bring up the rear and guard against any surprise attack from behind us."

"Roger," came two replies.

Colt bolted from cover and ran toward the large open door about midway down the chamber. Linda and Mack followed.

After Colt got close to the open doorway, he moved to the wall on his right, stopped, and pressed his back against it. He was on the right side of the large opening.

Linda followed, keeping about ten yards from Colt. She stopped and pressed her back against the wall.

Mack followed the procedure.

They continued to scan the surroundings, no opposition yet.

Everyone eased into position to peer inside the new chamber. More rows of stacked boxes dominated the area. The pungent odor was stronger.

As they continued to scan the area, the lights dimmed and then went out.

Everything was now pitch-black.

Colt held his SIG 556 in ready position with one hand and reached for his night-vision goggles with the other.

The goggles worked.

After a few minutes of studying the large chamber, Colt focused on a small opening about 50 yards in front of them.

"Some light coming from something," Colt whispered into his tactical comm unit, "to our right front."

"Got it," Linda said.

Mack responded accordingly.

Colt started toward the light, gesturing for Linda and Mack to follow.

They moved forward, their boots giving a slight echo from contact with the rock floor.

Within another minute, Colt stopped and studied the area closely. He soon moved to another steel door that had a white strip on it. This door was also locked.

Light came through a small transom above the door.

Colt waved Mack over to use his toolkit. Mack tried for several minutes without success.

Turning toward Colt, Mack asked, "Any clue how to get in?"

"Might be the same setup we had outside," Colt said. He took a penlight out of a pocket and scanned the walls.

He soon found what he was looking for.

Colt moved to a new position and put his feet on a couple of round spots on the floor while putting each hand in respective small indentions in the wall to the right of the door. There were some immediate hydraulic sounds and the steel door moved upward.

"You got it," Linda said. "Good job."

They peered through the doorway. A tunnel with dim lighting stretched forward for about twenty yards, brighter light dominated the far end of it. They removed their night-vision goggles and eased forward.

Linda held her SIG 556 in ready position and followed ten yards behind Colt.

Mack stayed ten yards behind Linda.

Other than faint sounds of boots scuffing on the smooth rock floor, there was no noise.

They soon came to a gigantic brightly lit chamber that looked about the size of a football field. There were more stacked wooden crates, rows and rows of them.

Elevated metal walkways stretched across the area above the rows of wooden crates.

"They probably know by now we're inside and I bet they're waiting for us, planning an ambush," Colt said. "Let's get in some better cover, we're going to hold up for a little bit."

Chapter 40

In the main conference room in his underground headquarters in Jamaica, Ivan scanned the faces around the table. He had summoned them for a critical discussion about addressing the new emergency he had just discovered a couple of minutes ago.

Sergei, Oleg, Maxim, Denis, Yaw, Wan, and Cham were all present.

Ivan pointed toward one of the large monitors on the wall and then looked at Yaw. “How did Randall and his taskforce get in here without a lot of alarms going off immediately?”

Yaw narrowed his eyes and said, “You were in a big hurry to move in down here. I worked hard to get everything accomplished quickly. I might have cut a few corners at one of the entrances.”

“Why didn’t you finish the job after we moved in?” Ivan asked.

Yaw shrugged. “I guess it slipped my mind. From the beginning you’ve insisted we launch the missiles as soon as possible. I’ve had all my engineers who remained after the initial construction concentrating on that.” He shrugged again. “I guess I was also concentrating too much on that.”

Glaring at Yaw, Ivan took a deep breath and exhaled slowly.

"I've been following your orders as well as I could." Yaw gestured toward Wan and Cham. "We all have."

Sergei looked directly at Wan. "Why did you tell me earlier you had installed an excellent warning system at every entrance and that anyone entering any of the underground areas without having keyed the proper access code would set off multiple alarms?"

"I was unaware we had skipped some parts of our plan," Wan said. "You just heard Yaw's explanation."

Sergei leaned closer to Wan and shook his head slowly. "Yeah we damned sure don't have loud sirens going off in multiple locations down here. In a sense, you all lied to us."

Wan made a dismissive gesture with his hands. "I'm sorry about this, but there's nothing we can do about it now. I regret the circumstances changed and we didn't finish installing all the extra equipment at that particular entrance."

Ivan looked at Yaw. "One of you should have informed me you didn't completely finish installing the alarm system. I would have wanted to be aware of that as soon as we moved in down here."

Yaw continued to shrug. "Sorry about that. Like I told you, I got so caught up in other priorities that I forgot about it. We've been giving all our attention and putting all our effort into getting the missiles launched and being able to hack into the Federal Reserve System." He looked at Wan and Cham.

Both nodded.

Ivan leaned forward toward Yaw. "What about the other secret entrance your engineers built? Does it have a functional alarm system?"

"Yes," Yaw said. "It leads directly into the room where the computers are. It was a higher priority than the other entrance and I made sure we got it done. Remember when we did the construction we took special care to construct the two special entrances in areas that had a lot of cover from satellite view. Making sure the entrances were hidden from any surveillance took a considerable amount of extra effort and consumed a lot of time." Yaw gestured with both palms up. "I just had too many things going on."

"What about the entrances originating in our embassies?" Sergei asked.

"Those were done early in the construction, and they definitely have working alarm systems," Yaw said. "If you remember, we decided to add the two secret entrances when everything else had been completed."

Sergei and Ivan each gave a slow nod.

Maxim's gaze focused on both Yaw and Wan. "One reason the secret entrance close to the computer area was built is that I insisted on being able to get to the computers quickly if we were outside somewhere."

"That you did," Yaw said, "but you were a little late in making the request and I had released some of my engineers to go back to China. We didn't have the manpower to work on both secret entrances at the same time. I concentrated on the most critical one."

Maxim didn't comment.

Yaw pointed at Sergei. "When you wanted an entrance built to lead directly into the storage area and I scrambled together the best team so I could get that done." He shrugged. "However, like I mentioned earlier, after we built that entrance my engineers' time got swallowed up with other priorities."

Sergei glanced at Ivan. "I think we've spent enough time on this. More discussion will do no good and it will waste time."

"Okay, enough about the failure of the alarm system." Ivan pointed at one of the monitors. "Randall and his group are inside, and we'd better do something about the problem we have right now."

"I have some assassins down there who're well prepared

to fight off an attack," Wan said. He looked at Oleg. "I think you have some too."

Oleg nodded. "I always keep a few down in the storage area."

Ivan's gaze took in Yaw, Wan, and Cham. "We need to deploy a lot of people between the storage area and the computer room just in case Randall gets past this first wave of our defense."

"I'll load up that part of our complex," Yaw said. "I'll also send Cham down there as a safety valve."

"Even if he gets past the computer room, Randall won't get past me for sure." Cham flashed another one of his massive grins. "Neither will any other members of his taskforce. I have a lot of ways to stop them."

Yaw nodded. "Cham is probably the most skilled warrior in the world when it comes to close-combat."

Ivan set his jaw as his gaze rested on the three Chinese sitting at the table. "One thing I've learned during the last year is that you can't underestimate Randall. You can't overlook any possibility. If there's any way he can get you he will."

"This time we'll get him," Yaw said. "We've had one little glitch on the installation of one segment of the alarm system, but you can rely on us. We've done well on everything else. Randall won't succeed in stopping us. We'll be able to launch the missiles and the new part in the guidance system will ensure we trigger the explosion at just the right spot when the position of the missile will produce the maximum damage."

Ivan narrowed his eyes and looked across the table at Wan. "And you've assured me that once we launch the missiles they're virtually unstoppable based on the depth they'll travel, right?"

Wan nodded. "By using underwater ramjets rather than propellers and traveling inside a bubble of gas to reduce friction, they'll move along in excess of 200 miles per hour."

He flashed a huge grin. "You're lucky you have us partnering with you. We've added a lot of advanced technology to everything you're doing to bring down the United States."

Ivan didn't reply as he shifted his gaze to Denis and Maxim. "So, you say you're sitting on ready to hack into the Federal Reserve System?"

"I think we can make it work without doing our last test run," Denis said. "We already know we can bypass all the financial safeguards the Americans have in place."

Ivan looked directly at Maxim. "Do you agree?"

"We're ready as far as I can tell," Maxim said.

Ivan narrowed his eyes and kept his gaze on Maxim. "Okay, you go with Denis and help him make a final check on the computer hacking software and then, if everything is okay, you go to the launch area and help Wan make a final check on the missile guidance system."

Maxim nodded.

Ivan gave a dismissal wave. "Go get started. There's no reason to wait any longer and we have no time to waste."

Denis and Maxim stood and rushed out of the room.

"Are you still going to use our supercomputer as part of the overall process to keep the money moving around?" Yaw asked.

"That's still the plan," Ivan said. "We'll use it to probe a variety of accounts all over the world that transfer funds to the Federal Reserve to make sure we haven't missed anything."

Yaw grinned. "You're lucky we're helping you out."

Ivan narrowed his eyes. "And you're lucky our scientists developed the Poseidon Missiles in the first place and planned all this. Our chess masters in Moscow have done an excellent job developing strategy. Now we just need to execute our plan before Randall and his taskforce wreck it"

"It's good we're on the same team," Yaw said. "The

United States is doomed. It's been a good team effort for us from the very start."

Ivan slammed a fist on the table. "Now we need to execute and give Randall a few surprises." He looked at the three Chinese sitting across from him. "Go make sure you keep Randall from interfering with the missile launches."

Yaw, Wan and Cham stood to leave.

"Randall will definitely get a lot of surprises that will eliminate him forever," Yaw said. "We'll get the missiles launched and also succeed in our computer hacking. I can guarantee you the United States will suffer a lot of damage and will cease to exist as a powerful nation."

Chapter 41

Colt noted a faint clank of metal echoed from a walkway above and ahead of him. "Down," Colt said, dropping to the solid rock floor and lying as flat as he could. He noted that Linda and Mack did the same.

Mack crawled up beside Colt. "See anything?"

"Not yet," Colt said, "but there was a distinct metallic noise on an overhead walkway in front of us."

The three warriors stayed in place for a few more seconds.

"Let's ease forward," Colt said. "Careful though, we might encounter the bastard who made the noise."

The three rose slightly and moved forward in a low crouch, while maintaining their spacing.

Colt kept his silenced SIG 556 pointed in front of him, barrel upwards at a 45-degree angle—his right hand on the rear pistol grip and his right index finger snug on the trigger. His mind flashed back to his Delta Force experience and the more recent training exercises. He prepared for a split-second reaction.

Two enemy combatants, rifles pointed down toward Colt, appeared in a raised area about twenty feet high to his left.

Colt cut the first man down with one shot. The man fell forward, his rifle clanging on the metal railing.

While swinging his rifle toward the other man, Colt heard some more soft pops. Before he could fire, the other man toppled forward and down to the concrete floor, hitting it with a loud thud.

Linda and Mack had reacted almost as fast as Colt had.

Neither enemy combatant had gotten off a shot.

Colt gave a thumbs-up and the three of them kept scanning the area, including the overhead walkway. Colt continued to keep his SIG 556 in ready position.

After scanning for a few seconds and not seeing any more threats, Colt scrambled over to the downed enemy combatants.

Linda and Mack followed.

"Each hit multiple times in the head," Colt said. "I guess we can say we did damn well."

Linda and Mack both nodded.

While the other two stayed on guard, Colt picked up a crowbar lying nearby and pried open the side of one of the wooden crates.

The smell they had been getting was suddenly overwhelming.

Colt stared at the inside of the crate for a moment. "What is it?"

Linda shook her head. "Not sure, but the white strips must be the markers for whatever it is."

"One strong smell," Mack said, "could be some extra strong form of marijuana."

Colt and Linda both nodded.

"And it could be a special stash for an exclusive market here in Jamaica," Colt said. "I guess any workers who come in here need a marker so they have an easy way to find where it's stored."

"Makes sense," Mack replied.

After hesitating a moment, the threesome moved forward again, using extreme caution.

They arrived at a bank of elevators and Colt spoke into

his tactical microphone, "Any action down there on the bottom level?"

"None yet for us," one agent said. "Should we keep going forward?"

"Has the tunnel stayed the same size?" Colt asked.

"Nothing has changed," the agent said.

Colt gave the seven agents on the lower level an update on what he, Linda, and Mack had experienced and then said, "Keep moving forward cautiously and report any action you encounter."

"Roger," the agents echoed.

Colt gestured toward the elevators. "Maybe we should check out where these lead to."

"We'll be taking a big chance. They must know we're here by now." Mack gave Colt a quick glance. "They could be waiting for us."

"Maybe not," Colt said. "The guys we shot didn't have any communications equipment. We're probably okay to use the elevators."

Mack and Linda each gave a slight nod.

Colt stepped forward and pushed a button. A metal door slid open and Colt walked in.

"We'll go one at a time," Colt said.

Mack and Linda didn't argue.

The state-of-the art elevator moved down rapidly in the underground facility. Colt flexed his knees as the elevator came to a stop and the door opened.

Colt kept his SIG 556 in ready position as he darted for the nearest cover and waited for Mack and Linda, who soon joined him.

All was quiet as the threesome looked around the corner of a wooden crate at the large chamber with more rows of stacked wooden crates.

"It took a lot of money and advanced technology to create multiple levels of large chambers down here," Colt said, with a touch of awe in his voice.

The threesome scrambled forward to the next row of wooden crates and studied the area.

"With China and Russia pooling their resources, they do have a lot of money and advanced technology," Mack said. "Creating all this wasn't a big financial hurdle or a big technological hurdle for them."

Linda made a sweeping gesture toward a lot of crates. "And they keep supplementing their finances with tons of money from illegal drugs."

Mack and Colt nodded as the three of them continued to scan the area.

It looked deserted to Colt. He hesitated for a moment and then waved everyone forward again.

They moved with great care and tried to make no scuffing noises on the stone floor.

Soon they came to an area of large metal containers.

Colt whispered into his microphone, "Spotted some movement about 50 yards ahead."

"Roger." Mack and Linda both replied.

Colt pointed at a row of metal containers to their right. They rushed toward them and took cover behind the first one in the row. Colt's internal alarms were going off as he peered around the corner of the large container.

"Three men moving this way," Colt said.

Two of approaching figures split off and went toward the other side of the area. One man continued forward.

Colt whispered into his microphone, "I'll take care of the one who's coming this way. You two take care of the others."

"The one coming this way is a bulk of a man, muscular, and looks about 250 pounds. Think you can you handle him without some help?" Linda asked.

"Yeah, I can handle him," Colt said. "I'm looking forward to some more action of this type. I also need the practice."

"Go get in your practice then," Linda said. "The other

two don't look too impressive. I'm sure we can handle them without too much trouble."

Linda gestured for Mack to follow and charged off to her right, down the aisle they were on.

Colt took a deep breath and prepared for action.

Chapter 42

In Tampa, in the main conference room at the FBI headquarters, Grant started his meeting to review the situation in Jamaica with the contingent from Boswic. Harlan, Jim, and Blake sat across the table from him.

"I got an update from Colt a few minutes ago," Grant said. "Our hi-tech phones are still working, and it looks like the taskforce is doing really well down there."

"So, as far as we know, the President is still going to keep the Military in backup mode?" Jim asked.

"As far as I know," Grant said. "If our taskforce fails, I'm sure he'll jump in. He knows we can't afford to let any of the Poseidon Missiles get launched. And remember Moscow denies having any involvement in any aspect of what's happening down there in Jamaica."

"How did the Poseidon Missiles get involved in this then?" Harlan asked. "I'm sure the Russian military owns them."

"According to the reports I've heard, Moscow claims they were stolen by a renegade group connected to China." Grant scanned the faces around the table. "Of course we know that's not true. We know both Russia and China are running all this behind the scenes, but they're doing it in a way to maintain their deniability."

Harlan laughed. "They're not fooling anyone."

"Yeah, but they can still deny having any involvement and they can accuse the United States of starting a major war," Grant said. "I've been constantly assured the President will use the Military to stop a missile launch if he needs to, but he'll only do it if our taskforce fails. I think it's a smart strategy."

"Is anyone keeping the President briefed on what's going on right now?" Jim asked.

"Yes, both Ken and Charles," Grant said. He gave a slight grin. "Of course they're depending on me to keep them briefed so they can give the President the latest and most accurate information." He glanced at his watch. "And I just briefed them ten minutes ago."

Harlan, Jim, and Blake all nodded.

There was a brief pause.

Grant scanned the faces across from him at the table. "Have any of you talked to Colt in the last few hours."

"He checks with us periodically," Harlan said. "So far it's only after he's talked to you. This time, we haven't heard from him yet."

"I told him about our meeting," Grant said.

Harlan grunted. "That would explain it."

"Do you sometimes get the sense that he's told you something I don't know?" Grant asked.

"When he calls, the three of us ask a lot of questions and he provides a lot of answers," Jim said. "On some of his answers we ask if you know that. Most of the time he says you do. Other times he tells us to inform you. We always do that."

"But you don't ask that question for every answer he gives you, right?" Grant asked.

Harlan grunted again. "I guess we could let some things slip through the cracks on occasion."

"We try not to let that happen." Jim narrowed his eyes and leaned toward Grant.

Grant nodded and gave a dismissive gesture. "And that

brings us to this meeting. We need to get together to discuss everything often and make sure we have all the latest information for Charles and Ken to use to brief the President."

Harlan, Jim, and Blake all nodded, and the meeting continued for another hour.

Chapter 43

In the J Edgar Hoover building in Washington DC, Ken stood and welcomed the three CIA agents from McLean into the main conference room.

Charles, Paul, and Nick settled into chairs across the large table from Ken, Frank, and Steve.

"I got the latest briefing from Grant less than an hour ago," Ken said, looking directly at Charles. "I called you over to review the latest details to help us stay in sync. One mistake by the taskforce could lead to some big problems."

"Have you talked to the President today?" Charles asked.

"Early this morning," Ken said. "After this meeting, we can both call him and make sure he's up to date on every aspect of what's happening down in Jamaica."

"Is the President still planning to keep the Military out of this if he can?" Charles asked.

"Yes, but he'll keep the Navy ships positioned to address the launch of any Poseidon Missiles," Ken said. "We all know we can't allow them to wreak havoc on us. They must be stopped."

"And that's the job of our taskforce." Charles stared at Ken. "I'm concerned we might not be able to pull it off. The President might need the Military to step in, whether he likes it or not."

Frank scanned the faces around the table. "Exactly how will the Military know if a missile gets launched?"

"The Navy has a lot of sophisticated underwater sensors," Charles said. "The President has told me several times he's asked the Navy to constantly monitor all the waters around Jamaica."

"The Poseidon Missiles are reported to be able to travel at a depth of 3,280 feet." Paul looked at Nick. "That's lower than any of our submarines can travel. How can the Navy detect one in the water at that depth after it's been launched?"

"That shouldn't be a big problem, and the missiles aren't going to start out in real deep water," Nick said. "They'll probably be launched at a depth of 100 feet or less. The Navy has a lot of ways to monitor what goes on in relatively shallow water and they can probably detect them in deeper water too."

Paul nodded.

"Does the Navy have a lot of sensors positioned in the waters around Kingston, Jamaica?" Ken asked.

"Remember, we know the general launch site," Nick said. "There's no problem knowing where to concentrate our attention. We'll know immediately if they launch any underwater missiles."

"We already know the Poseidon Missiles will be difficult to stop if they get launched," Ken said. "If the Navy detects one in the water and on its way, what can they do?"

"I'm not sure exactly," Nick said, "but they've told us they have a lot of options on things to try."

"So, it's possible there's something we can do to stop them once they're launched?" Frank asked.

"That's right," Nick said. "It's not definite, but it looks like we'll still have a chance to stop any of them that are in the water and on their way to a target." He paused. "We know for sure the Navy is keeping a close eye on things and have a lot of capability. If necessary, they're prepared to step in."

"Let's hope Colt and the taskforce succeed." Charles narrowed his eyes. "I think they're our best chance of eliminating the threat from Jamaica."

Chapter 44

In his underground headquarters in Jamaica, Ivan looked across the huge mahogany desk in his office at Sergei.

"Everything's moving close to completion," Ivan said. "If we can keep Randall from interfering, we should be able to launch the missiles within a couple of hours."

"Did you receive that information from Yaw and Wan?" Sergei asked.

"Yes." Ivan looked at his watch. "They're still down there in the launch area trying to expedite things. They're both experts on the missiles and they might be able to get the engineers to move things along more quickly. I should be hearing more details real soon."

Sergei gave a slow nod.

"Has Maxim finished checking the computer hacking software with Denis?" Ivan asked.

"Yes, why do you ask?"

"Maybe he should go on down to the launch area now. He might be of some benefit if he discusses things with both Yaw and Wan."

"In what way?"

Ivan gave a wry smile and then shrugged. "I just thought he might help speed things up."

"Are you talking about offering some advice to them?" Sergei asked, "Or by just being down there with them?"

Ivan shrugged again. "Maybe both, he can also keep an

eye on things and give us his opinion about how things are shaping up."

"You don't trust Yaw and Wan?"

"It never hurts to take some extra precautions when you're doing something this important," Ivan said.

"Yeah and we know the Chinese aren't always forthcoming about things." Sergei looked directly at Ivan and nodded slowly as he punched a button on his phone.

Chapter 45

In the area of Ivan Titov's underground warehouses in Jamaica, Colt waited for the muscular assassin who was walking toward him to get a little closer. Timing was critical.

Just at the right moment, Colt stepped out from the corner and leveled his SIG 556 at the assassin.

"Any further movement and you die on the spot," Colt said.

The muscular assassin shot a stunned glance at Colt. He dropped his weapon and raised his hands in the air.

"Looks like you have the advantage," the assassin said with a smirk. He didn't seem to be worried.

Colt spoke with a firm voice, "Lose the pistol. You know the drill, left hand, two fingers. That's right. Now drop it and step away."

The muscular assassin complied and stood motionless, glaring at Colt. "I know who you are Randall and you have this all wrong. You're the one who's going to die on the spot. It's not going to be me."

"That's something easy for you to say, but I might have a different opinion." Colt kept his SIG 556 trained on the assassin, who reminded him of a huge monster ready to pounce.

Colt had an urge to shoot him right there and be done

with it, a strong urge. He aimed at the muscular assassin's head but held his fire. The professional in him won out.

A hail of bullets kicked up pieces of the solid rock floor a few feet away. The sound was loud. Colt figured the shooter must be close.

Colt dropped flat, keeping his rifle trained on the muscular assassin.

The bullets kept coming.

Colt caught a couple of ricochets on his bulletproof vest, big impact, definitely high caliber bullets. Colt struggled to breathe. Not again, he thought, but he knew he had made it okay before.

Almost immediately, Colt heard silenced rifle fire in rapid bursts, long series of pops.

Then there was silence.

Linda's voice sounded in Colt's earpiece. "Action on railing above us, over to the right of the area, Mack and I are moving over there."

Colt tried to respond, but he couldn't. He couldn't draw a breath right at that moment. Colt realized the impacts to his chest had knocked the wind out of him. He continued his struggle to breathe.

"Colt, you okay?" Linda asked.

Colt managed to grunt well enough to give Linda a response that apparently was satisfactory to her. He figured she probably thought he wanted to remain silent due to what was going on around him.

Hearing more gunfire and more silenced responses, Colt lowered his rifle just a bit as he tried to rise to his knees.

The muscular assassin took advantage of the situation and bolted forward, launching a kick at Colt's head.

Colt rolled on the floor, avoiding the blow, but losing his rifle in the process.

Still struggling to breathe, Colt managed to launch into an upright position.

The muscular assassin charged again and made a karate-style kick toward Colt's right leg.

Able to finally gasp more air, Colt stepped back and avoided the kick.

The muscular assassin's momentum propelled him past Colt and onto the floor.

Now if I could only get my breathing back to normal, Colt thought.

Regaining his feet in an instant, the muscular assassin drew a double-edged combat knife from a sheath on the inside of one leg just below his knee. Holding the knife with the point upward and pointing forward, he moved directly toward Colt.

Not having any recent training in knife fighting, Colt tried to recall some of the techniques he had used several years ago. Feeling a bit rusty, he figured he might need a little good luck. At least his breathing was returning to normal.

The muscular assassin moved forward and waved the knife back and forth.

Keeping track of the knife with his peripheral vision, Colt focused on the assassin's chest.

The assassin feinted, making slicing motions across Colt's field of vision.

Colt didn't react. He was well aware he was just out of the assassin's reach. He figured it was best to wait for the assassin to get closer.

The assassin lunged and extended his knife toward Colt's heart.

Colt turned and slid to his left. The knife passed in front of him. Colt snapped his right forearm upward, blocking and guiding the assassin's wrist just enough to ensure that the knife continued on past.

As the knife passed in front of him, Colt grabbed the assassin's arm with both his hands trapping the knife hand. The thought he was as good as the assassin at knife fighting, and maybe better, flashed through Colt's mind. He didn't seem to be rusty after all.

Keeping a grip on the assassin's knife hand, Colt pivoted to his right and pulled the assassin forward and down, keeping him off-balance. Colt then reversed his own motion, stepping back with his left foot and twisting the assassin's knife-hand to the left.

Colt extracted the knife from the assassin's hand and snapped his elbow leftward toward the assassin's right temple. Colt's elbow was blocked.

Good move by the assassin, Colt thought.

The assassin seemed to gain some confidence.

Colt backed off a few yards and quickly reviewed his strategy. He needed to figure out a way to gain advantage. He guessed Linda and Mack were busy coping with the other two men.

Deciding some offense might work, Colt made a furious leap and targeted the assassin's legs just above the knees.

But the assassin dipped down and to his left just at the right time.

Colt still managed to deliver a glancing blow to the assassin's right side. But being deflected, Colt landed off balance and rolled on the floor. However, he bounced back to his feet quickly and dropped into a combat fighting stance, feet spread about shoulder-width, one foot slightly forward.

The assassin again went on the offensive. He seemed to think he was the better man.

Colt could feel a surge of adrenalin as the raging bull charged directly toward him.

The assassin launched a barrage of side-kicks.

None hit Colt.

All were diverted by Colt's crossed wrists.

The assassin launched more kicks. All were blocked. His energy was amazing. However, Colt felt he was doing okay himself on that score. He felt a degree of satisfaction.

Both men backed off a little and did some heavy breathing. The last round of blows and counterblows had been super strenuous.

The assassin looked irritated, good sign.

Colt backed off and stood in an Aikido defense posture, facing his opponent with his hands open and in front, just above his waist.

Since his offense hadn't worked so well, Colt decided to switch back to defense.

"Time for you to die," the assassin said. He charged forward.

At the last second, the assassin twisted and leaned his torso to the left and cocked his right leg high, bringing it around in a karate-style kick powered by his entire body.

It was obvious the assassin intended to connect his booted foot with the left side of Colt's head, but Colt saw it coming and stepped back just enough, catching the assassin's boot with both hands.

Twisting and levering up the heel of the boot while pulling down on the toe and pushing forward at the same time, Colt dumped the assassin backwards again, this time, a good eight feet through the air and onto the floor.

The assassin landed flat on his back.

Colt saw him tuck his head forward to keep from banging it on the stone floor. The assassin spread both forearms and absorbed at least some of the impact as he landed. It was an expert move.

The assassin regained his feet so fast that Colt didn't close in.

Colt backed up again to maintain a comfortable distance. He assumed a defensive posture and waited.

The assassin glared at Colt. "You're going down. It's obvious I'm the far better man. You won't last much longer."

Colt didn't reply. He continued to wait in a defensive stance. He noted the assassin seemed to be getting frustrated.

The assassin charged again. He slid in faster this time and leaned away at the last moment as he jumped sideways toward Colt.

Colt quickly made the necessary adjustment.

The assassin lashed out with the heel of his right foot towards Colt's left hip.

Avoiding contact, Colt slid to his right and then behind the assassin.

The assassin's foot flew by inches in front of Colt, but, as before, he landed on his feet and quickly turned toward Colt.

After surveying Colt for a moment, the assassin charged again. He was fast, but Colt was faster. All those action-packed years in Delta Force had sharpened Colt's reflexes to a high level and he had never lost that.

With perfect timing, Colt sidestepped and then leaped forward, grabbing the assassin's shoulders. Colt went with him to the concrete floor.

The two men rolled over and then got to their feet at the same time, both on balance and staring at each other.

Colt moved first this time and tried several kicks that met blocks. A few blows connected, but none did any real damage. Colt knew he had a tough challenge to make any headway.

Where were Linda and Mack?

The assassin counterattacked, but Colt managed to block his blows. Colt's confidence in his defense remained high, but what about his offense?"

Colt continued to use different moves, struggling to find an opening. Seconds seemed like hours.

After a few more unsuccessful kicks, Colt stepped back and took a deep breath.

It was good the assassin also wanted to rest for a moment, Colt thought.

Both men stood there staring at each other.

Colt was glad his breathing had returned to normal, but no help was available. What were Linda and Mack doing?

Keeping a defensive posture, Colt studied his opponent.

Colt took another deep breath.

The assassin seemed to want to rest a little more too. He stood still and continued to stare back at Colt.

Colt knew he had to come up with something to end the stalemate. What would a good tactician do? It was time to use some mental talent.

In a few more seconds, Colt rushed forward and faked a kick with his left foot.

The assassin shifted his position, obviously preparing to block the kick.

For a split second, Colt had an opening. He sent a crashing right hand toward the assassin's jaw, it connected.

The assassin staggered backwards but somehow stayed on his feet.

"Hold it right there!" someone said.

Colt glanced behind him. Mack had his SIG 556 pointed at the assassin. Linda was right behind him. Her rifle was pointed at the assassin too.

The assassin had to realize that he now faced insurmountable odds, Colt thought. This should be over.

"Hands in the air," Mack said.

The assassin raised his hands.

Again, a hail of bullets kicked up pieces of concrete all around them.

Colt, Linda, and Mack dove for cover, they had no choice.

After rolling behind some crates, Colt crawled to the corner and peered out. The assassin was gone. Shit!

However, Linda and Mack were okay. They were huddled behind a nearby stack of crates and were peering out in the direction the shots had come from.

Colt adjusted his tactical comm unit. It had been knocked loose but seemed to otherwise be intact. He whispered into his mike, "Mack and Linda, where were you guys?"

"Busy," Mack said. "Our men down below us had a big skirmish, Linda and I needed to give them some help. We tried to communicate with you, but I guess your mike wasn't working at the time."

"Yeah," Colt said. "It had been knocked loose early in my fight, any casualties?"

"Not on our side," Mack said. "We wiped about ten of them out. Several of the enemy ran. Our team down there is continuing their search."

Colt, Linda, and Mack took a few minutes to inspect the area. The people who did the shooting were gone.

"The assassin we just encountered might still be in here somewhere." Colt gestured toward a far wall. "But I'm guessing he left with the others."

"I think we can be assured of that." Linda glanced at Colt. "It looked like you were having a bit of trouble with the assassin. Remember, I was concerned about that."

"He's a damned good fighter, but he had a bit of trouble with me too," Colt said.

"Yeah, you did okay," Mack replied. "You probably shook off a lot of rust. You should do better in hand-to-hand combat from now on."

There was a brief pause.

"Let's open some of these metal crates," Colt said, "and take a look at what they contain." He glanced at Linda and Mack. "They probably have different cargo than the wooden crates."

They managed to open the one closest to them, but it was empty. They opened a few more. They were all empty.

"We damned sure found a huge stash of illegal drugs in the wooden crates," Mack said. "Looks like about a billion dollars worth of drugs we've found, and they'll probably continue to ship more in."

Colt nodded and waved everyone back the way they had come. "We'll hook up with the team below us and try to find the missile launch area as soon as we can. Stay on your toes. We could run into some more bogies."

"Should we also try to find the computer area as soon as

we can?" Linda asked.

"Both are critical," Colt said. "I'll summon our ten men who're outside to join us. We'll use two teams and do both at the same time." He gestured to Linda and Mack. "We should give our management a quick status report. We know our phones should work down here. I'll call Grant. Linda, you call Harlan. Mack you call Charles."

Everyone removed their secure satellite phones and punched a digit.

Chapter 46

In the main conference room at the Tampa FBI headquarters, Grant picked up his ringing phone. "It's Colt."

Harlan nodded as he also picked up his ringing phone.

Each man answered his phone at the same time.

"What's your status?" Grant asked. He listened for a minute and then disconnected.

After shooting a quick glance at Harlan, Grant saw that he had already finished his conversation too.

"Status report from Linda," Harlan said.

"You probably got the same information I did," Grant said, while keeping his gaze on Harlan.

Harlan grunted. "I didn't get any. I told her we were over here with you, and she just told me to check with you after you got the update from Colt."

Grant nodded. "The whole taskforce is moving forward in the underground tunnels and searching for the missile launching area. If they find the computer area first, Colt will dispatch some of the team to shut down the activity there. He and the rest of the team will continue searching for the launch area since that's the most critical one."

"Can't someone in one of the intelligence agencies do

something to help them in their search?" Blake asked.

"We've been trying," Grant said. "NRO has been making multiple sweeps with their various reconnaissance satellites. The satellites with the infrared capability haven't been able to penetrate the reinforced rock ceilings in most areas so they can't locate where the people are."

"What about NSA?" Jim asked. "Have they been able to intercept any calls and determine locations?"

"They've intercepted several and they're still trying to pinpoint the exact locations of the callers," Grant said.

Harlan leaned forward. "The callers who are in Jamaica?"

"There and other places," Grant said. "If we know the exact location of all the callers we intercept, we can put together a much more complete picture of everything that's going on."

Blake nodded. "I've been working with Steve and Nick on some of that. We've produced some useful results on several different aspects of the situation, both in Jamaica and elsewhere."

Harlan slammed a fist on the table. "Helping the taskforce find the damned launch site is the most important thing right now." He looked directly at Blake. "Have you helped any on that?"

"Maybe," Blake said. "Right before this meeting, I sent my analysis of a lot of data collected from the intercepted phone calls." He looked back at Harlan and then at Jim. "I think I pointed out some things that could help, especially if they have some collaborating data."

Harlan nodded slowly and didn't comment.

Grant looked at the Caller ID on his ringing phone. "It's Charles." He glanced at Blake before he answered. "Charles wouldn't be calling just to chat. Maybe Nick and Steve put all that analysis you sent them to good use."

Blake signaled a thumbs-up.

Grant pushed the button and answered.

Chapter 47

In the underground area serving as Ivan Titov's headquarters in Jamaica, Colt waved everyone forward.

As usual, everyone set their rifles on semi-automatic or single-shot firing mode. Since all the upcoming action would occur underground, the danger of ricochets made use of a multi-shot firing mode inadvisable.

In addition to grenades and the other weapons, every taskforce member had tactical communications gear, night-vision goggles and helmet-mounted infrared flashlights. If the lighting was insufficient inside any area of the underground structure, they still could navigate in dark areas.

If any area split into different direction, Colt decided they would operate in two teams of ten agents each. He would take team-one and move toward his left.

Mack would take team-two and move to their right.

Colt whispered into his comm unit and gave the instructions and the command to move forward in the large tunnel they now occupied.

"Roger," responded a chorus of voices.

Each team member was still outfitted in cotton and

nylon blend camouflage fatigues with a suit of tungsten disulfide-based nano-composite material, over five times stronger than steel, under the fatigues. The short-sleeved armor suits protected each person from neck to knee.

The two teams, team-one on the left side of the tunnel and team-two on the right, glided forward until Colt signaled a halt and gestured to Mack and Linda.

They rushed over to his position.

"Guard post ahead." Colt pointed. "I see only one person, and we could use a prisoner. Maybe we can pick up some valuable information about what's going on up ahead."

Mack and Linda nodded.

"Colt, you take care of this," Mack said. "You had the highest marks in your hand-to-hand combat exercises and you just got some more practice."

Glancing at Mack, Colt raised an eyebrow.

Mack shrugged. "I always study the records of anyone I team with. I studied Linda's too."

Colt looked back at the guard post. "All right, I'll give this my best effort. Make sure everyone stays on alert."

Mack and Linda both nodded.

Preparing for action, Colt felt an emotion of confidence mixed with extreme caution. He knew he had the exact skills for this.

As he moved forward, Colt reflected that all their rifles had sound suppressors (silencers). If any of his team did any shooting, they shouldn't alert any of the enemy in positions past the guard post.

Colt noted the guard wasn't looking in his direction. He seemed to be interested in activity to the side of him, over to his left. As Colt moved further forward, he could see the guard post was at an intersection of tunnels.

The guard raised his AK-74 and pointed it down the intersecting tunnel. Colt figured he must have spotted something.

Colt increased his speed, but he quickly realized he

wasn't going to get to the guard in time.

Damn, I can't let his gunshot alert all our enemies, Colt thought. We need a prisoner to interrogate for some information, but there's nothing I can do. He raised his SIG 556 and fired.

The guard fell, the only sound, a muffled pop.

"So much for taking him alive," Colt whispered into his tactical microphone. "At least we had the right idea."

"You're right about that," Linda replied. "Mack and I will join you. We'll figure out what to do with the body and then we'll keep on moving."

Colt checked the area. Everything looked clear at the moment down both tunnels. He wondered what had attracted the guard's attention.

"We'll stay on high alert and continue trying to find the missile launch area," Colt said into his tactical microphone. "My team will continue straight ahead. Mack, you take your team and search the connecting tunnel."

"Roger," Mack replied.

Everyone moved out quickly.

Colt hoped one of the teams would find the missile launch site quickly. As more time passed, that was becoming more critical.

Chapter 48

In the main conference room in their underground headquarters in Jamaica, Ivan looked across the large table at Sergei and Cham. The large Chinese warrior had rejoined Ivan after escorting Yaw and Wan to the area at the launch site.

Ivan pointed to one of the wall-mounted monitors. Colt Randall and his taskforce were congregated in the area around the guard post at the intersection of two of their most important tunnels. The guard was lying on the stone floor.

"We need to make a quick decision about this problem we need to address right now," Ivan said, shaking his finger at the monitor.

Cham's eyes gleamed. "I can take care of this without any help. I've wanted a chance to eliminate Randle, and I'll be glad to take care of this."

"There are twenty of them in the taskforce." Ivan narrowed his eyes and leaned toward Cham. "You won't be facing just Randall."

Cham pointed toward the monitor. "That guard post is at the intersection of two of our main tunnels, right?"

"What's your point?" Ivan asked.

"Probably ten men will go down each one of the tunnels," Cham said. "That would be a logical choice if they aren't sure where they need to go."

"Again, what's your point?" Ivan asked.

"You can keep me advised and I'll go after the group Randall is leading," Cham said. "I'll first shoot Randall and then I'll only be confronting nine people. I've fought a group that size many times."

Sergei grunted. "Nine seasoned warriors still amount to a lot of skills and firepower." He looked at Ivan. "Maybe Ludvig should join Cham."

Cham pursed his lips and looked at Sergei. "I don't need any help. I can do this alone. You and Ivan have my record of accomplishments."

Sergei shrugged. "Some extra help never hurts anything, especially in situations like this."

Ivan looked at Cham. "So, you think you can take on Randall and nine other warriors at once?"

Cham displayed another big grin and nodded vigorously. "I'll concentrate on staying in a good defensive position and knocking Randall off first."

"I don't know if that is going to work," Ivan said. "Even you will likely have trouble in this situation."

Cham narrowed his eyes and made no immediate comment.

"We have a lot of veteran warriors in the areas around the computers and around the missile launch site. And we don't know for sure Randall will find those areas." Sergei looked directly at Ivan. "We could deploy some of those assassins to take the offense against Randall and his taskforce."

"Those are our most critical areas to protect, especially the missile launch site," Ivan said. "We can overcome not hacking into the Federal Reserve System, but if we fail to launch the missiles, our whole mission fails miserably. We need every warrior we have left to protect those areas. We can't spare a single assassin who's there to ensure our missiles launch and our computer hacking activities aren't interfered with in any way."

Cham leaned forward. His eyes were gleaming even brighter now and his grin stretched even further across his face. "I keep telling you I can handle this. It's no big problem for me."

Sergei stared at Cham. "You might not be able to isolate Randall. How confident are you that you can handle ten of them by yourself?"

Cham continued to grin. "I've confronted larger groups of warriors than this many times. I'll have my AK-47 and plenty of extra ammunition. That's all I'll need."

"You'll be facing ten warriors with high powered rifles, probably SIG 556 models," Ivan said.

"I'll be careful." Cham's grin stretched larger. "I can crush them with my hands if I need to."

"You can't stop bullets from high-powered rifles," Ivan said. "You need a bulletproof vest, but we don't have one large enough for you."

"My mass of muscle provides a lot of protection. I've been through a lot of tests, and I don't think a few hits from 5.56 mm bullets will stop me." Cham stood and looked expectantly at Ivan.

Ivan made a dismissive gesture. "Okay go give it a try. We need to do something, and this looks like the only option we have at the moment."

Chapter 49

Cham stood in a well-lit tunnel and made a final decision on his strategy.

There weren't many hiding places available in this area, so he decided to move behind one of the wooden crates that were situated along the left side of the wall from his perspective. He took his position behind the first one in the long row of them which stretched for about 60 yards.

Unless they entered through the single outside entrance designed specifically for quick access to secure areas, Randall and his taskforce had to come along this route to reach the missile launch area or the computer area, Cham thought.

Cham glanced at his secure satellite phone. He knew Ivan and Sergei were watching the monitors and keeping close track of Randall's progress. He knew they would call him when Randall was drawing close.

He held his AK-47 in his right hand and waited. He had always preferred the AK-47 over the AK-74 because it had larger bullets, some more punch in his opinion.

The AK-47 used 7.62x39 mm ammunition while the newer AK-74 used 5.45x39 mm ammunition. The rate of fire for the AK-47 was 600 rounds per minute as compared to 650 rounds per minute for the AK-74, but that made no difference to Cham. His AK-47 could fire fast enough.

He knew Randall would be leading the taskforce when they arrived and Randall wasn't going to survive his first barrage of bullets. Cham laughed. This wasn't going to be difficult.

He would kill Randall and then decide how he would handle the others. Maybe he would stay behind cover and keep firing, or maybe he would charge down the tunnel and attack them more aggressively. He had a 40-round magazine, and he would make sure it was full before he charged out in the tunnel. He was carrying eight extra magazines, and he could change them in less than a second while he was running at full speed. He had practiced this many times.

Firing at a rate of 600 rounds per minute or 10 rounds per second should keep the taskforce hunkered down.

He wasn't worried about being shot a couple of times. He was highly resistant to bullets, especially the ones from the SIG 556 that were only 5.56 millimeter. And he was extremely fast, especially for his size. He would close on them before they could decide how to react.

Spraying his shots all around the area the taskforce occupied and closing on them quickly should work well for him. He laughed again. He was going to immensely enjoy this. He was glad Ivan was giving him this opportunity to use all his superior skills.

Cham leaned out from the corner of the wooden crate and looked down the tunnel. He could see clearly down the well-lit tunnel for the full 60 yards.

As soon as Randall appeared the egotistical American was going to die, Cham thought. Randall wasn't nearly as good as he thought he was.

This was fun.

Cham had his rifle set on full-automatic and he had all his spare magazines in a special container that served as a quick draw holster. He continued to laugh as quietly as he could.

Cham felt the phone in his pocket vibrate. He answered.

"Randall's almost to your area," Ivan said. "He's right where we expected him to be, leading the group. Get ready."

"I'm ready and you can be assured Randall will soon cease to exist."

"Don't be overconfident. Make sure you take precautions. You shouldn't allow yourself to be exposed to their gunfire for any more than a few seconds."

Cham continued to laugh. "Don't worry. I've got it all worked out. I know what I'm doing. I've been in this position many times."

Ivan said. "Okay, I'll let you take care of business." He disconnected.

Cham looked down the well-lit tunnel and waited. He was confident he would succeed. This time Randall and his taskforce were about to be eliminated for good. They would no longer be a threat to stop any missile launches.

Chapter 50

Colt moved forward slowly and carefully. Linda and the eight FBI agents behind her followed.

They moved in single file, five yards apart, along the left side of the well-lit tunnel.

"Down," Colt shouted as a spray of bullets kicked up fragments from the stone floor.

The ten warriors dropped flat on floor and rolled toward the wooden crates that were prevalent along the right side of the tunnel. Colt wasn't sure what their purpose was, but they were there.

"Anyone hit?" Colt asked.

All replies came back negative.

"We'll hold up here until we figure out what's going on," Colt said, as he peered into the well-lit tunnel ahead.

Colt noted a rifle protruded slightly from a corner of a wooden crate about 60 yards ahead and another burst of gunfire erupted. Stone fragments again flew around the area as well as fragments of wood. Colt stayed as flat as he could.

"I've only seen one rifle. I'm guessing there's just one of them behind that crate and he's trying to figure out how effective he's been," Linda said.

As soon as Linda spoke, a huge head appeared around the corner of the crate.

"No one move," Colt said into his tactical microphone.

"Roger," came multiple replies.

The rifle protruded from the corner of the wooden crate again and another burst of fire erupted.

Stone and wood fragments flew past Colt and the warriors on the floor.

"Anyone hit?" Colt asked.

"Negative," came back the replies.

"Count off," Colt said.

Everyone was accounted for.

Linda crawled up beside Colt. "What's our plan?"

"Get ready to open fire," Colt said into his tactical microphone. "As soon as a head shows around that crate again, let loose on it."

A rifle appeared from around the corner of the wooden crate and another barrage of shots kicked up stone and wood fragments around Colt.

Colt and the warriors around him fired back. The rifle went flying backwards and lay in the open around the wooden crate. Colt could tell it was an AK-47.

"Should we rush up there?" Linda asked.

Colt started to answer when a huge man emerged from behind the crate. Still about 60 yards away, he charged straight toward Colt.

"Looks like another one of those monsters our enemies have accumulated and he's coming after us unarmed," Linda said into her tactical microphone. "This one is the biggest yet."

Everyone rose to a kneeling position.

Colt grunted. "He's the Chinese assassin named Cham. I recognize him from photos I saw. He's seven feet tall and he weighs four hundred pounds, all muscle."

Linda looked directly at Colt. "I guess all these types like to kill people with their bare hands."

"He looks like he could do that pretty easily," Colt said.

Linda gave Colt a sharp look. "You couldn't handle the other one and this one is even bigger. We need to shoot him now."

"I was doing pretty well with the other one." Colt glanced at Linda. "You and Mack interrupted before I could finish him off."

"It looked like you were having a lot of difficulty, and this guy is a lot bigger." Linda looked at Colt. "We need to shoot him."

Colt watched Cham close to within about forty yards.

Linda narrowed her eyes and looked back at the charging monster and then again at Colt. "He looks agile and in great shape. Look how fast he's running. We need to shoot him now!" She pointed her SIG 556 at the charging monster and fired.

The bullets didn't seem to have any effect. Cham kept coming directly toward Colt.

Colt saw Cham flash a big grin and increase his speed.

"He acts like he recognizes me. I guess he's been well briefed," Colt said as he also fired at the charging monster.

Linda and Colt both continued to fire.

Cham veered toward a stack of crates about twenty yards away and disappeared.

"We're both good shots and I'm sure we were hitting him, but I didn't see any effect from being hit," Linda said.

Colt nodded and rushed forward. "He might be wounded though. Let's go get him."

They both charged toward the row of crates Cham had ducked behind.

As Colt and Linda slowed and approached the corner of the crates Cham had ducked behind, Colt said, "Move out a little wider."

They got to the aisle behind the row of crates and looked down it. Cham wasn't there.

With their rifles in position to fire, Colt and Linda

turned down the aisle.

As they continued forward, a huge hand from behind a crate grabbed Colt's rifle as another huge hand shoved him all the way across the aisle into the row of crates on the other side. Colt weighed 225 pounds, but he resembled a rag doll being tossed aside. He hit the stack of crates hard.

Several crates toppled onto the floor.

Cham, flashing a huge grin, charged out into the aisle toward Linda.

From five yards away, Linda fired multiple times at the monster's head.

The bull-like monster dropped to the rocky floor, thrashed around a few times, and then lay still.

Colt gave a thumbs-up as he regained his feet. He walked over to the downed bull and felt for a pulse. There was none.

Mack's voice came over Colt's tactical comm unit. "We've had no action. What's your situation?"

Colt explained.

"Wow, that's hard to believe those guys are that resistant to high-caliber bullets."

"They have a lot of tough muscle the bullets must go through," Colt said.

There was a brief pause.

"Are you still in the same tunnel you went down from the intersection?" Mack asked.

"Yes," Colt said. "And since Cham was here, it probably leads somewhere important. The right side of it is lined with the wooden crates we've become familiar with. We probably should open a few and see if they contain the expected illegal drugs."

"We've found nothing down this tunnel. I think it might be unused and put in for future use," Mack said. "We'll go back to the intersection and come join you."

"While we're waiting I'll give Grant an update and we'll open a few of the crates," Colt replied. "After you get here, we'll continue forward together and try to find the launch area and the computer area. Finding the launch area first will be our primary goal of course."

"Roger, we're on our way."

Chapter 51

In Tampa in the main conference room at the FBI headquarters, Grant disconnected from Colt's phone call and looked across the large table at Harlan, Jim, and Blake.

"Colt had some interesting information," Grant said. He explained.

"It looks like the Chinese have a lot of monsters like Cham they use as combat fighters," Harlan replied. "This is the second one Colt has fought in the last few minutes."

Grant nodded and reached for his phone. "I'll give Ken an update and he can inform Charles."

After his conversation with Ken, Grant said, "They're doing everything they can up there in Washington to figure out a way to help Colt find the exact location of the launch site, but they haven't had any success yet."

"So, the taskforce is on its own to find the exact location of the launch site in the underground area before it's too late?" Harlan asked.

"I guess that's sums it up accurately enough," Grant said. "However, Colt mentioned he was confident they were getting close. He'll keep us informed."

Harlan gave a slow nod. "He has a lot of capable

warriors with him. Hopefully they'll come through."

"The Russians and the Chinese have poured a lot of money into Jamaica to build that underground facility," Blake said. "But I'm sure we rushed them and they haven't been able to put all the finishing touches on it yet."

"What's your point?" Harlan asked.

"The area around the launch site probably isn't completely finished," Blake said. "It probably won't be obvious to Colt they're getting close until they actually get to it."

Grant nodded. "That goes along with Colt's report. He mentioned Mack and his team had figured they would get to a dead end if they had continued in the other tunnel they found."

"So, all twenty members of the taskforce are together?" Jim asked.

"That's correct," Grant said. "Once they find something they're prepared to split again in order to handle the computer site and the launch site simultaneously."

Harlan shook his head slowly. "We should be able to think of something that will help Colt out."

"We know the launch site has to be on the water," Blake said. "Do we have any way to find Colt's exact location right now?"

Grant reached for his phone. "I'll give Ken a call. He and Charles can confer with NRO and all their experts on that specific issue. Maybe there's some way the infrared cameras on some of our satellites can locate them."

After his call, Grant scanned the faces around the table. "Ken told me the infrared cameras still can't penetrate the top of the tunnel. Ken also mentioned we've implemented the new defensive shield our experts devised to protect the Federal Reserve System. That takes a little pressure off needing to find the computer area as fast as we find the launch area."

"With all the Chinese innovations, we know the

Poseidon Missiles probably have the most sophisticated technology available," Jim said. "They'll have no trouble hitting strategic spots in our country along any of our coastlines, even when they're launched from Jamaica."

Blake nodded. "We know the missiles now have a guidance system capable of maneuvering the Panama Canal."

"Jim tried to explain all that to me before, but I'm still not quite sure I got all the details." Harlan stared at Blake. "The Panama Canal has different levels because the Atlantic Ocean and Pacific Ocean aren't on the same level. Ships going through the canal must wait while the corrective actions are taken to allow them to go from one ocean to the other, right?"

"Right," Blake said. "But with all the Chinese improvements, we know the Poseidon Missiles can deal with all the complications."

"Exactly how can they do that?" Harlan asked.

"The water depth must be deep enough to handle the big ships. The missiles will have guidance systems smart enough to allow them to hover for long periods along the bottom and go through as the ships are going through," Blake said.

Harlan rubbed his chin for a few moments. "So, the Russians can hit our West Coast from Jamaica if they choose to or they can hit our East Coast. We can't consider any of our cities or strategic locations close to any of our coastlines to be safe from the attack of a Poseidon Missile."

"Right," Blake said.

Harlan looked directly at Blake. "We all know it's critical for Colt and the taskforce to stop any launch of those missiles. I'm now even more concerned about that. We might be running out of time."

"I share your feelings," Grant said. "Some data the FBI and CIA have collected indicates the missiles can normally travel underwater at a speed of 80 miles an hour," Steve said. "That's faster than our nuclear-powered attack submarines and also their anti-ship missiles. The Poseidon Missiles can also travel at a depth of 3,280 feet. That's far deeper than any of our submarines can go."

"Remember, there's another thing we should keep in mind," Blake said. "It's possible the Chinese have helped Russia improve the speed to exceed 200 miles per hour. They've added ramjet engines and have been able to create a bubble of gas for the missile to travel in. This reduces friction with the water."

Jim gave Blake a long look and then looked at Grant. "Have you seen any evidence of this being true?"

"I've seen several reports the Russians and Chinese have been working on improving the speed of the missiles by doing this," Grant said, "but none of our intelligence agencies know if they've perfected it yet."

Harlan narrowed his eyes and leaned forward. "Whether the Russians and Chinese have perfected that aspect or not, Colt and the taskforce damned sure better succeed down in Jamaica. We're going to have a hard time recovering from a successful Poseidon Missile strike."

Chapter 52

Ivan sat in the main conference room in their underground headquarters in Jamaica and looked across the large table at Sergei and Yaw, who had rejoined them.

Pointing to one of the wall-mounted monitors, Ivan said, "It looks like they're going to get to the launch area. We'd better be prepared."

Sergei turned fully toward Yaw. "Do you have our defense in position for the ambush?"

"Yes," Yaw said. "And during our construction we also installed an excellent intruder tracking system. Once Randall and his taskforce reach a certain point, we'll be able to monitor everything they do from there into the launch area."

Ivan set his jaw as his gaze rested on Yaw "I keep saying you can't underestimate Randall. You can't overlook any possibility. If there's any way he can get you, he will. Case in point, he just eliminated Cham."

"Cham was a great fighter, but he was only one person. My defense will hold," Yaw said. "Randall won't succeed in stopping us. We'll be able to launch the missiles, and the new guidance system will ensure we trigger the explosions at just the right spots for the missiles to produce the maximum damage."

Ivan narrowed his eyes and leaned toward Yaw. "Once we launch the missiles they're virtually unstoppable, right?"

Yaw nodded. "They'll be using our latest version of the supercavitating technology used by your current high-speed torpedoes. They'll use underwater ramjets rather than propellers and travel inside a bubble of gas to reduce friction. They'll travel at the maximum depth and achieve speeds in excess of 200 miles per hour."

"I'll check again with Maxim on the progress down there. I want to know precisely how soon the first missile can be launched," Ivan said. He grabbed his phone and punched a button.

Yaw flashed a huge grin. "I'm sure it will be very soon. We have a lot of experts on the job. You have many benefits from partnering with us. We've added a lot of advanced technology to everything we're doing here. We'll have no trouble bringing down the United States."

Ivan ignored Yaw's bravado as he heard Maxim answer.

"Are you ready to launch?" Ivan asked.

"We have the first missile on a rail car and it's now heading down toward the launcher," Maxim said. "It will be down there in five minutes. It will then take about twenty minutes to make the final preparations for the launch."

"So, the first missile will be in the ocean and on its way in twenty-five minutes?" Ivan asked.

"That's correct," Maxim said. "And the second missile is being moved out to another rail car now. The third will be close behind."

"Are you launching all three in succession like we planned?" Ivan asked.

"Yes," Maxim said. "Everything we planned is in process. Each of the three missiles has been programmed to hit its assigned target."

Ivan nodded in satisfaction and then disconnected.

Yaw grinned. "You're lucky we're helping you out."

Ivan narrowed his eyes. "And you're lucky our scientists developed the Poseidon Missiles in the first place and planned all this. Our chess masters in Moscow have done an excellent job in developing the overall strategy."

Yaw gave a slight shrug. "It's been a good team effort from the very start. It's good we're on the same team. The United States will soon cease to exist as it is now. Everything will come to a halt after three nuclear Tsunamis hit."

A brief silence ensued.

"If Randall and his taskforce somehow get into the launch site area, we can't let them shut us down like they've done on our previous initiatives," Sergei said. He stared at Ivan and Yaw.

"I wasn't involved before. I've already told you my defenses will stop Randall," Yaw said. "Our defenses will kick in hard. They're well positioned close to the launch area entrance. They'll stop Randall and his taskforce in their tracks."

"And you're sure they're in position now?" Sergei asked.

"Of course I'm sure," Yaw said. "They've all been in their final positions for several minutes now. They're all well trained and you can be confident they'll stop Randall and his group from getting into the launch area."

Sergei gave a slow nod.

Ivan studied Yaw for a few seconds. "Have you positioned any of your men inside the launch complex itself?"

"Yes, of course," Yaw said. "I did that just for extra insurance we'll get the launches off."

Sergei narrowed his eyes. "But you're still confident you can stop Randall from entering the launch complex itself?"

Yaw gave a wry smile and then shrugged. "I always prepare for the worst-case scenario, and I always have another alternative as a backup plan as an extra precaution.

It never hurts to have a lot of safeguards. I'm making sure we don't give Randall any chance to succeed."

"Let's hope your backup plan for this situation isn't needed," Ivan said. "Let's hope your defenses outside the launch complex eliminate Randall and his taskforce completely."

Yaw grinned. "I have a lot of confidence they'll do that. We have a great ambush strategy, and we'll execute it with precision." He looked directly at Ivan. "We'll even have various options for how we execute depending on how Randall and his group react to the first wave of fire."

Ivan nodded slowly and, after a brief hesitation, he said, "Okay, it sounds like you're as well prepared as you can possibly be. Now we need to give some consideration to an extra safety factor for the three of us in this room."

"You're thinking about an escape plan?" Sergei asked.

Ivan nodded. "It's always best to not take any chances on things going wrong."

Yaw threw both hands in the air. "An escape plan isn't anything we need to spend time on. I have everything covered. There's no chance Randall will survive the ambush, but even if he does, I have our insurance group in position inside the launch complex."

After a brief silence, Sergei looked at Ivan. "I would feel better having an escape plan for you and me. In this type of situation, we can't be too careful."

Ivan nodded. "Let's devise one. It would be the smart thing to do."

Chapter 53

Colt, with a full contingent of 20 warriors moved forward in the tunnel. The right side was still lined with wooden crates.

Linda pointed. "There's a huge metal door about thirty yards ahead. That must have some purpose.

The taskforce hugged the sides of the crates and moved toward the metal door.

Within less than a minute, they arrived at their target and Colt immediately inspected the stone wall around each side of the door. He spotted a couple of slightly discolored squares about a yard from the right side of the door and then inspected the wall above them.

About six feet above the floor were two small indentions two feet apart.

Colt put one foot on each of the squares and inserted his hands into the indentions.

A hydraulic noise came from above the door.

The door slowly lifted, exposing a lighted chamber about twelve feet high and twenty yards wide. The walls were metal.

Colt waved the taskforce forward toward the far end of the chamber which seemed about a hundred yards long.

Mack's voice rang in Colt's earpiece. "With all of their high technology, I'm surprised about the lack of advanced security all around this area."

"Maybe they're still in the process of installing it," Colt

said into his tactical microphone. "We probably got here a lot quicker than they expected."

"Yeah, that's a possibility," Mack replied.

Colt spoke into his tactical microphone. "Keep moving toward the far end, standard tactical formation."

"Thought I heard something," Linda said into her tactical microphone. "We might have some more company."

Everyone took cover and waited.

Colt's internal alarms were screaming. His instinct told him danger was present, but where were they?

Everyone continued to scan the area.

After five minutes, Colt gestured to move forward. "We can't stay here forever. Maintain a separation of about ten yards and let's keep moving."

Remaining on high alert and continuing to scan the large chamber, Colt led everyone forward in single file, about ten yards apart.

Colt saw some movement ahead. It was a rifle barrel.

"Down!" Colt followed his own command, but not fast enough—bullets tore the rifle out of his hands and sent it clattering across the stone floor.

Colt rolled toward the nearest wooded crate just as more shots rang out, showering him with splinters.

The other taskforce members also rolled behind the nearest crates.

"Everyone okay?" Colt asked into his tactical communications unit.

The rest of the taskforce answered in the affirmative.

Colt spotted his SIG 556 lying a few feet away and he had a strong feeling he would need it very soon. Staying as low as possible and pushing forward on his stomach as fast as he could, he retrieved his rifle and rolled back to cover.

No shots were fired.

Colt figured the original shooters must be shifting positions. That was a lucky thing for him.

He stood and pressed as flat against the crate as possible.

He peered around the corner of the stack of crates and scanned the area in the direction from which the shots had come.

No activity was visible.

Colt heard a lot of gunfire in multiple bursts and in multiple areas. All the shots were behind him.

Within less than a minute, Mack's voice rang loudly in the tactical communications unit in Colt's ear, "We've eliminated about thirty enemy combatants who came charging toward us from the rear. Guess they thought they could surprise us."

"Did you get all of them?" Colt asked.

"Think so," Mack said. "All of us back here compared notes. No one saw anybody retreat."

"We'll wait a few more minutes," Colt said. "If we don't have any activity, we'll move forward again."

After another five minutes, Colt stepped out from behind the crate. No shots were fired.

"Looks like we can move forward again," Colt said. "Let's go, same formation and guidelines."

Colt soon came to long stretch of glass-walled rooms. He stopped and Linda moved up to join him.

"Get behind some good cover and hold up for a bit," Colt said into his tactical communications unit. "Linda and I will inspect the area we've just come to."

"Roger," various replies echoed in Colt's ear.

Many of the rooms contained large quantities of electronic equipment, but no computer.

Scanning the area, Colt saw no people. There was no activity in any of the glass-walled rooms. The whole area reminded him of a large lab area in a hospital.

"They're waiting in ambush somewhere," Linda said, "but where are they hiding?"

Colt pointed toward some metal cabinets about 20 yards ahead. "That's a possibility."

The cabinets were positioned about five yards away

from the left sidewall.

"I don't think you could hide more than eight men up there," Linda said. "I would get behind those wooden storage crates sitting about ten yards out from the right sidewall. You could hide an army back there."

"They might use both," Colt said. "However, I would pick the crates. Let's check them first."

Linda frowned. "They can pick us off from the metal cabinets when we move toward the crates."

"Spread out and crawl. Stay as flat as possible," Colt said.

When they started crawling a hail of bullets bounced off the glass walls and rattled all around. It was obvious the glass was bulletproof.

"Looks like at least some are behind the metal cabinets," Colt said. "It's time to use our concussion grenades. We'll clean out the area behind the cabinets first and then move down to the crates."

Linda nodded.

"Let's get a little closer to the cabinets. Stay as low as you can," Colt said. After closing to within about ten yards of the target, Colt stopped and checked to be sure Linda was ready.

Linda gave a thumbs-up.

"I'll lob my grenade in the middle of the cabinets," Colt said. "You follow immediately. Don't be short. Bouncing your grenade off the wall behind the cabinets should work fine."

"Roger."

Colt lobbed his grenade. Linda's was on the way when his exploded. Keeping their SIG 556 rifles ready to fire, they crawled forward through the smoke and checked behind the cabinets. Eight bodies were scattered around on the floor. No one seemed to be alive. Colt and Linda checked to make sure they were all dead and then crawled back toward the crates along the other wall.

Knowing Mack and his team would stay alert for any further attacks from behind them Colt spoke into his communications unit, "The rest of team-one crawl up to where Linda and I are. We've cleaned them out behind the metal cabinets. We'll now concentrate on the wooden crates along the right sidewall."

After the eight men joined Colt and Linda, the ten warriors used the best cover they could find and stayed low as they moved toward the right sidewall and the row of wooden crates.

Colt called a halt about ten yards from the row of crates and surveyed the situation. So far no one had fired at them. Colt wondered if anyone was back there. If they were, maybe they were waiting for his team to come a little closer.

There was at least a twenty-yard distance between the top of the crates and the ceiling of the chamber, plenty of space to lob the grenades into.

Colt felt sure some enemy warriors were back there and decided to take no chances.

"Use your grenades to clean out behind the crates. Bouncing off the wall behind the crates works fine; just don't be short," Colt said into his tactical microphone, "everybody ready?"

"Roger," came multiple replies.

Colt immediately lobbed his remaining grenade. The other nine grenades were quickly on their way.

There were ten explosions.

Screams came from behind the crates. Smoke covered the area.

After readying his SIG 556, Colt charged forward. The other warriors followed.

Everyone ran a zigzag pattern toward the crates.

"Empty one magazine into the smoke," Colt said into his tactical mouthpiece. He started firing.

Everyone fired continuously for a few seconds.

Colt slammed in a fresh magazine and slowed to a walk.

As the smoke began to clear, he counted twenty bodies sprawled on the floor between the crates and the wall.

For a few moments, silence reigned; acrid smells permeated the air.

Colt saw a slight movement in the thinning smoke about fifteen yards in front of him. He fired at the movement.

A man tumbled off the top of the row of crates. His rifle bounced off the stone floor.

Colt and the nine warriors with him stayed low and moved forward toward the far end of the row of crates. Other than the ten members of his taskforce, there was no more movement in that area.

Colt spoke into his tactical mouthpiece, "Mack, we've cleared out the area behind the row of metal cabinets and the area behind the row of wooden crates. You can come up and join us. Stay alert though in case we missed something."

"Roger," Mack replied, "we're on our way."

In two minutes, the twenty warriors soon spread out and took cover down at the end of the large chamber.

"I think we got the whole group but stay alert; continue to look around," Colt said.

In a few more minutes, the taskforce ensured the area was secure.

Colt pointed toward another large metal door on the far wall. "That must lead somewhere important. Let's check it out."

The taskforce spread out some more and took cover as Colt, Linda, and Mack moved to the door.

Colt scanned the area around the door and determined it had the same opening scheme as he had used the previous times. He looked down along the stone for the discolored areas. He quickly found them and put a foot on each one while putting each hand in the respective small indentions immediately above him in the rock wall.

The door opened and revealed a well-lit tunnel about 12 feet high and 20 feet wide.

Chapter 54

Ivan sat with Sergei and Yaw at the large table in the main conference room in their underground headquarters in Jamaica.

Ivan scowled and stared at Yaw through narrowed eyes. "That didn't work out very well. I keep telling you Randall is tough to eliminate."

"That's why I have a lot of backup in place," Yaw said. "We'll still keep him from stopping the launches."

Ivan grunted and leaned forward. "It's time for the three of us to decide what our priorities are. We might need to make some quick decisions."

"I just checked with our defenses inside the launch chamber one minute ago," Yaw said. "They're waiting for Randall and his group."

"Are you still confident they can keep Randall from entering our main passageway?" Ivan asked.

"I have them positioned in two different areas toward the end of the tunnel leading into the launch chamber," Yaw said. "There's no way Randall or any of his group can sneak past them."

Ivan narrowed his eyes even further. "That's not what I asked you."

Yaw shrugged. "If Randall can't sneak past them, then he can't get into the launch chamber."

Ivan glanced at Sergei.

Sergei leaned toward Yaw. "Your defense hasn't stopped Randall yet. I'm not sure they can."

Yaw pursed his lips but made no comment.

"If Randall gets into our main tunnel, he'll know immediately it leads somewhere important," Ivan said. "It has better lighting than any of our other tunnels and the walls are a polished ceramic surface."

"We don't need to worry about Randall getting that far." Yaw reached for his phone and punched a button. "I'll check with my group leaders and make sure they're on full alert. Randall's not going to last much longer. Everyone in my remaining defense is a veteran fighter."

Ivan watched an impatient expression dominate Yaw's face and then Yaw furrowed his brow.

"No one is answering?" Ivan asked.

Yaw didn't comment. He quickly disconnected and punched another button on his advanced technology phone.

Ivan watched the same expressions dominate Yaw's face and then glanced at Sergei.

"This isn't good." Sergei turned fully toward Yaw. "If your men don't answer, they've obviously been eliminated."

"I just talked with them a few minutes ago," Yaw said. "They had their ambush all set up."

Ivan glanced at his watch. "A lot can happen within a few minutes in a war zone." He narrowed his eyes and jutted out his chin. "And that's exactly what we have here."

Yaw didn't comment as Sergei leaned toward him.

"Your men aren't among the living any longer. You need to admit that. It's obvious," Sergei said.

Ivan looked at Sergei. "You call Denis. I'll call Maxim."

Each man grabbed his phone and punched a button.

Yaw also punched another button on his phone.

"Is the first missile ready to launch?" Ivan asked.

"Like I mentioned before, we've loaded it on the rail car and it's down at the final launch point," Maxim said. "It should be in the ocean and on the way within a few more minutes."

"Precisely how many minutes are you talking about?" Ivan asked.

Maxim's voice echoed some concern. "Has something changed?"

"Damned right," Ivan said. "Randall might be paying you a visit at any moment."

Maxim's voice indicated he was feeling a wave of panic. "He's in the main tunnel?"

"Yeah and he'll be where you are real soon," Ivan said. "Go as fast as you can. We must get at least one missile launched."

"Wan must have just gotten the same message," Maxim replied. "He's running toward the rail car and yelling something in Chinese. I wish I understood the language."

"You don't need to understand the language," Ivan said. "I've told you what's going on. Go give him all the help you can. Make sure you get that missile launched."

"Yes sir, at least Oleg and Ludvig are both here with us."

Ivan disconnected and looked at Yaw. "So, you just informed Wan about the pending danger, right?"

"Right," Yaw said. "I decided to go along with your assessment of our situation down here. I don't want to take any unnecessary chances of Randall stopping us."

Ivan nodded and then looked at Sergei who had finished his latest phone conversation with Denis.

"Well?" Ivan asked.

"Denis told me he had a problem to resolve but would have everything ready to start their hacking attempt within ten more minutes. He mentioned he can go faster if Maxim can go back and join him."

Ivan shook his head and exhaled sharply. "Okay, I'll tell Maxim to go back and help Denis. I'll tell Oleg and Ludvig to stay in the launch area and help get the missile launched in any way they can."

"I explained the whole situation to Denis as quickly as I could," Sergei said. "He has a full understanding of the urgency."

"Is he handling it okay?" Ivan asked.

"He was calm enough. He told me they would be going as fast as they could," Sergei said. "He told me they really needed to concentrate hard to ensure the software functions correctly for the hacking attempt. He emphasized that Maxim would be a big help in resolving the unexpected problem."

Ivan shook his head slowly and then scanned all the wall-mounted monitors. He pointed at one of them.

"There they are," Ivan said. "Randall and his taskforce are now in the final passageway leading to the launch site."

Sergei looked at Ivan and stood. "I don't think we should stick around down here. We can use the elevator at the emergency exit and take the boat to the airport. Finland will be a good place to get back to."

Ivan also stood.

"I'm going to join Wan," Yaw said. "I'm not letting Randall barge into the launch area and disrupt things without a big fight."

Ivan grunted and waved to Yaw as he and Sergei moved toward the emergency exit and the elevator.

Chapter 55

Colt entered the well-lighted tunnel and waved everyone forward. He noted the walls were a glossy ceramic of some kind. They've really put the finishing touches in this area, he thought. We're definitely getting close to at least one of our main objectives.

The taskforce moved along cautiously with everyone in single file and ten yards apart.

Colt saw two large metal doors about fifty yards in front of them. He looked back at Linda, pointed toward the doors, and said into his tactical microphone, "I'm betting one of those is to the launching area and the other is into the computer area."

Linda nodded. "We should concentrate on the launch area first."

"That's the critical area alright," Mack said, "and I'm guessing you're going to need a lot of help in there. I'll send four of my team to the computer area and the rest of us will help you in the launch area. Putting a stop to the computer activity as soon as we can is important too."

Colt nodded as he approached the two doors and

inspected the area around them. It was immediately obvious they could be opened using the same process as he had for the other doors. He chose the one to his left and quickly heard the familiar hydraulic sound.

Mack opened the door on the right.

Colt looked in and saw a giant chamber below him. The entrance was on a rocky ledge. A stairway led down to the floor level.

"We have a large room with some computers over here," Mack said. "No people are in sight. I'm sending four of my men in to check things out. The rest of us are going to join you in the launch area."

"Roger," Colt said. "No one is in sight over here either. It's a giant chamber and we're on a ledge. We're proceeding down a stairway to floor level. Join us down there."

"We're on our way," Mack replied. "Don't walk into another ambush."

Colt gave a short laugh. "That's the number one thing on my mind right now. We're proceeding with caution."

In less than five minutes, Colt and the other fifteen warriors with him were on floor level and in good cover.

Linda and Mack eased up to Colt's position.

"This chamber must be for future use," Colt said. "There's nothing in here and no people are around."

Mack pointed toward a far wall. "There's another door."

Colt told five of his group to spread out, find some good cover, and guard the area. Mack and the other five agents with him followed Colt, who moved toward a large metal door like the others.

Chapter 56

Bing Yaw stood with Ludvig Glinka, Oleg Rowan, and Chen Wan alongside the first Poseidon Missile to arrive in the launch area.

Five other men were working frantically to make the final adjustments so they could soon send the missile on the way to its target and then start preparing the second missile which had just arrived on the rail car.

Yaw thought about the third missile which was still back in the initial preparation area. He knew it wouldn't be far behind. Speed was of the essence, but there was nothing they could do to help the five technicians complete their tasks quicker, Yaw reasoned. They would only be in the way.

"A couple of us should have stayed in the initial preparation area," Oleg said.

Yaw shrugged. "This is where the launch occurs. We need to ensure at least one of the missiles gets launched."

Wan nodded as his gaze took in both the Russians. "Your bosses have left to go back to Finland."

"That doesn't concern me," Ludvig said. "They wouldn't be in here fighting with us anyway."

"Right, and that's okay. I just want my chance to knock off that bastard, Colt Randall," Oleg replied. "Launching the missiles and eliminating him is all that concerns me right now."

"Your bosses could offer support," Yaw said. He gestured toward Wan. "I always do that with my subordinates, especially when the situation takes a turn for the worst. That's why I'm here."

Oleg narrowed his eyes and looked at Yaw. "You're a fighter and that makes a difference. My bosses aren't fighters."

Ludvig nodded. "I agree with Oleg. Our bosses never get into physical fights. The fights they get into are ones they plan from an office somewhere. Their fights are always on a larger scale." He shrugged. "If they were down here with us, they wouldn't be of any real help. I doubt they've ever fired a pistol or a rifle. Even if they have, they probably can't shoot straight."

"I'm glad they're not here to mess things up." Oleg pointed toward the upper level of the descending rail system. "Now let's decide what we're going to do if Randall and his group show up in here."

"I suggest we find a good place to hide and let Randall and everyone with him get completely in here," Yaw said. "Then we ambush them."

Ludvig looked around the large chamber and gestured toward the far wall opposite the wall with the descending rail system, opposite where they expected Colt Randall to come from. "We have a lot of large equipment, tools, and supplies stored over there and we have a long row of large metal cabinets. We can spread out and wait for them to come in. It's obvious by now someone in Randall's group knows how to get our security doors open."

Oleg pointed at the technicians working on the missile. "What about the workers? Shouldn't we do something to protect them?"

"They need to continue their work," Yaw said. "We don't know how soon Randall will get here. Maybe they'll finish in time to move the missile completely into the launching mechanism and push the trigger."

"Should we give them some weapons?" Ludvig asked.

"They aren't fighters," Yaw said. "If they haven't finished, they'll just have to be sacrificed."

Wan and Oleg walked closer to the missile and looked closely at the details of the fine-tuning process. Wan made no comments to the workers and they seemed to pay no attention to their primary supervisor looking at what they were doing.

"I think they're almost finished," Wan said, looking at Oleg. "They should be ready to push the missile fully into the launcher within about five minutes."

Oleg nodded.

"Let's go over to the tool area and select our best options for ambush and get setup." Yaw looked carefully at the other three standing beside him. "We need to have a well-thought-out plan and be ready when they show up down here. Let's go get ready."

Wan gestured toward the workers. "Don't we need to say something to them?"

"Its best we don't interrupt their work," Yaw said. "They might finish on time and get the missile launched before Randall gets down here."

Oleg narrowed his eyes and looked at Yaw. "Maybe they deserve some kind of a break. They've done a real good job for us, and we can be certain Randall will indeed come storming in here."

"They're all Chinese. We have a lot more like them, an oversupply in fact," Yaw said. He made a dismissive gesture with his right hand. "They're expendable. We don't need to go out of our way to protect them. Besides, they'll be okay if they get the missile launched in time. Then they'll have a chance to get out of here."

Oleg wrinkled his brow and didn't comment.

Yaw turned toward all the equipment along the far wall

and waved everyone forward. "Come on let's go. We need to get setup before it's too late."

"Give me a chance to shoot Randall first," Oleg said. "He's been a large pain in the ass."

"What makes you think you'll succeed?" Yaw asked.

"I just know I will," Oleg said. "I'm a great shot."

Yaw grunted. "We'll let you post up in front of the rest of us, so you'll get an early look. However, if any of us get Randall clearly in our sights, we're going to take him out."

"Fair enough," Oleg said. "All I want is a good chance to have the first hit on him."

Chapter 57

Colt and the other ten warriors with him stopped in the well-lighted area around the large metal door.

The door appeared to have the usual opening scheme. Colt moved to the right side of the door and put his feet on a couple of discolored tiles while putting each hand in respective small indentions immediately above him in the ceramic wall.

The familiar hydraulic sound ensued, and the door opened to reveal another large chamber.

"We'll go in two at a time and immediately take whatever cover we can find," Colt spoke into his tactical microphone. "Flat on the floor will be the best option if we don't find any cover."

"Roger," came several replies.

"We'll form two lines, one on each side of the doorway. Mack, you and your group get on the left. The rest of us will get on the right," Colt said. "Okay?"

Everyone nodded.

The warriors lined up on each side of the doorway and waited for Colt to give the command.

"Go," Colt said. He and Mack bolted through the wide doorway on opposite sides and took immediate cover.

After the eleven warriors moved silently into cover behind metal cabinets and various pieces of equipment, Colt peered around the corner of the cabinet he had taken cover behind.

Even though he thought he was prepared for the sight, Colt gasped as he looked at the large missile on the rail car. The front of it resembled the nose cone of a large jet, but it was much more menacing.

Colt knew the dimensions of the Poseidon Missile, but what he was looking at appeared even bigger. Looming like a monster ready to pounce, it sat directly in front of them on a rail car. He took a few moments to adjust to the sight before he resumed his activity.

"As far as the opposition is concerned, I don't see any," Colt said into his tactical microphone. "Anyone see any people around?"

All replies came back negative.

Colt studied the rail system that led downward and around a corner. The bottom part of the rail system wasn't in view.

"The actual launch area has to be down at the bottom where the rails lead to," Mack said.

"They're probably waiting for us to show up down there," Linda said. "There will likely be plenty of cover for them to stage an ambush."

Colt nodded and left two of his warriors to watch the area as he waved everyone else forward.

The nine remaining warriors with Colt proceeded with caution, single file, ten yards apart.

Colt turned the corner and immediately saw that the rails extended downward to a large flat area. Another Poseidon Missile sat on a rail car at the end of the rails.

Five Chinese workers labored feverishly over a third missile sitting just in front of what appeared to be the launch mechanism.

As he continued to scan the area, Colt waited for Linda

and Mack to come closer.

"None of the workers have guns," Colt said. "And I don't think they've seen us yet. They seem to be concentrating hard on what they're doing."

Linda looked at Colt. "We need to get down there and stop them immediately, but we need to be cautious." She pointed toward a row of large metal cabinets and various large pieces of equipment along a far wall of the flat launch area.

"There's not much cover for us," Mack said. "If they're behind those cabinets, we'll be sitting ducks."

Colt spoke into his tactical microphone, "Everyone except Linda and me should have a grenade left. Mack, you select two men who will do a low crawl toward opposite ends of the row of cabinets. When they're both close enough to throw a grenade, they'll coordinate with each other and throw at the same time."

"Roger," Mack said. He selected the two warriors and repeated the instructions.

Colt watched as the two warriors executed perfectly.

Two large explosions occurred simultaneously behind the row of cabinets.

As the taskforce members waited for the smoke to clear, the only sounds came from the Chinese workers scurrying for cover.

The two warriors who threw the grenades rushed up to check behind the row of cabinets. They immediately gave the all-clear signal.

"Looks like no one was immediately behind the cabinets," Mack said.

Colt rose to a standing position. The other six with him also stood.

No one fired at them from the flat area below.

"We'll secure the immediate area where the missiles are and then check on what's further back behind the cabinets," Colt said. "Mack, we'll use four of your men to round up the

Chinese workers and maintain security. They'll also need to make sure no missile is launched."

"Roger," Mack replied. He gave the order and deployed two more of his men to join the two standing around the cabinets.

"Now, let's go see what's closer to the wall," Colt said. He waved Linda, Mack, and the remaining two warriors standing with him forward.

The four men from Mack's group started rounding up the workers while Colt's group moved toward the row of large metal cabinets.

"They're probably set up for an ambush as soon as we go around the cabinets." Linda said.

Colt spoke into his tactical microphone, "Linda and I will go to the left end of the row of cabinets. Mack, you and the other two warriors go to the opposite end. Stop and check out the area as best you can before you round the corner and then we'll compare notes. We'll take a couple of minutes."

"Roger."

Colt peered around the corner of the metal cabinet he was behind and studied the area for several minutes. Several rows of large crates and large pieces of equipment sat between the cabinets and the wall.

No enemy was evident.

Colt glanced at his phone and saw he still had a signal. He figured the Russians and Chinese had arranged for that throughout the underground area to enhance their coordination when they were moving supplies. He punched a digit and heard Grant answer. He immediately gave Grant a quick update.

"So, you're going to continue to check the area with all the supplies and equipment you're in right now and you're expecting more trouble?" Grant asked quickly.

"Yeah, we figure there are still some of them left and we're going to be very cautious," Colt said. "We'll stay prepared for an ambush."

"We have good satellite surveillance of the area around Kingston. We'll know if any activity occurs outside," Grant replied. "Keep me posted as well as you can on how things go inside. Good luck."

"Roger," Colt said.

Chapter 58

Ludvig, Oleg, Wan, and Yaw huddled behind a large piece of drilling equipment close to the wall.

Oleg had reported he had taken a position behind a large wooden crate closer to where the missiles were and well to the left of where the other three men were located. He had explained he would wait there for Randall's group to make an appearance.

Each man in the foursome was equipped with tactical communications gear and with AK-74 rifles. They had all heard the explosions and they knew the enemy was now in the immediate area.

Randall was probably in the group, Oleg thought. That was good. They would now have a good chance to eliminate him and get him completely out of the way.

Everything was now quiet as Oleg scanned the well-lit area in from of him. No enemy was in sight at the moment. But he knew some number of them would soon be coming in his direction and he would be prepared to eliminate them quickly, especially Randall.

Yaw stared at Ludvig. "I still think it's a bad thing your bosses have left to go back to Finland. I think they should have stayed and done something to try to get at least one of the missiles launched."

Wan nodded. "Their decision is going to send a real bad message to my bosses."

"Oleg and I keep telling you they aren't fighters," Ludvig said. "They wouldn't have been able to make any difference at all in trying to defeat Randall and his taskforce. No matter what happens here its best they get back to their stronghold off the shore of Finland and remain capable of taking some more action in the future when needed."

"Consider us unconvinced," Yaw said with a scowl.

Ludvig leaned toward Yaw and Wan. "We need to concentrate on the ambush. If we wipe Randall and his force out, we can go back and get all the missiles launched."

Yaw continued to look irritated but made no comment.

Wan also remained silent.

In a few moments, Yaw looked at Ludvig and gestured toward Wan. "Well, we still have one big thing in our favor: if we lose all our technicians, he can get the missiles ready to launch."

Ludvig nodded. "And Oleg can help him. First, we need to get Randall and his taskforce out of the way."

Yaw narrowed his eyes and looked at Ludvig. "We're giving Oleg his chance to eliminate Randall. I just hope he's good enough to do it."

"I know he's had a lot of practice with rifles and other weapons, but he hasn't had to use them in the field against opposition. I'm not sure how good a shot he is but I think he'll do well enough," Ludvig said.

Yaw gave a slight shrug. "Well at least there are four of us. If Oleg doesn't get Randall right away, we'll still have a chance to get him from our positions which will all be in good cover." He looked at Ludvig. "And you're a true assassin. If the rest of us don't get Randall first you'll have a chance to do your job."

There was a brief silence.

"We need to agree on our strategy and get in our final positions." Yaw said.

After a brief discussion, Yaw pointed to some large crates to his right. "Wan and I will select a couple of positions over there. I suggest you go to the left and move closer to Oleg."

Ludvig gave a thumbs-up and began to move.

"Oleg, I'm coming over in your direction," Ludvig said into his tactical mouthpiece, "but don't worry, I'm not going to interfere with anything you do. You'll still have your chance to knock Randall off first."

"Roger," Oleg replied. "I'm sitting on ready and I'm going to nail that bastard as soon as he gets within range."

"Someone needs to eliminate Randall and I'm okay with you being the one who does it. I'll function as your backup. Aim carefully and don't get overanxious."

"Roger."

Chapter 59

Ludvig moved into a position where he had good cover and the best view of the surrounding area.

He could see Oleg about twenty yards ahead of him and slightly to his left. If Oleg didn't get Randall then he would finish the job.

Oleg might be a weapons expert, but he wasn't a talented assassin like he was, Ludvig thought as he shrugged mentally. He would try to be patient and give Oleg the chance he wanted.

But one thing for sure, Randall had to be eliminated.

Ludvig continued to scan the area around him. No activity yet, but he was certain Randall would be coming.

As Ludvig waited, he thought about Ivan and Sergei probably being on their way back to their stronghold in the islands just off the shore of Finland. That was a good thing.

If he and the other three with him didn't stop Randall and didn't get the missiles launched, then Ivan and Sergei would have more chances do the necessary damage to the United States.

Ludvig hated Americans. He always had. Helping to destroy the United States had always been a passion.

He knew Russia had more Poseidon Missiles so this wouldn't be the only chance they had to get some launched. It was always good to have more options in case things didn't work out at first.

But one way or the other, they were going to work out, Ludvig thought. He would make sure of that.

Ludvig heard Yaw's voice in his earpiece.

"Wan and I are in our positions," Yaw said. "We're both about ten yards away from the wall now and about fifteen yards apart. We both have excellent vantage points, and we're fully prepared for action. We should be able to eliminate any enemy force that shows up."

"Good," Ludvig replied. "We're all set to make sure Randall and his taskforce get eliminated and we can continue preparing for the launch. Oleg, I'm about twenty yards behind you and a little to your right. I'll give you the first chance to get Randall unless he pops up right in front of me. Then I'll take him out."

Oleg's voice boomed in Ludvig's earpiece. "That's fair enough, but don't be too quick on the trigger. I might see him too and shift position a little to get a better field of fire."

"Don't be too slow. We don't want to miss a good chance to get rid of him for good."

"I see him now. He's moving directly toward me!" Oleg exclaimed with obvious excitement. "Hold off until I get him."

Chapter 60

Colt and Linda stayed alert as they moved forward slowly. Colt was about five yards in front of Linda. Mack and the two warriors with him were about 20 yards to Colt's left and also moving forward.

Several loud booms occurred as splinters flew off a large wooden crate a few feet in front of Colt. He dropped and pressed flat against the stone floor alongside some metal barrels.

"Linda, you okay?" Colt asked into his tactical microphone.

"Yes, and I'm flat on the stone floor like you are. Did you take any hits?"

"No."

More splinters flew into the air around Colt's position and then some stone fragments flew past him.

"Shooter's finding the range, stay low," Colt said.

After the flurry of bullets stopped, Colt stayed as low as he could and crawled forward.

Peering around the edge of the barrel he was behind, Colt saw a rifle protruding from behind the corner of a large wooden crate well ahead of them.

"Do you see anything?" Linda asked.

"A rifle sticking out from behind a wooden crate about

50 yards in front of us," Colt said. "Apparently the shooter got a little anxious and fired too soon, lucky for us."

"Yeah," Linda replied, "lucky for us."

Colt spoke into his tactical microphone, "Mack, the shooter is about 50 yards in front of Linda and me. We'll try to take him out. Are you still moving forward?"

"Yep, and we'll stay alert over here and offer any help we can," Mack said. "Good luck to you and Linda."

In less than a minute, multiple gunshots rang out to Colt's left front. Some were loud and some were soft pops. It was clear both sides were shooting. Colt was glad to hear more soft pops than loud bangs.

Colt peered around the edge of the large barrel again.

A figure was charging hard toward him. The figure had his rifle pointed forward and he was only about twenty yards away.

Being careful to stay as much behind the metal barrel as possible, Colt aimed and fired multiple times.

The figure staggered forward another yard or so and then fell. He thrashed around for a few seconds and then lay still.

Keeping his rifle in ready position, Colt moved out around the barrel and toward the prone figure.

Linda followed.

Colt noted the high-powered bullets had torn several holes in the enemy warrior's chest. He obviously wasn't wearing any bulletproof clothing.

More loud bangs sounded.

Colt felt several big impacts to his chest, stomach, and shoulders. He went down. The flexible bullet-proof nano-composite material he wore under his fatigues had saved him but many of his muscles were throbbing. He couldn't move his right arm.

The loud bangs continued.

As more bullets kicked up stone fragments around him, Colt stayed as flat on the stone floor as he could. He tried to move his right arm to return fire, but it was numb. In desperation, he twisted on the stone floor and reached for his SIG 556 with his left hand.

Colt could see a large figure about thirty yards away charging toward him and closing fast. Bullets were hitting all around him.

The figure obviously couldn't aim very accurately while running fast, Colt thought. But he was drawing closer rapidly.

Colt felt his adrenalin surge as he stayed as flat as he could and stretched toward his rifle.

The bullets stopped for a second.

Seeing the charging figure was in the process of inserting a new magazine, Colt had grabbed his rifle with his left hand, and he struggled to get it into firing position. He had to do something. He could see the figure was still closing fast and had inserted the new magazine.

The figure was now within about ten yards, and he was in the process of pointing his rifle back toward Colt.

Colt heard a multitude of soft pops erupt behind him. He knew Linda was firing at the charging figure.

The figure plunged toward the stone floor in a rolling flurry. His rifle flew out to the side as he came to rest in a motionless heap.

"I could tell he was concentrating on you," Linda said. "I took a chance and stood up to aim while he was reloading."

Cold gave a thumbs-up with his left hand.

"Are you okay?" Linda asked as she drew closer.

Colt pushed off the floor with his left hand and got to his knees as Linda moved closer to him. He slowly rose to a standing position.

Both stayed alert and scanned the area as they moved back behind cover.

"I'll be okay. I'm beginning to get full movement again," Colt said. "I got hit about four times in vital areas.

The bulletproof clothing we wear under our fatigues saved my life. That guy was a really good shot from a distance. I'm glad he decided to charge toward us and not stop and aim." He looked at Linda. "Thanks for taking care of things."

Linda gave a thumbs-up and continued to scan the area.

Colt heard Mack's voice in his tactical earpiece.

"What's your status?" Mack asked.

Colt explained.

"We eliminated two others, two Chinese," Mack said. "We've checked around a bit. I think we have them all cleared out. The two other guys with me are still searching the area just in case."

"Good job," Colt said. He removed his secure satellite phone from a pocket and punched a digit. "I'll give Grant a report."

Linda stayed on alert and continued to scan the area.

After a brief conversation with Grant, Colt disconnected and spoke into his tactical microphone, "Grant told me the President has changed his thinking a little and is sending a Navy contingent from the Reagan to do the cleanup and secure the area. They'll get the Poseidon Missiles moved to the appropriate military facility."

Linda pumped a fist in the air. "Great!"

"And another thing," Colt said. "As soon as the Navy force gets here, we've been ordered to go home."

Chapter 61

The next day at his headquarters on an unnamed island just off the western shore of Finland, Ivan Titov sat with Sergei at the round conference table in his office.

"Well, that was definitely a setback, but we survived and we'll have more chances to bring the United States down," Ivan said.

Sergei nodded slowly. "Maybe Russia should try to be more independent next time we launch a big project."

"China provides a lot of funding and a lot of technology," Ivan said. "That's all very useful."

"It didn't work out this time, and we lost three of our top assassins. We also lost our top expert on international banking, along with one of our top experts on computers."

"We still have our moles in the United States Government. They all have close connections to China," Ivan said. "They can still keep things moving on bringing down the United States and they can keep things moving with China if we want to continue that relationship."

"Does the Kremlin want to stay closely connected with China?"

"I'm not sure." Ivan wrinkled his brow. "I'm confident the Kremlin will let us know what they want us to do after they decide how they want to progress. I know they're still discussing things with China. They each want to bring down the United States, and our continued cooperation could be very valuable to both countries."

Sergei gave a slow nod.

"We're in the process of manufacturing a lot more Poseidon Missiles and they all have the new guidance system. We can thank China for that," Ivan said. "And we still have the two missiles being built in China that are 80 feet long and will likely carry a much larger warhead, maybe up to 100 megatons."

Sergei leaned forward. "Where in China are they?"

"Beijing," Ivan said. "And they'll stay there until their entire manufacturing process is complete."

Sergei narrowed his eyes. "Then the Kremlin will move them back to Russia?"

Ivan leaned back in his chair and gave a short laugh. "Of course they will. And the Kremlin will soon be able to launch again from a more secure site."

"Won't China copy our Poseidon Missile and have it in their arsenal going forward?"

Ivan narrowed his eyes. "Of course they'll do that. That was something we knew would happen, but our gain will be more than our loss. China contributed enough technology to give us a much more advanced missile to keep in our arsenal for future use and so what if they do have their own versions of our Poseidon Missiles. They won't use them against us."

"Are you sure about that?"

Ivan narrowed his eyes and didn't comment.

"Since both Russia and China want to dominate the world, what's going to happen when we bring the United States down?"

"The Kremlin will have to figure that out."

"Are they working on that?"

"Yes," Ivan said, "and I know they've already worked out a lot of details."

Sergei nodded slowly.

Ivan held a fist high in the air. “Cheers for Mother Russia to be the dominating country on the planet. The Kremlin will find a way to bring down the United States and then I’m sure they’ll have a way to keep China from attacking us and taking us over.”

Chapter 62

In the main conference room at the Tampa FBI headquarters, Grant reviewed the current situation with the contingent from Boswic. Colt, Linda, Harlan, Jim, and Blake sat across the table from him.

Grant looked at Colt and Linda. “You did a great job down there in Jamaica, thanks.”

Colt and Linda each gave a thumbs-up.

“Ken called earlier this morning and gave me an update,” Grant said. “The Navy has completely inspected and secured the whole area Titov used for his operations in Jamaica. The warehouses remain secured and the underground facility in Jamaica that served as the headquarters for Ivan Titov has now been impounded. The Navy has loaded the three Poseidon Missiles onto one of their ships. They’re taking them to Guantanamo Naval Base in Cuba for a thorough inspection.”

“What about the Russian and Chinese embassies down there?” Linda asked.

“Ken told me the President has all the right people taking care of any necessary details,” Grant said. “We don’t need to get involved in any of that."

There was a brief silence.

Harlan leaned forward. "Once we thoroughly inspect all the technology the Poseidon Missiles have inside them maybe we can figure out a real good defense against a future strike."

Grant nodded. "We have a lot of experts ready to do that."

After giving everyone more details on the current status of events, Grant activated a large monitor on the wall and pointed to it.

"Those are live pictures of the missiles being moved into our Guantanamo Naval Base," Grant said. He stared at the monitor for a few seconds and then scanned the faces across the table. "Anyone have any questions?"

"Will they be secure there?" Jim asked. "We signed a lease with Cuba in 2003 for the land our base is on, but I understand Cuba has a change of heart and is no longer accepting payments for the lease."

"Ken mentioned that and he assured me all of our top officials are keeping a close eye on that situation," Grant said. "If any problems crop up, we'll move the missiles to another location."

"Do we know what Ivan Titov and Sergei Nikitin are up to now?" Harlan asked.

"We know they're back in their headquarters on their island base just off the shore of Finland," Grant said. He pushed a button on a device resting on the table and pointed at another monitor. "We have the satellite footage of their arrival earlier today. Incidentally, we have footage of them leaving the Russian Embassy yesterday." He pushed another button.

Colt looked at the monitor and watched Ivan and Sergei move from a side door of the Russian Embassy to some docks nearby. He saw both men disappear into a large boat.

"Well, I guess we're going to be keeping a close watch

on that area off the shore of Finland," Colt said. "They're certain to get involved in another project to bring us down."

Linda nodded. "And China will probably be helping them again."

"We know for sure China is involved in a lot of schemes to tear down our economy," Blake said. "I've completed a lot more research and I'm close to being able to provide some interesting details on that."

"We know they're still cooperating directly with Russia on some things, and I figure they're cooperating on a lot of other things too," Grant replied. "China might also be cooperating directly with Mexican drug lords; they have some mutual interests. They both like the cash flow they get from the activity. Also, the continued influx of illegal drugs into the United States will help destabilize our country, something Russia and China both love."

"We'll have to figure out all the details of their next operation before it's too late," Harlan said. "At least we've avoided being hit by an underwater nuclear missile so far."

Colt narrowed his eyes and nodded slowly. "Yeah, at least we've done that for the moment. We're going to have to stay on our toes. I'm sure the Russians will build a lot more of them and China will now have them too. And we can be sure all the new models will incorporate all the latest advanced technology developed by the Chinese."

A brief silence ensued.

"We'll have to stay alert on many fronts," Grant said. "I suspect the Russians will soon be mounting a lot more big initiatives to increase their supply of gold. We think they have less than a thousand metric tons of it, about half of the amount China has. We need to be alert to various things they'll do along that line. They might partner with China on that too and try to empty Fort Knox."

Harlan nodded. "Damned right, I'm sure they'll go after our supply of gold, and they have a lot of options as to how they can do that."

"There are a lot of rumors that Fort Know is already empty," Blake said. "Steve and I have discussed those rumors a few times and he thinks they might be true."

Grant gave a dismissive wave. "Steve has mentioned those rumors to me too, but we'll talk about that another time. We have some other things to concentrate on right now."

"Russia and China might continue to partner on some mutually beneficial projects, but I think the Russian leaders probably feel at a distinct disadvantage to China on several things. They now probably want to gain ground on China in as many ways as they can," Blake said. "They definitely don't want China to be able to take them over."

Grant again scanned the faces across the table and then leaned forward. "Yeah, I understand the consensus at the CIA is that Russia will continue attempts to gain more international clout in any way they can. Bringing us down is just one of their many goals. If they need help from China they'll probably accept it."

"Moscow likely has a strategy for using the multitude of islands between Finland and Sweden to promote many of their upcoming initiatives," Colt said. "I'm guessing there are a lot more Russian bases on those tiny islands than we've found so far."

Harlan grunted. "The Russians will do whatever they can to gain wealth. I agree the Russians will try to increase their gold supply for a lot of reasons and we haven't figured all of them out yet. The known Russian bases off the shore of Finland all have helipads. Maybe they're planning to start transporting gold there with helicopters."

"I'll ask Ken to have his analysts do more study on that possibility." Grant looked at Blake. "If Harlan and Jim agree, I suggest you do that also."

Blake gave a thumbs-up and explained that the total amount of gold that had ever been mined worldwide was around 142,000 metric tons. At 1,000 dollars per ounce, that would amount to about four and a half trillion dollars. He went on to say that wouldn't even cover the amount of money in circulation in the United States.

"So, what's your point?" Harlan asked.

"The Russians want to increase their total wealth any way they can," Blake said. "Just increasing their gold supply isn't going to get them to where they need to be. They'll constantly try to increase their wealth in a lot of ways. Partnering with Mexican Drug cartels will be one of them. We'll be fighting Russians on a lot of fronts for a long time."

Grant nodded. "The Russians definitely have a variety of activities in mind. We'll continue to stay alert for all the advantages the Russians and Chinese are trying to create to promote their attempts to defeat us. We'll counter as many of their moves as we can. We'll constantly strive to study all the possibilities and stymie all progress they're trying to make toward being able to take us over."

There was a brief silence.

"We'll probably see more activity from Ivan Titov and Sergei Nikitin soon," Grant said. "I'm guessing they want revenge for what just happened." He looked at Colt. "They'll probably come after you in every way they can."

"I'll stay alert," Colt said. He scanned the faces around the table. "I'm sure we'll all stay alert."

Everyone gave a thumbs-up.

www.ingramcontent.com/pod-product-compliance
Lightning Source LLC
LaVergne TN
LVHW052253200926
848481LV00002B/353